EVEN MORE FANTASTIC FAILURES

TRUE STORIES OF PEOPLE WHO CHANGED THE WORLD BY FALLING DOWN FIRST

WRITTEN BY

LUKE REYNOLDS

ALADDIN
New York London Toronto Sydney New Delhi

BEYOND WORDS
Portland, Oregon

FOR FOUR EXTRA SPECIAL PEOPLE
WITHOUT WHOM THIS BOOK WOULD NOT EXIST

JENNIFER REYNOLDS
TYLER REYNOLDS

TAMACHA EMMONS

CONTENTS

INTRODUCTION

Success.

Yes.

It's the best!

Except . . . well . . . when it isn't. Or when the success you get isn't exactly what you had in mind. Or when you're on the ground, face covered in dirt or shame, staring up ahead at what you wanted slipping slowly (or quickly!) away.

Right now, chances are that you see a lot of success all around you. Teachers in your schools may highlight certain students for good grades or sports ability or other achievements. Your parents or guardians may talk about siblings who have done truly astounding things. Your social media feeds may feature friends and enemies alike who all (*all!*) are doing some truly amazing things, in some truly amazing places, with some truly amazing people—and doing most of it much better than you and me.

But wait.

These versions of success are two things, guaranteed: (1) They're not the full story. (2) They're maybe not even the versions of success you want.

I remember when I was growing up long, long ago, in a galaxy far, far away called Windsor, Connecticut, baseball seemed like the only way for me to prove myself as a boy. Many of my friends were really into baseball, loved it, and played it pretty darn well. Enter Luke Reynolds. I would get up to bat, take a breath, and then proceed to strike out.

Over and over again, I'd strike out.

I remember standing at the home plate in my tight, tight pants (that itched uncontrollably!) and being terrified that a pitch was going to hit me. I would have much rather written a poem about the death-intent fastball than been standing at the plate waiting for it to come right at me.

But writing a poem about a fastball didn't seem like a viable version of success for me as a young boy. Baseball was what it was all about. Baseball was where triumph was won.

Need to overcome fear?

Baseball was the way to do it!

Need to show leadership?

Baseball again, yeah!

Need to learn the power of community and working together?

Yup. You guessed it. Baseball.

And so, I tried my hands again and again at that epic terrain, hoping to learn and then showcase these successful life skills.

Yet every Saturday, as I waited for fastballs that I believed mocked me ruthlessly en route to the home plate, all I could really think about doing was writing poetry. I would have much rather been up in the tree fort that my dad had built, where I hammered in some stray boards to build myself a little corner desk facing what I thought, at the time, was a stream (it was actually a sewer), writing . . .

Poetry.

But in my boyhood, baseball was cool. Baseball was where one proved oneself.

Poetry was not.

What I needed to learn, standing there on that baseball field, was that sometimes, our versions of success need to change in order for us to embrace the experiences we actually want to pursue.

In the book you're now holding, you'll see this theme emerge, with amazing people like Alan Naiman, Mindy Kaling, and Grace Hopper, who all had to reject society's version of success for them in order to break into their own definition of what it means to succeed, in their own way, and using their own unique set of skills and abilities.

But getting honest with ourselves about what we really believe we need to pursue is no guarantee that triumph is going to arrive because of it.

I eventually stopped playing baseball (or should I say, trying to play baseball) and started writing more and more poetry. But that didn't mean that the *New Yorker* or any other revered magazine was about to come knocking at my door saying something like . . .

Luke!

We have heard the oft-told tales of your heretofore mentioned struggles with the athletically inscribed activity known as "baseball" and how you finally chose to relinquish your pursuits in the heretofore mentioned arena and instead pursue the subsequent desire to write poetry. Ah, what a lovely and courageous choice! We would now like to publish any poems that you craft, but may we humbly suggest that you write your first poem to be published by us about a death-intent fastball that mocks you en route to the plate?

Sincerely,
the New Yorker *Poetry People*

Nope. A letter like that never came. Instead, an awful lot of failure and rejection came with poetry (and every other kind of writing I've ever attempted!).

You'll find that the stories of every single one of the people (and places and things!) profiled in this book had the same basic trajectory. Why? Because there is an important commonality among us all regarding what it means to be human (or, in the case of places and things, run by humans): we all fail.

We all make mistakes. We all struggle.

Those struggles look vastly different, and not all struggles are equal in their intensity or in their scope. But I guarantee you this: none of the pictures on social media tell anything close to the true story of a person's journey. Behind the seemingly happy and perfectly placed photos, there are stories of struggle, of failure, of confusion, of fear, of hurt, and of wonder.

I know this not because I am a sage but because I know myself, and I know the students I have taught for almost twenty years in high school, middle school, adult education programs, and now college. And I've learned one basic thing from all of them: we fail.

What is powerful about our human condition is not that we somehow gain an ability to live without failing or without making mistakes or without being rejected but rather that we can learn how to embrace failures and struggles as part of our story, so that we can move on from them.

The people profiled and explored in this second volume of Fantastic Failures are admirable and beautiful to me not because they've done things perfectly but because they have grappled with their own struggles with honesty and resolve. These are people I admire, appreciate, and want to emulate. I share their stories here, with you, in the hope that you will understand that you are not alone;

those profiled in this book need help to keep moving forward, just the way you and I do.

Welcome to the human family. None of us gets it right the first time, but by being honest about that, we can have a lot more fun (and hope) along the journey. See you out there in the dirt, and let's both be ready to extend a hand and help the other up. After all, we're family, right?

1

BARACK OBAMA

Consider the scene: a young man flanked by well-connected parents is announced as the forty-fourth president of the United States of America. Cue the crowd. The country is united, and Barack Obama's journey to the microphone onstage fills him with reminders of how seamless—how truly easy—the quest has been. Red carpets were rolled out for him and his wife, Michelle, everywhere they went. Widely respected, he never had to deal with attacks on his character or his name. And all of his previous races for office—at the state and national levels—were met with resounding successes as well. Indeed, this night is a fitting capstone to a journey marked by victory after victory. Obama takes a deep breath, thankful that he has not had to deal with heartrending defeat and rejection, and he begins his acceptance speech.

Not!

Barack Obama was indeed elected as the forty-fourth president of the United States of America, beginning his term in 2008. But his path to reach that pinnacle included far more failure and rejection than we can imagine. Case in point: In 2000, Obama attempted to be the Democratic nominee for the First District from the state of Illinois for the United States House of Representatives. This race would decide who would run for the House for the Democratic Party, and Obama was hoping he'd be the choice. Instead, he lost the race by thirty percentage points to his rival, Bobby Rush. Obama received a total of 31 percent of the votes in the election.[1]

Think about that. In the year 2000, running for the House of Representatives, the man who would become *president* of the *entire country* only eight years later received less than one-third of the support of one district in Illinois. This is after he had campaigned hard, knocked on door after door to introduce himself to people, given countless speeches, and participated in endless fundraisers.

Consider studying hard for a big test that's coming up. It's huge. You've got the date marked on your calendar. Circled. Your teacher has said repeatedly that this test counts for a lot of your final grade. So, it's go time! You study night after night, work with friends, memorize and talk the ideas through, and practice, practice, practice (and then practice some more). The big day finally arrives. You take the test, feeling like you gave it all you had. And after your teacher tallies the results, there is a big *31%* on top of the first page, circled in bloodred marker.

Ugh.

What gives?!

You feel floored. Defeated. And, let's be honest, kind of hopeless. You gave it your all, and what did you receive in return?

Thirty-one percent.

Like Obama.

So, how do you think that made him feel? Do you now think you can imagine it?

But when a friend of his tried to re-inspire Obama by suggesting a trip to the Democratic Convention later that year, where Al Gore would be officially announced as the candidate for president, Obama agreed that maybe it was what he needed to reignite the spark.

There was just one problem: he had no money.

Okay, actually there was a second problem: no one knew who he was.

Okay, actually, to be completely honest, there was a third problem as well: he couldn't even get into most of the convention.

After Obama's flight landed in Los Angeles, he went to the rental car desk because he next had to drive to the convention at the Staples Center. Unfortunately, the attendant at the counter informed Obama that he would not be able to rent a car. His American Express credit card had been maxed out! He had used his last bit of available credit to buy the plane ticket to LA, but once there, it looked like he might not even be able to make it the last part of the journey to the convention center![2]

Imagine a deep passion of yours—whether art or basketball or ballet—and using your last bit of energy to get to the art show or the championship game or the dance recital. You were not going to be in the show, game, or recital, but you wanted to be in the audience because you knew that passion was a part of you and what you still hoped to do in the future. But then you got turned away before you could even arrive at the site!

Obama finally convinced the sales associate at the car place to let him rent a car, and Obama finally made it to the Staples Center and the 2000 Democratic Convention. Whew! Now that he was there, people would realize that he was a truly gifted individual.

Right?

They would realize that *here* was a person who could one day be president!

Right?

They would realize that they should definitely let him in to interact with the leaders of the party and the nominee for president, Al Gore.

Right?

Wrong. Obama made it to LA and then to the Staples Center and the convention, but he still couldn't get inside the actual doors. He couldn't hear the most important speeches, and he even left before the final day, when Al Gore officially accepted the nomination and gave his acceptance speech. In an interview with David Axelrod, who would become Obama's senior advisor during his presidential run, Obama noted, "They [gave] me the pass that basically only allows you to be in the halls. The ring around the auditorium doesn't actually allow you to see anything."[3] Obama later wrote about the experience, "I ended up watching most of the speeches on various television screens scattered around the Staples Center."[4] With a wife and young daughter back at home in Chicago—and another baby on the way shortly—Obama had no money, no direction, and was literally standing outside the doors of the career he had passionately thought he wanted.

I ended up watching most of the speeches on various television screens scattered around the Staples Center.

—Barack Obama

So, a brief recap: Obama had lost his 2000 congressional primary race to represent Illinois in the US House of Representatives. He had earned only 31 percent of the vote. Because of the extreme effort and energy required during this fierce campaign, he had used essentially all the money he had and had maxed out his credit card as well. Then, when he attempted to attend the national convention, he wasn't even allowed into the room. Dick Durbin, the US senator representing Illinois, commented about Obama at the 2000 convention, "I have no memory of him there. It was a disastrous trip for him."[5]

> ## FROM WEAK TO PEAK!
>
> Even though she lost her political race for a state senate seat in Illinois, Ida B. Wells accomplished astronomical amounts while working toward justice: as a newspaper editor at the turn of the nineteenth century, Wells bravely wrote about lynching and demanded justice for victims. She also established programs for kindergartners, a women's group, and a suffrage organization for African American women.

How did all this feel? What did it make Obama think? He shared, "I felt as if I was a third wheel in this whole thing. I ended up leaving early, and that was the stage when I was really questioning whether I should be in politics."[6]

I felt as if I was a third wheel in this whole thing. I ended up leaving early, and that was the stage when I was really questioning whether I should be in politics.

—Barack Obama

The eventual forty-fourth president of the United States of America, who was elected not once but *twice* to the highest office in the country, once felt like he was a third wheel. Like he didn't belong. Think about what that means for you and me, and for your best friend, Jada. (How did I know your best friend's name was Jada? This book involves a lot of research, so I research everything!) That means that if you or I (or, yup, your best friend, Jada) feel like a third wheel in something, it doesn't necessarily mean that we don't belong. And it *definitely* doesn't mean that we'll never belong. All it means is that in one precise moment, we feel ignored.

Rejected.

Unseen.

Unappreciated.

Unknown.

But we are not alone! Obama felt that way, too, yet he found a way to keep moving forward. You may be standing at the doors of your own convention center right now, trying to find a way in and hearing those in power tell you, "Sorry, you don't have the right credentials. You're not allowed." They may even slam the door in your face.

You may find yourself relegated to the hall, where you watch the action on a television set rather than in real life.

That's okay.

That's part of the journey. And if that convention center is a place you know you want to be, or a place where you *know* your voice needs to be heard, represented, paid attention to—then you won't give up. You won't politely allow those in power to tell you to back off, to go find somewhere

NOT DIMINISHED...FINISHED!

Louisa May Alcott became a sensationally successful author when her novel *Little Women* was published, but it took her years of struggle and rejection before she was able to break through with this novel, which is still widely read today.

else to frequent. No, you'll learn, you'll grow, you'll keep using your voice (or creating your art, or dribbling your basketball, or doing your pirouettes), because you know that one day you'll come back to those doors with a voice so powerful that no one will be able to ignore you anymore.

That's exactly what Obama did. Over the years, he hadn't just lost political races and been turned away at conventions. He had grown accustomed to being pulled from airport security lines because of the sound of his name, and he had become used to people wondering, *Who is this guy? Never heard of him!*

But in 2004, the day after Obama gave the keynote address for the Democratic Convention at the Fleet Center in Boston, Massachusetts, a story long in the making took a fascinating turn. One of his advisors, Robert Gibbs, shared this revealing moment about the aftermath of Obama's rousing speech: "We got close to the Fleet Center and a group of Boston cops walked over to shake his hand, having heard the speech the night before."[7]

HAVE GRIT—DON'T SPLIT!

Author J. R. R. Tolkien, who would create the phenomenon Lord of the Rings trilogy, struggled with his academics at the University of Oxford until he switched into the study of languages. He also served on the front line in World War II and had to overcome his wartime trauma to eventually craft his masterpiece.

Instead of locking Obama out, police officers charged with providing security for the convention were seeking Obama out to shake his hand. They were grateful for his message! His words had been heard; he had found his mission and his place.

Your own journey will look different from Obama's, and the place where you feel rejected or like a third wheel may not be the exact place where you later thrive. Sometimes, as you will read in other chapters, failure and rejection help us find new passions, new opportunities, and new stories to explore. Other times, as it happened for Obama, failure and rejection help to birth resolve in our hearts, so we can eventually push open the doors before which we once found ourselves barred.

As you face closed doors and your own longing to belong, remember that this is temporary. This situation—this rejection, this failure—is not permanent. Keep moving forward, keep using your voice, keep making your art, dribbling your basketball, and turning your toes to help your body rise. Closed doors are not the end of your story, but rather, just one chapter of your journey.

★ The Flop Files: **Ta-Nehisi Coates** ★

Now a massively famous writer and intellectual whose work and words are cause for celebration and fierce debate, Ta-Nehisi Coates once used to wonder where his next meal was coming from.

In 2007, Coates was thirty-one years old, had never graduated from college even though he attended Howard University earlier in his life, and was trying to figure out a path forward for himself, his wife, and their son. He had wanted to be a writer—but putting food on the table as a writer wasn't easy. Additionally, he had lost all three of his most recent jobs. In short, nothing really seemed to be working out. Coates later wrote, bluntly, "This story began, as all writing must, in failure."[8] Instead of surging toward his hopes and dreams, Coates was collecting unemployment money from the government to help get by, and because of this, he took a government-sponsored seminar. He found himself sitting in a state office building in New York City, listening to people expound upon the need to work hard and take responsibility for yourself. He was trying to do just that! His wife had a job, and he hoped that he could soon find a way to make enough to not need the government checks. But nothing was working out.

However, a year later, in 2008, his first book, *The Beautiful Struggle*, was published.

A book deal!

Success! Exactly the thing Coates had been longing for!

But the publication did little to change things. Sales were low, and people didn't seem all that interested in or excited by the book. But Coates kept writing and continued to hope that his work would take off. When *The Beautiful Struggle* was rereleased in paperback, the tide slowly began to change. Readers took note, paid attention, and followed his work. It helped, too, that he began writing for the large, mainstream magazine the *Atlantic*. One of his most compelling and widely circulated articles for the magazine, "The Case for Reparations," explored his argument that America needs to make amends—in the form of money due—to descendants of those who were kidnapped, tortured, and enslaved throughout this country's history and making.[9]

The piece catapulted his words and his work and soon led to the publication of another book, *Between the World and Me*. Unlike his first book, which caused little stir or acknowledgment, his second sold out before it reached many bookstores! Orders flew in, and the books flew off the shelves.

Colleges began assigning it to incoming freshmen; readers and intellectuals began debating it; and soon it became part of—and started, in some cases—a national conversation about race and racism in America.

While walking the streets of New York in 2007, Coates felt a deep sense of fear, shame, and despair. These emotions did not last forever. Instead, out of failure, his story took a turn toward something that would shake a nation and stir up discussion, debate, and possibility.

But Coates wasn't content with only intellectuals and academics debating his work. Instead, he also accepted an invitation to become a writer for new issues of the Black Panther comic books series. He is also writing a screenplay, entitled *Wrong Answer*, to be directed by Ryan Coogler (read more about him in chapter 6!) and to star Michael B. Jordan.[10]

Coates may once have wandered in despair, but now he is creating and articulating with flair.

NOTES

1. Ashley Alman, "Barack Obama Was a Nobody at the 2000 Democratic National Convention," *Huffington Post*, December 26, 2016, https://www.huffpost.com/entry/barack-obama-2000-dnc_n_586143a3e4b0eb586486da83.
2. Alman, "Barack Obama Was a Nobody."
3. Caroline Kenny, "Obama's Other DNC Moment: His Credit Card Got Declined," CNN, December 27, 2016, https://www.cnn.com/2016/12/27/politics/president-obama-axe-files-credit-card-dnc/index.html.
4. Jeff Zeleny, "Once a Convention Outsider, Obama Navigated a Path to the Marquee," *New York Times*, August 26, 2008, https://www.nytimes.com/2008/08/27/us/politics/27obama.html.
5. Zeleny, "Once a Convention Outsider."
6. Kenny, "Obama's Other DNC Moment."
7. Zeleny, "Once a Convention Outsider."
8. Ta-Nehisi Coates, *We Were Eight Years in Power* (New York: One World Books/Random House, 2017), 5.
9. Jordan Michael Smith, "The Education of Ta-Nehisi Coates," *Chronicle of Higher Education*, October 2, 2017, https://www.chronicle.com/article/The-Education-of-Ta-Nehisi/241356.
10. Concepción de León, "Ta-Nehisi Coates and the Making of a Public Intellectual," *New York Times*, September 29, 2017, https://www.nytimes.com/2017/09/29/books/ta-nehisi-coates-we-were-eight-years-in-power.html.

2
KEHKASHAN BASU

As a young girl growing up in Dubai, Kehkashan Basu decided from a very young age that she wanted to use her life to help the environment. Knowing that the scope of the problem was large, she enlisted the aid of adults in her community and beyond who had always respected both her gender and her age. Others who had already achieved great things viewed her fondly and encouraged each step she took, whether she organized tree-planting missions or became the leader of her own environmental start-up. Male leaders, especially, were deeply glad to see such a young girl desire to be her own CEO of the organization she started; they encouraged Basu every step along the way!

*W*ellll . . . not exactly.

Kehkashan Basu *did* know from an incredibly early age that she wanted to make a difference in the world through environmental causes and progress. As she has told the story, her birth on June 5, 2002, was a significant factor in her knowing she was meant to change the world through her support of the environment. June 5 is World Environment Day, and by the time she was only eight years old, she had decided her mission.[1]

Basu began by planting one seed—a single seed—right outside her own busy apartment block in Dubai. Then, she decided to plant more seeds, and more seeds, and more seeds. She enlisted the aid of friends and classmates and started leading them on excursions to plant seeds wherever they could. They also cleaned up areas that had become overrun with pollution and waste. At first, her friends thought this might be boring work, but they soon came to see how important and thrilling it could be, as Basu led them on foot or, sometimes, in kayaks. Wherever she went, trees sprang up, contributing a powerful offset to the dangerous levels of carbon dioxide filling the ozone layer.[3]

HOLD THE BOLD!

In 1969, star outfielder Curt Flood became the first baseball player to argue for what would come to be known as free agency. An African American player, Flood endured a variety of trials throughout his time in Major League Baseball, and when his team wanted to trade him, Flood powerfully responded, "After 12 years in the major leagues I do not feel that I am a piece of property to be bought and sold irrespective of my wishes."[2]

Four years later, by the time she was twelve years old, what had begun as an informal tree-planting mission for Basu and her friends had bloomed into a massive enterprise, including her starting her own nonprofit organization, called Green Hope (greenhopefoundation .com). Green Hope's mission would bring Basu's commitment to a whole new level and spread her efforts worldwide. With over 15,000 members, and still under Basu's leadership, the organization continues to plant trees but also has expanded to include work with refugee populations, assisting children in poverty, and fighting for the rights and voices of girls and women. Such efforts grew out of Basu's own journey to fight for what she believed was both right and essential.[4]

When she started Green Hope, she heard criticisms against her because of her age and her gender. Basu was often asked why she wanted to lead an organization that had grown so large and become connected to areas all around the world. To many people, it made no sense for a young woman to lead such an organization, and they encouraged her to let a man lead instead. Leadership was "something for males," they told her.[5] This kind of attack was nothing new for Basu. Before she started Green Hope, even before she planted that first tree at age eight, Basu had wanted to be a pilot. People responded with incredulity, reprimanding her, saying that such a career goal was, again, something for males, not females.

Leadership was "something for males," they told her.

But instead of relinquishing control of her organization or heeding such attacks on her ability because of her gender, Basu fought harder and spread her message, her work, and her mission even further.

By the time she was sixteen years old, in 2018, she had won the International Children's Peace Prize for her work aiding the environment, refugees, children, and girls and women. Later that same year, she was one of the featured speakers at the One Young World Summit in The Hague, Netherlands. Instead of listening to her critics, she turned their attacks into fuel to forge forward.[6]

If you've ever been told you cannot pursue something because of your gender or age, Basu is a powerful ally for you to consider. Just because certain roles in your community, town, city, state, or country may have been occupied by people of one gender or by people older than a certain age, that doesn't mean it will inevitably remain that way. Before Basu led her own huge nonprofit, she didn't have an example of a young woman doing the same. That didn't mean it was impossible; that meant it hadn't been done before in a way that she could replicate. Just because you do not know someone who identifies as your specific gender doing what you envision yourself loving doesn't mean it can't (or won't!) happen.

PLUCK ENOUGH!

The Nobel Prize in Medicine is a pretty big deal. Actually, it's the biggest deal within medical research and practice. When Dr. Harold Varmus won it in 1989, it was especially powerful because Harvard Medical School had rejected Varmus from admission not once but twice. The second time, the dean of the medical school told Varmus he was "inconstant and immature."

It may just mean you need to fight to be the first.

The journey to walk against the words of others who seem to know better, appear wiser, or claim the mantle of expertise is difficult, to be sure. It never feels good to be told you're doing something wrong or that you're messing up the way things should be. But by following your passion to make the world better, you become part of the world's unfolding story of people who resist suffocating boxes to create more opportunities for *all* of us.

That's what Basu has done and what she continues to try to do.

Adults tended to be cynical, even dismissive. However, children were the opposite.

—Kehkashan Basu

If you've ever shared a big vision, idea, or hope with someone older, and heard a response that included something like "That's not really how the world works," you are in good company! As Basu led Green Hope to a variety of places and spaces, she often heard adults who disregarded or criticized her mission. She shared, "Adults tended to be cynical, even dismissive. However, children were the opposite."[7] Many adults had become used to understanding the environment a certain way and viewed any attempts to change the current trajectory with an air of defeat and impossibility. But instead of accepting this premise, Basu found that young people still believed in the potential to change the effects of carbon dioxide, the health conditions of the world's cities, the status of refugees, the

CRAVE THE BRAVE!

Ever wanted to make a team or get into a special program, only to have the powers that be tell you no? You are in good company. Among those who have heard a resounding *no* from their first-choice colleges are United States presidents Barack Obama and Harry Truman and actors Tom Hanks and Tina Fey. They got into other schools . . . and ended up doing pretty well anyway.

poverty rate among children, and the way girls and women are viewed in countries all over the world.

None of these things, for Basu, are static. None of them are immovable or unchangeable. Instead of lamenting the state of what is, Basu constantly fights to develop what *could* be, even if that fight appears, on its face, to be simple or insignificant: She plants a tree. She helps a refugee child among the Rohingya. She hands out a solar lamp.[8] She talks to another teen, sharing how they can join the effort. In this way, fear turns into hope and paralysis turns into action. Basu explained, "You actually need to go out into the field and do something physically. Even if you can't physically do it, work with someone who [can]."[9] Basu believes that if you want to change the world, you have to remain close to the seed, and you have to continually get your hands dirty, digging that hole and planting it. Never lose sight of the need to stay actively involved with what you long to change.

You actually need to go out into the field and do something physically. Even if you can't physically do it, work with someone who [can].

—Kehkashan Basu

Older people may try to diminish your vision or your idea because they simply haven't seen it before or because they don't think you have enough expertise or information. But here's a powerful truth: no one does—not even the adults! There is always more to learn, and people who call themselves experts still have a lot of learning to do. (In fact, sometimes the people who think of themselves as the very *best* experts have the *most* learning to do because their heads can get so full of what they know that there is little room to be proven wrong, to perceive a new way, or to entertain a new idea).

Your work in this world is crucial. If you're young, then we desperately need *your* ideas, *your* experiences, *your* view, because you might bring a new way of understanding or doing something that we have never before considered. You might find a way through the problem, a breakthrough that can help *all* of us. Your age is no detractor from your ability; instead, it enhances what you might do in this world, as Basu has proven, and continues to prove, with her work and voice.

NOTES

1. Helen Nianias, "Dubai's Teen Eco-Warrior: 'It Was Preordained that I'd Take Care of Mother Earth,'" *Guardian*, December 15, 2016, https://www.theguardian.com/global-development-professionals-network/2016/dec/15/teen-eco-warrior-activist-dubai-climate-change.
2. William C. Rhoden, "Like Jackie Robinson, Baseball Should Honor Curt Flood's Sacrifice," The Undefeated, April 15, 2019, https://theundefeated.com/features/like-jackie-robinson-baseball-should-honor-curt-flood-sacrifice.
3. Nianias, "Dubai's Teen Eco-Warrior."
4. Green Hope Foundation, https://greenhopefoundation.com.
5 Nianias, "Dubai's Teen Eco-Warrior."
6. Tahmeed Shafiq, "'Think Global, Act Local': U of T Students Kehkashan Basu, Quinn Underwood Discuss Grassroots Activism, Launching Startups," *Varsity*, January 14, 2019, https://thevarsity.ca/2019/01/14/think-global-act-local/.
7. Kehkashan Basu, "Why Youth Are Key to Sustainable Development," filmed February 9, 2019, TEDxDonMills, 5:05, posted April 9, 2019, https://www.youtube.com/watch?v=bKxckiMIP0Q.
8. Sarwat Nasir, "Dubai-Based Students Spend Winter Break at Rohingya Camp," *Kaleej Times*, January 8, 2019, https://www.khaleejtimes.com/nation/dubai/dubai-based-students-spend-winter-break-at-rohingya-camp.
9. Shafiq, "Think Global."

3
ALAN NAIMAN

Dressing in shoes so spiffy and shiny you could see the whole world reflecting in them, Alan Naiman was a guy who knew the definition of success. Getting his start as a banker, Naiman invested his money wisely so that it grew, and grew, and grew, and . . . you get the point. This guy had a *lot* of money. And even though he was rich, he still did his part to help others, working as a social worker as well. He always made sure to dress to impress, including with Rolex watches, and he drove a high-class Porsche 718 Boxster, which cost $60,000—mere change in the deep pockets of Naiman. He worked hard, at some points in his life taking on three jobs at a time! Naiman was a man who knew what success meant and knew how to show others that he had, indeed, made it.

In fact . . . no!

While Alan Naiman did get his start as a banker, and he did also transition to a career as a social worker, he lived nothing like that first paragraph represents. Actually, quite the opposite. Friends of his even commented that rather than buy a pair of new shoes when his old ones got holey and wore out, Naiman preferred to repair them with duct tape and keep using them.[1]

Duct tape.

Duct tape!

Imagine looking down at your feet and seeing holes pulling open in your shoes. If you can afford new ones, is your first thought, *I wonder if anyone at school has some duct tape I can borrow to tape these up because I don't want new ones?* That, in a symbol, was Alan Naiman.

While he did start off his career as a successful banker, after a few years, he transitioned to become a social worker in the state of Washington. His job included finding homes for children whose parents were unable to care for them. He worked hard and often put in overtime to make sure every kid had a safe place to live.[2]

People who knew Naiman considered him a quiet, kind soul who did his job diligently and with the belief that it mattered. Kids loved and appreciated him, and the adults he contacted to help take

SWERVE WITH NERVE!

Rodney Stotts is an inspiring licensed falconer, but his path to get there was both long and arduous. Growing up surrounded by gangs and drugs, Stotts said he made a lot of mistakes and was often confused about his direction. When an owl named Mr. Hoots landed on his arm during his work with Earth Conservation Corps, things changed. Stotts now conducts training and educational programs and inspires a new generation of earth-friendly, falcon-loving people.

care of the kids in his case files viewed him as sensitive, thoughtful, and hardworking.

One friend joked that Naiman was also incredibly frugal, never wanting to spend more money than he absolutely had to. Once, Naiman even boasted that he had gone an entire day—and had a lot of fun—without spending a single dime. Finding free ways to enjoy his life, Naiman appeared, to everyone's eyes, to be a humble man just doing his best to get by and make as much of a difference as he could.[3]

Not exactly a ringing endorsement of what modern culture tells us about success, right? Do you ever see commercials or hear epic pop, rock, or hip-hop songs that have any version of the following message:

FAIL...THEN PREVAIL!

Astronaut Neil Armstrong's first mission with NASA, the Gemini VIII, had to abruptly stop and return to Earth because of complications. Armstrong and fellow astronaut David Scott had made it to Earth's orbit, but after a brief eleven hours, they found themselves crashing into the Pacific Ocean in need of rescue. Three years later, on July 20, Armstrong would become the first person to step onto the surface of the moon.

Money? No, thanks, no way!
Fame? Be gone yesterday and today!
I just want to do a little job,
Eat some corn on the cob,
Duct tape on my shoes,
Listen to some blues.
Don't want to be rich
(No No No)

Don't want to be famous
(Whoa whoa whoa)
Just want to be humble,
Just want to bumble.
Twitter followers?
NO, THANKS.
Bank account?
NO, THANKS.
Suave clothes?
NO, THANKS.
Reputation?
NO, THANKS!

You get the picture. (Did you make up your own rhythm and jingle as you read those mind-shattering lyrics? I sure did.)

Our society celebrates money, fame, style, reputation, appearance, and social media numbers and equates all of these with success. Don't have some of those? You can still work harder to get them. And you better get working, fast! Quick, post loads of stuff on social media and try to get everyone to follow and share! Don't have *any* of these things? Then you might be viewed as a failure, our culture roars.

But Naiman debunked this whole concept of what it means to succeed. Instead of pointing to a massive social media following,

FROM WEAK TO PEAK!

Struggling with a writing assignment you've got to do? Hang in there. Critically acclaimed author Ali Benjamin has said that when she was writing her bestselling novel *The Thing about Jellyfish*, she was there too: "I was so frustrated with my own ability to get it right, I literally walked around holding a pencil between my teeth in order to stay positive."[4]

an insanely expensive sports car, a mansion, his own reality television show, or anything else like that, he quietly helped kids find homes.

Naiman quietly treated other people with dignity.

Naiman noticed his shoes were breaking, quietly grabbed a roll of duct tape, and then bent down to fix them.

Naiman noticed his shoes were breaking, quietly grabbed a roll of duct tape, and then bent down to fix them.

And when he died, early in 2019, Naiman quietly left approximately $11 million to a variety of charities that work to care for kids in need.[5]

ELEVEN MILLION DOLLARS.

The only time he revealed how wealthy he was—just how big his bank account really had gotten—was after his death.

No one could thank him.

No one could do a story that he would hear and see for himself on the news.

He couldn't do a big social media post and reveal to the world how awesome and cool and famous he should be for his actions, thereby ensuring loads of social media followers and shares and reshares, and reshares of those reshares, and reshares of those reshares of those reshares, and . . . you get the point.

One of the organizations that received some of this massive gift was the Pediatric Interim Care Center (PICC). Devoted to caring for babies who are born with drug addictions due to the mother's use, the PICC helps the babies break the addiction and tries to restore their health. Founded by Barbara Drennan, this group receives about two hundred babies a year from hospitals and slowly nurses them back to health. The PICC had a big mortgage on their building and a need for some new wheels to help get the babies from the hospital to the interim care site. But after Naiman's gift, those needs were filled. Drennan, after learning of the gift, said, "We would never dream that something like this would happen to us. I wish very much that I could have met him. I would have loved to have had him see the babies he's protecting."[6]

We would never dream that something like this would happen to us. I wish very much that I could have met him. I would have loved to have had him see the babies he's protecting.

—Barbara Drennan

Naiman wasn't after the kind of success our culture so typically celebrates. He wasn't after fame and recognition. He wasn't angling to be seen making grand promises and gestures and stepping boldly to a microphone to lead the way.

Sometimes, genuine success and leadership are quiet.

In a world where noise and action and flurry and *turning up the mic* are often portrayed as the only way to be successful, Naiman showed an alternate route. Can you imagine what people might have thought as they watched a man wearing duct-taped shoes rush with a bunch of kids in tow, one place to the next?

What would *you* think?

Probably not: That's my idol right there! I want those shoes! I want that life!

There is nothing wrong with dreaming big, with embracing the microphone, and with sharing about your brave deeds or kind actions. There is nothing wrong with striving and working hard and dreaming of the big stage.

However, this is not the *only* form of success.

If you find that the stage and the spotlight don't make your heart beat fast, if you find that earning lots of money and amassing social media followers don't actually bring you much deep joy, then please hear this: *there is nothing wrong with you!*

Your version and your vision of success may look like failure to many in the world. But what's wildly popular can sometimes lead you away from who you truly are, rather than toward your authentic self.

Naiman may have looked to the world like a walking antonym of success, but the kids he helped to find homes for and the charities he sustained by the generous gifts after his death know differently. They know better.

Naiman may have fallen, according to many of the world's standards. But by the standards of his own heart, he was wildly, brilliantly successful.

How might *you* be wildly, brilliantly successful according to your heart's standards, rather than the world's?

★ The Flop Files: **Virginia Apgar** ★

When a new baby comes into the world in any hospital in America, one of the first things that happens is that the baby is assessed to see how they are doing. Within one minute of life, the baby is ranked and rated based on something called the APGAR score, created in 1949. As a dad of three—soon to be four—I can tell you firsthand how crucial this score is to knowing how safe and healthy the baby is! The word *APGAR* is an acronym for the five characteristics of the baby that the score measures: appearance, pulse, grimace, activity, and respiration.[7]

But the word *APGAR* also names a person, and an amazing one at that.

Virginia Apgar went to Mount Holyoke College. To pay for her classes, she worked a variety of jobs, including as a waitress and a stray-cat catcher! When she left Mount Holyoke in 1929, she went to medical school at Columbia University, graduating with her degree in 1933. Out of the class of ninety people, there were only nine women, and she was one of them.[8]

Apgar wanted to become a surgeon, but her mentor at Columbia rejected her pursuits. He explained, as Apgar recounted, "Even women won't go to a woman surgeon."[9] Apgar refused to cease her medical career because of this rejection. Instead, she became interested in anesthesiology. At the time, it was seen as a lesser-than pursuit in the medical field, and Apgar worked hard to change that perspective. With her help, its status eventually elevated so that anesthesiology became its own area of study.

This huge growth for the field—and her own initiative and involvement in this change—would seem to guarantee her position as a leader in anesthesiology, right?

Not so much.

Columbia University, from which she had graduated with a medical degree, didn't hire her to lead the burgeoning field. As Apgar's friend, Melinda Beck, claimed, "She was passed over for a man to head the new department at Columbia."[10] This second rejection *still* didn't slow down Apgar, though.

Instead, she became a professor at Columbia's medical school and continued her own studies alongside her teaching. Then, a groundbreaking moment occurred in a seemingly quite normal way: She was eating lunch in the school cafeteria when a student inquired about what should be done to figure out if a newborn baby was healthy and doing okay or not. Apgar began writing down, off the cuff, some notes of what a doctor should look for.

One thousand babies and two years later, these notes became the APGAR score criteria. By 1952, the score was becoming more and more legitimized and was used in ever-widening circles.

The brilliant woman who had been rejected from becoming a surgeon and been rejected from leading a department of anesthesiology had instead revolutionized the way medical staff evaluated and responded to newborn babies. And in a truly ironic twist, while her name was rejected from academic posts and job positions, it also became one of the most common words used by medical staff around the country The APGAR score is ever-present, even though the doctor with that name wasn't always recognized or accepted by those around her.

NOTES

1. Sasha Ingber, "Social Worker Led Frugal Life to Leave Nearly $11 Million to Children's Charities," NPR, December 29, 2018, https://www.npr.org/2018/12/29/680883772/social-worker-led-frugal-life-to-donate-nearly-11-million-to-childrens-charities.

2. Sally Ho, "An Intensely Private Social Worker Who Duct-Taped His Shoes Left a Surprise $11M to Kids," USA Today, December 28, 2019, https://www.usatoday.com/story/news/nation/2018/12/28/social-worker-left-surprise-11-m-childrens-charities/38807249/.

3. David Williams, "A Frugal Social Worker Left $11 Million to Children's Charities in His Will," CNN Heroes, December 29, 2018, https://www.cnn.com/2018/12/28/us/frugal-social-worker-leaves-millions-to-charity-trnd/index.html.

4. Ali Benjamin, "FAQ," official author website, accessed October 29, 2019, http://alibenjamin.com/site/faq/.

5. Ingber, "Social Worker Led Frugal Life."
6. Ho, "An Intensely Private Social Worker."
7. Fiza Pirani, "Who Was Virginia Apgar? Google Honors Trailblazing Doctor Who Saved Millions of Babies," *Atlanta Journal-Constitution*, June 7, 2018, https://www.ajc.com /news/national/who-was-virginia-apgar-google-honors-trailblazing-doctor-who-saved -millions-babies/lGLeu37G1oUcZoUZTb4VVN/.
8. Pirani, "Who Was Virginia Apgar?"
9. Melinda Beck, "How's Your Baby? Recalling the Apgar Score's Namesake," *Wall Street Journal*, May 26, 2009, https://www.wsj.com/articles/SB124328572691452021.
10. Beck, "How's Your Baby?"

4

NICK FOLES

In February of 2018, quarterback Nick Foles became the MVP (that's *Most Valuable Player* in sports speak) of Super Bowl LII (that's *fifty-two* in Roman-numeral speak) when his team, the Philadelphia Eagles, beat the New England Patriots in a riveting come-from-behind victory. But this moment—this sweet, thrilling, satisfying moment—was a given. Everyone knew it was coming. Foles had been the number one draft pick for the Eagles five years earlier. He had led the team to winning seasons year after year. Foles was a person who did not doubt. He did not fear. He had played season after season with the utmost confidence and dedication, always mentally visualizing the moment when he'd be crowned MVP in the Super Bowl.

Wrong!

Rather than a steady, successful, confident climb toward the 2018 Super Bowl victory, Nick Foles endured heartbreaking seasons, confusion, doubt, and indecision. He was, in fact, drafted in 2012 by the Philadelphia Eagles. He had played a promising college career in Arizona and was selected as the eighty-eighth pick in the 2012 NFL (National Football League) draft. There were seven quarterbacks selected prior to Foles, so even at the inception of his professional football journey, he was never the top choice. His initial role for the Eagles, in fact, was to be the backup quarterback for their starter, Michael Vick.[1]

Though Foles played fairly well when he stepped in for Vick, he never became a star. Foles never leaped off the screen or the stats page. Then, in 2014, Foles broke his collarbone. During his healing and recuperation, Foles got a call from Eagles coach Chip Kelly letting him know that he would no longer don the Eagles jersey: he was being traded to the St. Louis Rams.[2]

So, in two years of professional football, Foles had collected a status as a backup quarterback, a broken collarbone, and a trade.

However.

However!

NOT DIMINISHED... FINISHED!

John Thompson took on the role of head coach of the Georgetown University Hoyas in 1972. The previous year, the men's basketball team had won only three games and lost a staggering twenty-three. Thompson began his new job by telling the squad that the program would win an NCAA championship. They did. Thompson is now in the Basketball Hall of Fame for his epic career.

With the Rams, Foles would have a shot to lead an NFL team and prove that he could be a star player. He had worked hard to get there, to recuperate, and he was now ready to show the Rams, the league, and viewers what he could do.

Or not.

After half of the season, the Rams decided to bench Foles, relegating him, again, to status as a backup quarterback. His teammate, Case Keenum, would take over the Rams as the main quarterback. Foles watched the rest of the season flash before his eyes, feeling the bench beneath his bum rather than the field beneath his feet.[3]

And when the season ended in 2015, Foles came face-to-face with a tough question: Should he just leave football?

He'd had a chance to lead an NFL team, and he felt as though the opportunity had been squandered. Maybe it was time to leave the game and find something else to do.

For a week, Foles seriously contemplated quitting. He felt exhausted. He felt drained. And he wondered if perhaps it was time for a new direction. Often, failure and struggle can lead us to new paths. And sometimes, it is important to quit something—to walk away from something and use struggle and failure to fuel a new pursuit.

Sometimes, failure and struggle help us dig deeper into the exact journey we're on. Other times, they help to reveal a new opportunity or path. For Foles, he took a week, went camping with his brother-in-law, talked and processed with his wife, and eventually decided

HAVE GRIT—DON'T SPLIT!

Priyanka Chopra recalls being fired from movies and being intensely criticized by directors when she was starting her acting career in Bollywood as an eighteen-year-old. However, she said, "I taught myself confidence. I learned it's what you do after failure that makes you a success."[4]

to stay in the NFL. "It wasn't an easy decision . . . It wasn't like it was 100%," Foles said.[5] This is crucial for us to contemplate: *it's not usually 100 percent.* Very few times, when we're battling struggles, failure, and rejection, do we feel a 100 percent sense of direction.

It wasn't an easy decision . . . It's not like it was 100%.

—Nick Foles

It's *normal* to struggle with our decisions about struggle!

It's *normal* to question which direction we need to go.

It's *normal* to decide and then to not necessarily feel a complete, 100 percent certainty about it. Why are all of these emotions and struggles normal? Because we're human. We are not preprogrammed computers or machines. It's okay to wonder, to question, to explore, to figure it out as we go.

And that's exactly what Foles did. He came back for the 2016 season with the Kansas City Chiefs, and his ultimate goal was a remarkably simple one: have fun. The injuries and the rejections Foles had endured throughout his career had taken their toll, and now that he was coming back to play again, he wanted to find the fun of the game again. He wanted to remember that playing a sport was first and foremost a prospect to be enjoyed, not endured. Foles said

HOLD THE BOLD!

Though not the biggest player on his youth football team, ten-year-old Lane Bridges certainly knows how to give an inspiring pregame talk! One of his team speeches has gone viral, with over 3 million views, and his mom said that "all Lane wants is for everybody to believe in themselves."[6]

of that time in his life, "When I decided to play, the ultimate goal was to find the joy of football again. It wasn't to win a starting job. I simply wanted to have joy again when I played the game of football."[7]

When I decided to play, the ultimate goal was to find the joy of football again. It wasn't to win a starting job. I simply wanted to have joy again when I played the game of football.

—Nick Foles

With this new paradigm in mind, Foles didn't necessarily have a breakout season with the Chiefs. He didn't even play all that much. However, what *did* happen was Foles found the love of playing again. He remembered why he had started playing in the first place, and as that joy returned, so did his drive and his confidence.[8]

Both of these attributes would be hugely important the next season, when Foles would be traded back to the Philadelphia Eagles, take over for star quarterback Carson Wentz at the end of the season, and proceed to do something that stunned football fans everywhere. Foles marched his Eagles through a postseason schedule that included record-breaking passer ratings, and then Foles met up with another quarterback, named Tom Brady, and the Patriots in the Super Bowl in 2018. Most fans and sportswriters conjectured the Patriots would cruise to victory.

However, Foles had been preparing for this moment, without even knowing it, for many years. All those years riding the bench, recuperating from injuries, and soul-searching about his next steps seemed to come together and provide a resounding answer on the field for Super Bowl LII. Foles would lead his team to a 41–33 victory, throw 373 yards, catch a touchdown pass (as a quarterback!), and be named MVP of the game.[9]

When we deeply love something, rather than working harder or digging deeper, sometimes what matters most is reconnecting to why we love it. What about its pursuit helps us hope or enables us to feel fully alive? For Foles, his amazing comeback story is catalyzed not by a determination to work harder but rather by his commitment to find joy again. How can joy journey with you as you pursue your own path forward?

★ The Flop Files: **Fireworks** ★

Historians aren't certain about the specific time and location fireworks were invented, although many trace the invention of the widely used explosives back to 200 BC in China, when a cook mistakenly dropped a bit of saltpeter into an open fire. He was simply trying to cook, but what happened mesmerized him: colorful, unnatural flames emerged.[10]

People began using the concoction to make colorful flames to celebrate events, until bamboo was added to the mix. As bamboo burned, it became especially volatile and eventually produced a loud sound. Some in China believed the loud sounds would keep away potentially dangerous spirits and therefore provide safety to those who burned the bamboo.[11]

Bamboo became a way to house some of these volatile ingredients, so the concoction would not only produce mesmerizing colors but also yield a loud noise at the same time. The combination of these two effects seemed startlingly impossible and had a certain element of otherworldliness to it.[12]

In the tenth century AD, a Chinese monk named Li Tian living in the Hunan province (where massive amounts of fireworks are still produced today!) became the first person to wrap paper around explosive ingredients, including sulfur, potassium nitrate, and charcoal. When heated, the tightly wrapped mixture yielded dramatic and colorful results, as well as a loud burst or bang.[13]

Fireworks were born!

Li Tian is still celebrated in China every April 18, and his invention has traveled far and wide. Each year in America alone, approximately $1 billion is spent on fireworks, equaling about 268 million pounds of fireworks used.[14]

What has become a worldwide way to mark significant or celebratory occasions was created by mistake, only over centuries eventually narrowing more and more into its current usage.

NOTES

1. John Seabrook, "Why Philly Loves the Eagles' Big Nick Foles, the N.F.L.'s Best Backup," *New Yorker*, January 11, 2019, https://www.newyorker.com/culture/personal-history/why-philly-loves-the-eagles-big-nick-foles-the-nfls-best-backup.
2. Seabrook, "Why Philly Loves."
3. Seabrook, "Why Philly Loves."
4. Aravind Peesapati, "Directors Used to Yell at Me and Throw Me Out in the Early Days: Priyanka Chopra," Xappie, September 9, 2019, https://www.xappie.com/entertainment-view/directors-used-to-yell-at-me-and-throw-me-out-in-the-early-days-priyanka-chopra-23784.
5. Kimberley Martin, "A Wing and a Prayer: Nick Foles Turned to Higher Power Before Returning to Eagles," *The Washington Post*, January 17, 2018, https://www.washingtonpost.com/sports/a-wing-and-a-prayer-nick-foles-turned-to-higher-power-before-returning-to-eagles/2018/01/17/31d284d6-fbc5-11e7-a46b-a3614530bd87_story.html.

6. Rachel Paula Abrahamson, "5th Grade Football Player Goes Viral with Pre-Game Pep Talk," *Today*, October 10, 2019, https://www.today.com/parents/10-year-old-lane -bridges-goes-viral-football-pep-talk-t164397.

7. Adam Teicher, "Nick Foles Lost His Love for Football; the Chiefs Helped Him Find It," ESPN, September 5, 2019, https://www.espn.com/blog/kansas-city-chiefs/post /_/id/26630/nick-foles-lost-his-love-for-football-the-chiefs-helped-him-find-it.

8. Mark Abadi, "The Eagles Quarterback Who Defeated Tom Brady to Become Super Bowl MVP Nearly Retired 3 Years Ago—and His Career Path Is One of the Wildest in Recent Memory," Business Insider, February 5, 2018, https://www.businessinsider.com /nick-foles-career-super-bowl-2018-1.

9. Abadi, "The Eagles Quarterback Who Defeated Tom Brady."

10. Anne Marie Helmenstein, "History of the Invention of Fireworks," ThoughtCo., September 1, 2019, https://www.thoughtco.com/invention-of-fireworks-607752.

11. Susanah Cahalan, "How Fireworks Exploded into History—and Became an American Symbol," *New York Post*, July 2, 2017, https://nypost.com/2017/07/02/how-fireworks -exploded-into-history-and-became-an-american-symbol/.

12. Jennie Cohen, "Fireworks' Vibrant History," History, last modified July 3, 2019, https:// www.history.com/news/fireworks-vibrant-history.

13. Simon Quellen Field, *Boom! The Chemistry and History of Explosives* (Chicago: Chicago Review Press, 2017).

14. Brittany Shoot, "Firework Facts: Americans Incinerate $1 Billion in July Fourth Fireworks Every Year," *Fortune*, July 29, 2018, https://fortune.com/2018/06/29/july-4th -fireworks-billion-dollar-burn-injuries/.

5
EMMA GONZALEZ

Making a huge speech on the steps of the Lincoln Memorial in Washington, DC, on the impact of gun violence, Emma Gonzalez had the unanimous support of an entire country. As she stood at that podium, she could recount all the ways Americans had come together to support her, encourage her, and believe her as she and others detailed the trauma of gun violence. Furthermore, all emotional impact and trauma had completely faded from her life, which was a huge relief. To change the world, she only had to say those words.

Wrong—100 percent.

Emma Gonzalez, a survivor of the horrific February 14, 2018, attacks at Marjory Stoneman Douglas High School in Parkland, Florida, has endured more than many of us can imagine. That day, Gonzalez heard the shouts of "Code Red!" over her school's intercom system and saw the confusion erupt, the panic spread through the students around her. She crouched between seats in the auditorium of her public school, holding the hands of her friend Lenore and another friend, refusing to check the news because it might cause her to panic.

Afterward, she saw the toll: seventeen of her fellow students had been shot and killed by a lone gunman in the school.[1]

Measures that might have protected the students at Stoneman Douglas—as well as at many other horrific shootings at schools across America—had been ignored by the United States government for years. Measures such as more extensive background checks to ensure that those who buy guns are mentally fit to use them? Not established by the US government. Bans against extreme assault-style rifles—the kind that are used by soldiers on the battlefield? Not established by the US government. Laws prohibiting the sale of guns to those who have been convicted of domestic violence? Not established by the US government.[2]

I do believe that an AK-47, a machine gun, is not a sporting weapon or needed for defense of a home.
—President Ronald Reagan

And so, Gonzalez crouched in that auditorium, knees against the cold, hard floor, as a student with an assault-style rifle murdered seventeen other students. Nothing had prevented the shooter from obtaining a gun. Nothing had been put in place to make such a decision difficult for the shooter.

But Gonzalez's story did not end there. Nor did the stories of Marjory Stoneman Douglas High School or of the many other students who have been traumatized by gun violence in places where their sole job was to learn. Gonzalez decided to make a courageous decision in the face of the American government's failure to protect its children.

Gonzalez decided to act.

Along with some of her classmates, Gonzalez founded the March for Our Lives movement, which included two main purposes: to spread awareness about the need for common-sense gun control and to plan a massive march to help bring the voices of young people together so that adults might be forced to listen to their plea for protection.

As Gonzalez began speaking out about these two drives, she was not unconditionally accepted. She was not even fully respected. After enduring the trauma of the Parkland massacre, she also had to then experience vicious attacks from commentators, media personalities, and many anonymous online social media users. Gonzalez, along with some of her classmates who also spoke out to try to raise awareness of gun violence protection efforts, was attacked and called a "child actor," implying she had been hired to act upset.[3]

PLUCK ENOUGH!

Quarterback Colin Kaepernick failed to gain any offers to play in the NFL in 2017, in 2018, and in 2019. This is despite Kaepernick having the sixth-best touchdowns-passes ratio *of all time*, as well as leading the charge for his previous team, the San Francisco 49ers, to reach the Super Bowl in 2013. Kaepernick took a knee during the national anthem to protest racism in America and was unafraid to speak out for what he believed, even though it cost him his job.

A survivor of America's seventieth mass shooting (that's right: the shooting at Stoneman Douglas was the seventieth mass, public shooting in America), Gonzalez then had to listen to people claiming that she didn't go through what she had just gone through. Over and over, commentators and social media users labeled her and her classmates child actors, asserting that the shooting was a hoax, or that the trauma these students endured was simply scripted and performed.

> ## CRAVE THE BRAVE!
>
> Karuna Riazi said that when she was a kid, there weren't any books with Muslim girls featured on their covers. Now, she has changed that. When her first novel, *The Gauntlet*, was published, Riazi recalled, "The first time I saw the cover I actually cried . . . There are going to be kids who look at the cover and feel that they see themselves."[4]

Additionally, others purposely mischaracterized Gonzalez's stance on guns in America. Many quickly used fearmongering to claim that she—and her classmates—were after something they had never said or supported: getting rid of all guns everywhere in the country. Instead of abolishing the second amendment of the US Constitution, Gonzalez is after creating safer and more reasonable laws—such as a ban on assault-style rifles, about which conservative President Ronald Reagan once said, "I do believe that an AK-47, a machine gun, is not a sporting weapon or needed for defense of a home."[5] Critics pounced instead of listening to the plea for logical protection of children—and adults—in America, twisting her words or simply inventing lies.

Gonzalez could have thrown up her hands in defeat, exhaustion, and exasperation with how she was treated. She could have chosen to speak no more, to step away from the microphone, and to stop trying to change a system that allows children to be murdered in their schools again, and again, and again.

But instead?

Gonzalez chose to do her best to ignore those who tried to bully her into silence. She asserted, "I haven't actually said anything to any of my critics."[6] She chose to ignore the lies and focus on being proactive—including helping to lead a massive effort to register young people to vote. She even has a T-shirt of an American flag that includes a QR code that can be scanned to then direct young people how to register to vote in only two minutes![7] Speaking out to raise awareness about the effects of gun violence, working to change unjust and dangerous laws, and helping to register young people to vote are a few of the major efforts Gonzalez is currently leading.

And she has no plans to back down. Instead, she wants people of all backgrounds to understand their own power. Even though critics will emerge to attack, bully, lie, and demean, Gonzalez encourages others to not stop moving forward because of those words. Instead, she has argued, "Women have the power to do anything men can do, just as black people have the power to do anything Hispanic people can do, and gay people have the power do anything that straight people can do, and trans people have the power to do anything that cis people can do. This country's government was made to work slowly, but if we elect the right people and keep moving as fast as we have been, we will change our world for the better."[9]

You and I may not have endured the kind of trauma Gonzalez has faced. We may not have the same microphone or the same audience

SWERVE WITH NERVE!

Antoine Hunter was ridiculed for being "different" as a kid, recalling, "I was betrayed and bullied just because I'm deaf." But he found the art of dancing, worked tirelessly at it, and learned to reject these hateful and false attacks from others. He started the Urban Jazz Dance Company and now has said, "I'm black, I'm deaf, and I'm proud."[8]

she has had, but we, too, have causes to work toward, efforts to make this world a better place. And like there is for anything that's worthwhile, there are critics and bullies ready to shout at you until you go back to being silent.

Women have the power to do anything men can do, just as black people have the power to do anything Hispanic people can do, and gay people have the power do anything that straight people can do, and trans people have the power to do anything that cis people can do.

—Emma Gonzalez

Maybe you notice something in your classroom or your school that seems unfair. Are there two sets of standards or rules—one that seems intended for one gender or another? Are there circles of gossip that target another student? Are there areas where those in power aren't listening to the people they are supposed to be leading or supporting?

Bullies—whether young or old—are always invested in your silence. They retain power by belittling others, so they can continue on unopposed. If you believe in something that has the potential to help others and yourself, be prepared to face off with your own fair share of bullies. You may be lied about online or called names or hear things about you that have no basis in any fact. This simply means that the bullies are scared of you. Your voice, your actions, your power scares them. Instead of returning to silence, talk to others. Enlist more friends, family, or classmates to help you. It sometimes takes immense effort to convince people to see your point of view—both about the big stuff and the little stuff. Gonzalez has joked that she once had to give her parents a PowerPoint slideshow to prove why she should be able to wear her hair in a buzz cut![10]

To whom might you give your presentation—showing why it's okay to be you, why it's okay to speak what you know to be true, and why you need their support to do so? Gonzalez's parents, siblings, and classmates are some of her most ardent supporters, and they help sustain her on this long journey toward justice.

Against the bullies who would silence you, support is essential. Reach out, ask for help, and, taking the hands of the people beside you, march forward for what you believe in, knowing that the world does, indeed, need *your* voice to help it grow and change for the better.

★ The Flop Files: **The Fifty-Fourth Massachusetts Volunteer Infantry Regiment** ★

In Boston Commons, in the heart of Boston, Massachusetts, I stood before a large stone memorial to the Fifty-Fourth Massachusetts Regiment, and their colonel, Robert Gould Shaw. Etched in my own memory, as it is on the massive stone picture of the regiment, is part of the poem that appears there:

> *But the high soul burns on to light men's feet*
> *Where death for noble ends makes dying sweet.*

In the throes of America's civil war, from 1861 to 1865, North and South battled each other in the deadliest war ever fought by Americans. Escaped slave and prodigious speaker and leader Frederick Douglass, among others, argued at the time that the Union (representing the North) should include an African American regiment. It was unheard of, and there were many who rejected the idea immediately. However, with time and pressure, by 1863, the US government had agreed, and the Fifty-Fourth Massachusetts Volunteer Infantry Regiment was established.[11]

Shaw, who was an abolitionist, agreed to lead the regiment, and Douglass had two of his own sons join.

Naysayers believed the regiment would not be able to fight or would be ineffective on the battlefield. Even while these six hundred brave African American men were fighting to end the scourge of slavery in America, they endured racism even from the very side they were fighting for, the Union. Their military-issued uniforms and weapons—along with what little respect they were given—were all far more tattered than those of any other regiment in the war.

But they trained hard, and on July 18, 1863, the Fifty-Fourth led five thousand Union troops in battle at Fort Wagner in South Carolina. Confederate troops were holding the fort, and the Fifty-Fourth led a valiant charge toward the hill where Confederate soldiers waited. It was a death trap.[12]

Confederate soldiers fired indiscriminately. Colonel Shaw pulled his men together, but rather than retreat in the face of pervasive gunfire in a truly uphill battle, the men surged forward again, directly into the line of fire, without hesitation. Colonel Shaw roared out in the early morning to his men, "Forward, Fifty-Fourth!" and forward they went.[13]

By the end of the battle, the charge to take Wagner would fail. The Union would be forced to retreat. And the brave men of the Fifty-Fourth would lose almost half of their regiment. Of the six hundred men on the battlefield that day, 280 were killed, Colonel Shaw included.[14]

However, the valiant and seemingly fearless charge became a testimony to the spirit of these men, the first African American regiment in the war. Their example lifted the spirits of the Union army, and their bravery was without comparison.

Their failure ensured an eventual victory for the Union army and the ultimate end of the civil war. America would abolish slavery and work to become a better nation. While the men of the Fifty-Fourth endured racism and unfair treatment, they fought for victory on an even larger battlefield than Wagner: they fought for respect, equality, and freedom.

NOTES

1. Claudia Eller, "Emma Gonzalez Opens Up about How Her Life Has Changed since Parkland Tragedy," *Variety*, October 10, 2018, https://variety.com/2018/politics/features/emma-gonzalez-parkland-interview-1202972485/.
2. Maureen Groppe, Matt Wynn, and Jason Lalljee, "Poll: Americans Don't Expect Congress to Act on Gun Laws," *USA Today*, September 9, 2019, https://www.usatoday.com/story/news/politics/2019/09/09/gun-control-most-americans-dont-expect-congress-pass-new-laws/2151086001/.
3. Mari Uyehara, "The Sliming of David Hogg and Emma Gonzalez: How a Campaign to Discredit the Parkland Survivors Went from the Right-Wing Fringe to the Conservative Mainstream," *GQ*, March 30, 2018, https://www.gq.com/story/the-sliming-of-david-hogg-and-emma-gonzalez.
4. Beth Whitehouse, "Hofstra Student Hebah Uddin Writes YA Book with Muslim Hero," *Newsday*, March 27, 2017, https://www.newsday.com/lifestyle/family/hofstra-student-hebah-uddin-writes-ya-book-with-muslim-hero-1.13323182.
5. Uyehara, "The Sliming of David Hogg."
6. Eller, "Emma Gonzalez Opens Up."
7. Eller, "Emma Gonzalez Opens Up."
8. Darielle Britto, "Deaf American Dancer Finds His Rhythm in Silence," *Deccan Chronicle*, August 1, 2018, https://www.deccanchronicle.com/lifestyle/books-and-art/010818/deaf-american-dancer-antoine-hunter-finds-his-rhythm-in-silence.html.
9. Eller, "Emma Gonzalez Opens Up."
10. Eller, "Emma Gonzalez Opens Up."

11. "54th Massachusetts Regiment," National Park Service, accessed September 19, 2019, https://www.nps.gov/articles/54th-massachusetts-regiment.htm.
12. "54th Massachusetts Regiment."
13. "54th Massachusetts Regiment."
14. "54th Massachusetts Regiment."

6
RYAN COOGLER

Many years before he directed the record-breaking smash-hit superhero film *Black Panther*, Ryan Coogler knew he wanted to work in the movies. His parents have joked that, as a baby, he only ate food that matched the colors worn by his favorite superheroes. By the time he was four, he had already directed two movies, using friends from his school as the actors and producers. And by the time he reached the old age of ten? You got it: Coogler had already attended various conferences, seminars, workshops, and countless mentoring sessions with expert filmmakers and teachers. He would be ready! He would break Hollywood records! He would have clear, immediate direction in his life and stop at nothing to reach a preordained set of goals from the time he was very, very, young.

Yeah!

N*o!*

There are only two true statements in the previous paragraph. Can you guess what they are? Kudos to you if you got the first one: *Black Panther* was, in fact, a record-breaking movie. Released in February of 2018, it garnered the record for the highest-grossing opening for a February release, the highest-grossing opening for a single-character Marvel film, and the highest-grossing opening of a film directed by an African American person. Ryan Coogler accomplished something special and profound with *Black Panther*.[1]

Did you discern the other true statement? A caveat: it might be difficult to find because it is only half-true. Something significant did happen to Coogler when he was four years old—*but* it wasn't that he directed his first film using school friends. In fact, it was quite the opposite. Coogler started school early and as a four-year-old was often mixed in with students who were five and six years old. Partly due to this age difference, partly due to his size, Coogler shared, "I was doing fine academically, but I was having a tough time because I was smaller than the other kids . . . I didn't fit in."[2]

I was doing fine academically, but I was having a tough time because I was smaller than the other kids . . . I didn't fit in.

—Ryan Coogler

Coogler soon found a passion for football—a sport that allowed him to process some of his anger at not fitting in. By the time he started high school in the Bay Area of San Francisco, Coogler had playing professional football as his main goal. As a talented and hardworking player who also maintained high grades and found solid achievement both in and outside the classroom, Coogler thought that goal seemed entirely attainable.[3]

Recruited by a variety of colleges—including places like Harvard University—Coogler eventually chose to attend Saint Mary's College in Moraga, California, because it wasn't far from his family, with whom he was very close. As a freshman who played for the college's football team, Coogler struggled with how to keep up with everything. The football practices were relentless, and the labs and coursework for his major, chemistry, were just as relentless. It seemed that no matter how hard he tried, he couldn't keep up with everything.[4]

And then something entirely unexpected happened. Coogler was in a creative writing class that was a core requirement for the college when he happened to write a story about a deeply emotional time in his life with his dad, Ira. The professor, Rosemary Graham, herself an author of YA books, read the story and then asked Coogler to come into her office for a meeting. On the first day of class, Coogler had already decided that he wasn't going to like the professor because of the way she spoke about football players, and so he assumed she had asked him to her office for some negative response. Instead, the story had left an indelible impression on the

FAIL...THEN PREVAIL!

More than anything in the world, Maria Tallchief wanted to make it as a dancer. After struggling to break into the industry as a teen in California, she moved to New York, along with her family, where she auditioned for many ballet companies. Over and over again, she was rejected because she was Native American. Refusing to quit—or to change her last name, as some advised—she eventually became an internationally acclaimed ballerina and later started and led the Chicago City Ballet.

professor, and she challenged and encouraged Coogler to spend his life writing screenplays and making movies.[5]

That seed remained planted in Coogler's heart, even though it would still be a while before it grew and blossomed. When Saint Mary's shut down their football program, Coogler decided to transfer to Sacramento State, where he played football, changed his major to business, and started taking as many filmmaking and screenwriting classes as he could. His hunger to tell stories through film grew bigger and bigger, eventually leading him to apply to the graduate film school at the University of Southern California (USC). While there, Coogler learned all he could and directed short films, basing his work on true stories and the lives of people he saw throughout his own journey. During this time, he even lived out of his car for a semester to help make ends meet financially![6]

FROM WEAK TO PEAK!

Rhiannon Owens loved drawing superheroes, but an art teacher told her that there was no way she would ever be able to make a living doing that. She now draws superheroes for Marvel and DC (and makes a living).

Does this sound like the legacy of a soon-to-be Hollywood blockbuster director? Not what you imagined? How often have you convinced yourself that if you want to achieve something awesome, you need to have decided that from a very, very young age? How often have you allowed yourself to dream *beyond* an original goal you might have set for yourself? Sometimes, you might think you know *exactly* what you want to be or do. You may have already decided you want to be a groundbreaking fashion designer, or a highly skilled emergency room doctor, or a ready-to-rock firefighter, or an environmental activist, or a world-renowned painter. And all of these are amazing, beautiful goals. By all means, pursue them with passion and determination!

However.

However!

Sometimes the things you think you want to do with your life change. You may be surprised at a passion or hunger you find later. You may be surprised by an ability you have that you previously didn't even notice. You may have an opportunity to do or pursue something you never before imagined. This, too, is a beautiful thing. Because your journey may not always be a straight line. Sometimes, as in the case of Coogler, you may be pursuing one thing (or two things, or three things . . .) and find that deep inside you, there is something entirely different that you long to do.

Coogler decided to finally go all in on his new pursuit. He created his first full-length feature film, entitled *Fruitvale Station*. It stars Octavia Spencer and Michael B. Jordan and tells the true story of an unarmed black man named Oscar Grant who is killed by a white police officer. At the prestigious Sundance Film Festival, *Fruitvale Station* won both a Grand Jury prize and the Audience Award. [7]

After *Fruitvale Station*, Coogler harkened back to his childhood, when he and his dad would watch Rocky movies together. They were profoundly important for him, and he saw a spirit of determination, hard work, and hope in the films and the characters. But a question kept popping into Coogler's mind: What about the racial implications of the film series? Coogler began to think about Apollo Creed, the friend of Rocky Balboa, and epic character in his own right, who is killed in a boxing match. What if Apollo Creed's son was stuck inside a juvenile detention center, feeling angry and lost? Having himself worked in a juvenile detention center, and having grown up with a father who worked there as well, Coogler had a deep empathy for and understanding of kids who are stuck in the juvenile detention system, and the idea for the Rocky spinoff film, *Creed*, was born.[8]

Again working with actor Michael B. Jordan, Coogler went on to create an epic new film about the son of Apollo Creed, Adonis, whom we see first in a juvenile detention center. Serving time for fighting, the film implicates, we follow Adonis as he is later mentored by Rocky and learns to claim the power and the truth of his own name, his own creed. A wide success both financially and critically, this film served as a springboard for Coogler landing the job as director of the Marvel superhero film *Blank Panther*.[9]

Now, Coogler hopes that his success does not become an anomaly. Instead, he hopes that the movie industry truly breaks open—revealing opportunities for people from diverse experiences, cultures, and perspectives to finally have more opportunities to tell stories. To see the world through the lens of differ-

NOT DIMINISHED... FINISHED!

Kohei Horikoshi created the worldwide phenomenon My Hero Academia, a manga series exploring the journey of Izuku, a character with zero super-powers, even though most everyone else in the world has them. Since 2014, My Hero Academia had been published in a weekly newspaper and totals nineteen volumes of manga. However, Horikoshi still makes mistakes in his writing, and he went on Twitter to point out some spelling and content mistakes he made in a recent compilation. Fans love the series and love Horikoshi even more for naming and claiming the mistakes!

ent views is so crucial to both art and life. Rather than wondering if more feature films will be made by underrepresented populations, Coogler has shared, "What I hope, for this industry, is we're transitioning from it even being a question that movies made by people of color or minorities are a risk."[10]

What I hope, for this industry, is we're transitioning from it even being a question that movies made by people of color or minorities are a risk.

—Ryan Coogler

Coogler's journey as a director was not clear, nor was it straight. It included detours, struggles, some confusion, a searching for direction, and—eventually—a home. You are not alone if you pursue one thing and then change your mind. You are not alone if you're uncertain about whether the goals you now have will be the ones you'll hold on to five years from now. And that's okay. Sometimes, hard work and determination *need to* include tangents and opportunities to change course. Sometimes, you need to be surprised. And there can be just as much beauty and power in changing course as there can be in staying the course.

★ The Flop Files: **George Lucas** ★

While the epic Star Wars franchise of films now boasts endlessly enthusiastic countdowns for each new movie that releases, it wasn't always that way. In fact, before the release of the first Star Wars film, *A New Hope*, it looked to be the biggest flop cinema had ever seen.[11]

George Lucas, the writer-director of the film, was thirty-three years old in 1977, and he had spent two years bringing his vision to life. His cast consisted of entirely new actors who hadn't yet done big feature films. The special effects had been concocted in a massive warehouse using new and risky techniques, and the sounds of space and intergalactic fighting included combinations of all kinds of unique things: construction noises, alarms, bells, and more.[12]

While thousands of movie theaters existed in the United States in 1977, guess how many agreed to show the premiere of the original *Star Wars*?

Thirty-two.

That's right. That's less than 1 percent of the theaters that could have shown it. Consider the sheer insanity of that statistic. More than 99 percent of movie theaters that had an option to show *Star Wars* thought the movie was going to be such a flop that they passed. And it wasn't just their perspective, either. Even the studio that hired Lucas and produced the movie with him, Fox, was embarrassed by the film and thought it was going to be a huge dud.[13]

No one would like it, they thought. And so their goal was to have the movie play at a few theaters and then be over and done with, before critics and fans alike screamed at them in anger for making such a movie.

Well, fans and critics alike *did* scream, but not in anger. Lines to get into the thirty-two theaters that *did* play the movies stretched far and wide. Word spread fast, and before long, 1,750 theaters had picked up the movie. *Star Wars: A New Hope* would remain in theaters for about a year. Oh, and it would also go on to win six Academy Awards.

The man who at first seemed like he was going to become a disgraced filmmaker, and the movie that seemed like it was poised to plummet, ended up changing cinematic history and inspiring a massive and sprawling universe of his own.

NOTES

1. Eliana Dockterman, "Ryan Coogler: In a Year Marked by Division, the *Black Panther* Director Proved that a Movie Can Bring People Together," *Time*, https://time.com/person-of-the-year-2018-ryan-coogler-runner-up/.
2. Kelly L. Carter, "'Black Panther' Director Ryan Coogler Got Ready for His High-Intensity Life on the Gridiron," The Undefeated, January 29, 2018, https://theundefeated.com/features/black-panther-director-ryan-coogler-prep-college-football-star-sacramento-state/.
3. Scott Macaulay, "Ryan Coogler," 25 New Faces of 2012, *Filmmaker Magazine*, 2012, https://filmmakermagazine.com/people/ryan-coogler/.
4. Carter, "'Black Panther' Director Ryan Coogler."
5. Tony Hicks, "'Creed': Ryan Coogler's Bay Area Roots Play Big Role in 'Rocky' Film," *Mercury News* (San Jose, CA), November 23, 2015, https://www.mercurynews.com/2015/11/23/creed-ryan-cooglers-bay-area-roots-play-big-role-in-rocky-film/.
6. Courtney Connley, "How 'Black Panther' Director Ryan Coogler Went from Living in His Car to Becoming Marvel's Youngest Filmmaker," CNBC, February 23, 2018, https://www.cnbc.com/2018/02/23/ryan-coogler-became-marvels-youngest-filmmaker-with-black-panther.html.
7. Macaulay, "Ryan Coogler (25 New Faces of 2012)."
8. Dockterman, "Ryan Coogler: In a Year Marked by Division."
9. Connley, "How 'Black Panther' Director Ryan Coogler."
10. Dockerton, "Ryan Coogler: In a Year Marked by Division."
11. Brian Jay Jones, "Column: George Lucas Feared 'Star Wars' Was Flop," *Fredericksburg*, February 26, 2017, https://www.fredericksburg.com/opinion/columns/column-george-lucas-feared-star-wars-was-flop/article_4d0169be-ccbb-50ec-863a-309b24b3b960.html.
12. Jones, "Column: George Lucas."
13. Pamela McClintock, "'Star Wars' Flashback: When No Theater Wanted to Show the Movie in 1977," *Hollywood Reporter*, December 9, 2015, https://www.hollywoodreporter.com/heat-vision/star-wars-flashback-no-theater-wanted-show-movie-1977-846864.

7
BOYAN SLAT

With the ocean drastically bombarded by garbage and other debris on a daily basis—much of it dangerous plastic—a young Danish inventor named Boyan Slat decided that he would clean up the world's massive water supply lickety-split! He figured, correctly, that all you really needed was a big vacuum. Scratch that. Make it a *really* big vacuum. Wait, scratch that too, and make it a massive, gargantuan, really, really, *really* big vacuum. Good? Okay, great! After that groundbreaking idea, Slat simply got a few friends to build a big vacuum and bam: clean oceans for everyone! Hooray!

*N*o *way!*

Sometimes, even after you make headlines and the world (or your own small corner of it) has admired something you do, failure ensues.

Sometimes, in fact, failure takes root and reveals itself well after you've already proven yourself successful at something.

Ever have an experience where you've won a big game—played well, scored a lot of points, or collected a lot of blocks—only to play downright *awful* the next game?

Or maybe you won the spelling or geography bee for your school one year, only to lose in the first round the next year?

Or maybe one day you feel on top of the world: you've got a great group of friends with whom you sit, and it seems like nothing can break this incredible bond you all have with each other. But the next day, scandal and betrayal break out and—*bam*—what seemed untouchable the day before now makes you feel confused and angry.

Or (last one, promise!) maybe you get a math test or a big essay assignment back with a huge A+ circled at the top of your page, and you're feeling energized and confident. *You get it! You know the game, and you're onto how to ace this thing called schoolwork!* But then the next math test or essay comes back, and there's a big D on top, confusing you beyond belief because you feel like you did it the same way you did the previous assignment?

HAVE GRIT—DON'T SPLIT!

Robert Goddard is sometimes called the father of modern rocketry for his work in developing the science that allowed rockets to blast off. However, before his breakthroughs, many of his peers thought his ideas were ludicrous and impossible.

If you can relate to any of these, then you'll want to know the story of young inventor Boyan Slat. Noticing that the ocean was becoming more and more filled with plastic garbage—so much so that it created literally miles and miles of floating debris—Slat decided that he was going to use his passion as an engineer to do something about it.[1]

Knowing full well that the problem was old and he was young, he expected pushback from other experts. However, Slat forged ahead with his aim to rid the Pacific Ocean of this massive amount of plastic garbage. Critics said it couldn't be done. The trash was just too enormous.

HOLD THE BOLD!

Elizabeth Rona was a Jewish scientist working in the areas of chemistry and radioactivity. Even though she received death threats and frequent rejection of her ideas based on her gender and religion, Rona persisted, and her work spans sixty years of groundbreaking research.

How enormous?

Enormously enormous. Consider the state of Texas. It measures 268,597 square miles. That's *a lot* of miles. And right now, as I write these words (and as you read them, unless a wonderful and miraculous change has occurred), there is heap of plastic trash floating in the Pacific Ocean (between California and Hawaii) that is about double the size of Texas.[2]

So, a quick recap:

1. Texas is really, really big.
2. The trash heap of plastic floating in the Pacific Ocean is Texas times two.

Researchers have actually given this heap of garbage an official name. They call it the Great Pacific Garbage Patch. That's right.

Slat desired to do something about a situation that had been hopelessly getting worse and worse for the last sixty years. No other researcher could devise a solution. So, Slat created a nonprofit called the Ocean Cleanup and, with a team of researchers, eventually developed a solar-powered trash-collecting system that would be released near the Great Pacific Garbage Patch. Using the power of the sun, the system would bring trash into its two-thousand-foot-long tube system, where it would then retain it until it could be brought to shore and properly disposed of, thereby eventually cleaning all the estimated 1.8 *trillion* pieces of trash in the Pacific Ocean.[3]

Hooray!

Trash?

Be gone!

Garbage hurting the ocean animals and destroying the natural waters?

See you! Wouldn't want to *be* you!

Right?!

Yeah?!

I mean . . . *right?*

Um . . . *yeah?*

Well, the story isn't so simple. Even though Slat designed a state-of-the-art system that managed to win the respect of a slew of professional inventors and researchers, and even though he managed to get funding from crowdsourcing and a few wealthy individuals who shared his passion to clean up the ocean, there was just one slight problem.

The system didn't work. It hit a few obstacles, including allowing some of the debris it collected to reenter the ocean. How did Slat respond to this failure of function? He said, "I'm confident that, considering we created this problem, we should also be able to solve it."[4]

I'm confident that, considering we created this problem, we should also be able to solve it.

—Boyan Slat

Even before that early run, Slat's system encountered a problem. During its initial launch into the Pacific Ocean in 2018, it couldn't even try to gather some of the 1.8 trillion pieces of plastic garbage into its tubing—because the infamous Great Pacific Garbage Patch seemed to have a better idea than to wait around and be destroyed. It would escape!

The Great Pacific Garbage Patch has been floating at a faster rate than the system can move. There's an easy solution, right? Just speed up the system.[5]

Nope, because speeding up the system seems to impede its ability to function. It can't position itself exactly where it needs to be to use its energy properly and do its work efficiently. While Slat had enormous success designing the system, starting his own nonprofit, leading a brilliant and audacious fundraising drive to build the system, and winning the respect and support of researchers and experts, he struggles with the failure of the system's launch and has had to continue tweaking and changing the system to try to get it to function properly.[6]

Is Slat ready to call it quits and throw in the towel on his ambitious hope? Not at all. Not even close. Instead, he has said, "What we're trying to do has never been done before. So, of course we

PLUCK ENOUGH!

Patsy Sherman was hired to work as a scientist at the 3M company in 1952. To get to this point, she'd already had to prove her high school teachers wrong—she was going to go on to college, and she was not going to aim to be a housewife alone. And prove them wrong she did! Sherman ended up inventing Scotchguard, the first substance that could protect materials from stains. Yet the invention occurred by mistake, when an assistant in the lab with her dropped a beaker filled with a latex solution. When it splashed on her shoes, Sherman noted that the substance was impenetrable, and the new idea was born!

were expecting to still need to fix a few things before it becomes fully operational."[7] What a beautiful response to critics who might watch you fail! Imagine if you could memorize Slat's lines and repeat them anytime someone questioned or criticized you for trying something new, attempting to solve a difficult problem, or take on a big challenge. Imagine if you had Slat's lines ready to go for the barrage of criticism.

What we're trying to do has never been done before. So, of course we were expecting to still need to fix a few things before it becomes fully operational.

—Boyan Slat

Critic: Well, sure looks like that was a *massive* mistake on your part to design an airplane whose seats can rotate throughout the flight so that no one has to remain in the exact same section of the plane as when they boarded. Ready to quit?

You: What we're trying to do has never been done before. So, of course we were expecting to still need to fix a few things before it becomes fully operational.

Critic: Well, *definitely* looks like your idea of developing a new sport called Fuddlehumdinger is a nonstarter. No one even came to your big launch event! *Wipeout!*

You: What we're trying to do has never been done before. So, of course we were expecting to still need to fix a few things before it becomes fully operational.

Critic: You seriously thought it was possible to walk on Mars . . . and in *that* ship and in *that* suit? Seriously? I mean, the idea actually went through your head that *you* could do that? Now, have you learned any better? Ready to let that pipe dream go?

You: What we're trying to do has never been done before. So, of course we were expecting to still need to fix a few things before it becomes fully operational.

Critic: Thought *you* could get the principal and the school board to change the whole structure of the way the school day is run? You thought movement and fresh air were crucial enough to warrant two whole hours of the school day? *And* you thought standardized testing wasn't the best way to measure growth and skills? Now that your crazy idea has flopped, ready to go back to the way things have always been?

You: What we're trying to do has never been done before. So, of course we were expecting to still need to fix a few things before it becomes fully operational.

Okay, okay. You get the point.

Like Slat, sometimes you're going to have amazing ideas, and you're going to work really hard on them. And sometimes, you're going to achieve some truly awesome and beautiful things. But just because you've achieved some awesome and beautiful things doesn't mean that you'll never encounter failure, struggle, mistakes, or rejection again.

You will.

The key question is, like Slat, will you be able to respond that you simply need to fix a few things, and keep moving forward? If so, then there's no limit to the good you, too, might do.

NOTES

1. Francesca Paris, "Creator of Floating Garbage Collector Struggling to Capture Plastic in Pacific," NPR, December 18, 2018, https://www.npr.org/2018/12/18/677663325/creator-of-floating-garbage-collector-struggling-to-capture-plastic-in-pacific.
2. Paris, "Creator of Floating Garbage Collector."
3. Paris, "Creator of Floating Garbage Collector."
4. Aria Bendix, "A 25-Year-Old's Mission to Clean up the Great Pacific Garbage Patch Relies on a Giant Plastic-Cleaning Device. Here's How It Works," Business Insider, September 13, 2019, https://www.businessinsider.com/how-boyan-slats-ocean-cleanup-device-works-2019-9.
5. Paris, "Creator of Floating Garbage Collector."
6. Bendix, "A 25-Year-Old's Mission."
7. Paris, "Creator of Floating Garbage Collector."

8

THE REGGAE GIRLZ (THE JAMAICAN WOMEN'S NATIONAL SOCCER TEAM)

Consistently enjoying the deep support of its governing body, the Jamaican women's national soccer team has dominated news channels and broadcast stations. Enjoying some of the finest benefits professional sports has to offer, the team travels on a first-class private jet everywhere they go, even if the match would take a mere one hour by bus. Instead of driving that whole hour, the team hops on its private jet for a cool and comfortable nine-minute ride. Additionally, their uniforms are made of gold. Literally. The expensive nylon threads are dipped into fourteen-karat gold, so that each uniform demonstrates the intense commitment of this hardworking soccer team. Go, Reggae Girlz!

*U*m . . . *not quite.*

In 2014, Jamaica—a small country of 3 million people—decided that it no longer had the funds to support a national women's soccer team, which is called football there. The governing body for national sports in the country, the Jamaican Football Federation (JFF), argued that the women's team wasn't drawing enough fans or selling enough T-shirts to support itself. Plus, the JFF argued, the team had never qualified for a World Cup.[1] Therefore, did the team really need to continue on?

Facing annihilation—after having its funding reduced six years earlier, in 2008—the team rallied and raised its own funds to keep itself alive. Additionally, with the help of Cedella Marley, the daughter of epic singer Bob Marley, and a single she released, "Strike Hard," the team grew in its reach and recognition. While the women's team was cut off from national funding, Marley noted that the men's team continued to receive funding, even though they had not qualified for a World Cup since 1998. Said Marley, "For me everyone should have the right to go after their dreams and passions without gender being a factor."[2]

For me everyone should have the right to go after their dreams and passions without gender being a factor.

—Cedella Marley

This insistence provided the hope and determination the Reggae Girlz used to catapult them along a highly unlikely journey, culminating with the rare distinction of being one of only twenty-four teams worldwide to make it into the 2019 World Cup for women's soccer.

Besides a lack of funding, the journey of the Jamaican women's national soccer team was marked by setbacks, struggle, and uncertainty. Once Marley signed on to help raise both funds and awareness for the team, the battle was far from over. Not even the necessities of a national sports team could be taken for granted on this journey.

Think about uniforms. If you have ever played soccer—or baseball, basketball, volleyball, or any other sport—you might remember getting your T-shirt with your team logo on the front, and maybe even a number on the back if your town league splurged for such expenses. Even though I played decades ago, I remember the tingle of excitement when I was a kid and my coach would pass out the uniforms. I wasn't the best player (in any sport I played as a kid), but wow, did I *love* uniform day. It made me feel like I was a part of something—like I belonged to this group that was trying to get better and to play better and to work harder.

CRAVE THE BRAVE!

Gertrude Benham bravely sought endless adventures as she attempted to summit as many of the world's big mountains as she could. Having climbed over three hundred of them, she lived on little money and saw success as an act of simplicity. One of these mountains, in Alberta, Canada, Mount Fay, was named after a fiercely competitive climber named Charles Fay—even though Benham reached the peak of that mountain before he ever did!

Now, as a dad and a coach for my kids' teams, I see the same light in the eyes of players when it's uniform day:

"Can I have number twenty-one?!"

"Whoa—green! Yeah, that's my favorite color!"

"Look how big these shirts are—awesome!"

I still get tingles when I pass out the uniforms to players as young as five years old. It's still a way of saying, *You belong. You are a part of this team, and we need you and want you here.*

Now think of a *national* team and consider that the Reggae Girlz, a cast of highly talented, ambitious women, was not funded enough to be able to have team uniforms. However, facing steep challenges was no surprise to hardworking and resilient player Kadija Shaw. Shaw knew that her team faced battles simply to get *to* and *on* the playing field. She shared, "We've faced a lot of setbacks and adversities so that's nothing new to us."[3]

We've faced a lot of setbacks and adversities so that's nothing new to us.

—Forward Kadija Shaw

SWERVE WITH NERVE!

After a stunning professional soccer career, including earning a World Cup title and two Olympic medals, soccer player Abby Wambach tried sports commentating. In her initial broadcast, she said, she failed horribly. However, the experience led her to her activism, speaking, and writing about leadership and equality.

But the challenges didn't stop with funding struggles and a lack of uniforms. Another basic need of a sports team is a coach, right? Consider that the Reggae Girlz had such little funding that they could not afford to hire a full-time coach to lead their mission. Instead, Marley once again came to the aid of the team and persuaded Hue Menzies, who had previously coached in Orlando,

Florida, to take on the challenge of leading the team. The only problem was that there was not a salary for Menzies and his assistant coaching staff: Lorne Donaldson, Andrew Price, and Hubert Busby Jr. But instead of demanding money, Menzies saw something special in the opportunity, and took the job for free, on a volunteer basis.[4] It wasn't until 2019—when the team qualified for the World Cup—that Menzies and the coaching staff finally received full-time salaries.

In addition to team necessities such as a coach and uniforms, any national team also has to deal with costs related to travel and lodging for games in other countries and tournaments all around the world. For the Reggae Girlz, this, too, was a cost often passed on to team players, or eventually, covered by fundraising and the campaign led by Marley.[5]

No aspect of this team's journey to the 2019 World Cup was easy, nor was it ever a sure thing. Having their national funding slashed in 2008, being officially disbanded by the Jamaican governing body for the sport in 2014 . . . the Reggae Girlz have faced enormous odds. But the one consistent theme the team never lost was their determination to stay alive.

Sometimes, refusing to quit is the greatest form of victory. You may not be able to ensure that circumstances around you are fair. You may not be able to ensure that you are treated with complete respect. You may directly *witness* others being treated better than you, and that may frustrate you to no end. Sometimes, the powerful may make you feel as though you are powerless. But the Reggae Girlz embody a profound truth: others can manipulate the circumstances to try to make you give up, but they cannot fully force you to give up. When you choose to stand back up again, and again, and again for something about which you are passionate, the governing bodies of your school or your town or your sport or your club or your country will eventually be forced to face you.

And if you have used the setbacks to grow stronger, more determined, and more passionate than you ever were before, when challenges do arrive, you will see that there is power in refusing to quit. The Reggae Girlz honed this power, drew people to their mission, and eventually made the world see them and their story in 2019 when they qualified for the Women's World Cup.

The world needs your story too. So, if you're facing enormous setbacks about something for which you have a deep and abiding passion, don't stop. Ask for support, draw other people to your cause, and keep standing until others, eventually, see the power that is unmistakably yours.

FAIL...THEN PREVAIL!

Billie Jean King is the acclaimed tennis star who beat Bobby Riggs in the epic tennis match that came to be called the Battle of the Sexes on September 20, 1973. While she lost her share of matches over the years, she powerfully claimed, "For me, losing a tennis match isn't failure, it's research."[6]

The Flop Files: **The United States Women's National Soccer Team**

On July 7, 2019, the US Women's National Soccer Team made history for winning their fourth World Cup.

That's right: *fourth.*

In the final match, they faced the Netherlands, and won by a score of 2–0. Throughout the tournament, Megan Rapinoe led the women with an incredible array of offense and a fighting spirit that seemed never to wane. The entire team surged time and time again, refusing to play lightly even in matches where they had strong leads—such as when they beat Thailand 13–0 in the opening round of the World Cup tournament. For this fighting spirit and refusal to do any less than their very best, they were often critiqued as rude or bragging. Writer Mariah Burton Nelson has claimed that the criticism of the women's team for playing at their highest level, no matter what, is founded on a fear of successful women. She said, "It has to do with the female apologetic. If women are going to be strong and successful, they need to balance that with also being feminine and nice. If they don't do that, it makes people uncomfortable."[7] Perhaps this need to be "nice" also feeds a consistent inequality that has persisted for many years: the big difference in how much their male professional soccer counterparts are paid by the United States Soccer Federation.

Five members of the US women's team began the fight in earnest when they filed a complaint in 2016 about the unfair pay practices. That complaint did not result in any action or even response, and so the team is now involved in a twenty-eight-member class-action lawsuit against US Soccer, alleging that their male counterparts can earn up to $13,166 per game played, while they can only earn up to $4,950 per game. Additionally, the lawsuit focused on the years between 2013 and 2016, when men received $55,000 if they were able to make and join the national squad, while women received $15,000 for the same exact feat. This huge discrepancy, the women argue, should not exist. The argument becomes especially strong when considering that the men were unable to qualify for the 2018 World Cup—and have never won a World Cup—while the women have now won four.[8]

However, one other interesting caveat helps the cause: The US men's soccer team is fully in support of the women's mission for equal pay. Their statement in agreeing with the women reads, "The members of the United States National Soccer Team Players Association once again stands with the members of the world champion Women's National Team in their pursuit of fair compensation for their work as professional soccer players. . . . The Federation downplays contributions to the sport when it suits them."[9]

Though the women have failed thus far in their bid for equal pay, they refuse to stop fighting. On the field, they have proven themselves champions. In courtrooms, they soon hope to do the very same.

NOTES

1. Jason Beaubien, "Underdog 'Reggae Girlz' Make History at Women's World Cup," NPR, *All Things Considered*, June 8, 2019, https://www.npr.org/sections/goatsandsoda/2019/06/08/730413093/jamaica-didn-t-really-care-about-soccer-then-came-the-reggae-girlz.
2. Beaubien, "Underdog 'Reggae Girlz' Make History."
3. Beaubien, "Underdog 'Reggae Girlz' Make History."
4. Michelle Kaufman, "Here's Why Jamaica's Reggae Girlz Could Become Women's World Cup Fan Favorites," *Miami Herald*, May 24, 2019, https://www.miamiherald.com/sports/mls/article230804324.html.
5. David Cox, "Jamaica's Reggae Girlz Seek Change in Culture through World Cup," Al Jazeera, June 8, 2019, https://www.aljazeera.com/news/2019/06/reggae-girlz-hope-world-cup-change-jamaica-sporting-culture-190608100109583.html.
6. Ken Sundheim, "The Sport of Writing Your Resume Where the Job Description Left Off," Business Insider Australia, August 6, 2011, https://www.businessinsider.com.au/the-sport-of-writing-your-resume-where-the-job-description-left-off-2011-5.
7. Nancy Armour, "Opinion: Here's What's behind Criticism of U.S. Women and World Cup Celebrations," *USA Today*, June 15, 2019, https://www.usatoday.com/story/sports/columnist/nancy-armour/2019/06/15/criticism-us-women-celebrations-rooted-sexism/1464858001/.

8. Emily Kaplan, "U.S. Women's Soccer Equal Pay Fight: What's the Latest, and What's Next?" ESPN, November 9, 2019, https://www.espn.com/sports/soccer/story/_/id /27175927/us-women-soccer-equal-pay-fight-latest-next.

9. Kaplan, "U.S. Women's Soccer Equal Pay Fight."

9
LIN-MANUEL MIRANDA

If you want to truly do something beautiful and impactful in the world, always remember one key word: fast. Good things happen fast! Like lightning! Like a waterfall! Like a jet! Like a world-record-breaking Olympic sprinter! Don't believe me? Consider the amazing journey of playwright and actor Lin-Manuel Miranda—the force behind the smash hit musical *Hamilton* and, before that, *In the Heights*. Both were Broadway successes, garnering Tony Awards and showing in front of sold-out crowds. But consider that Miranda wrote each hit musical in about one month. He simply furiously wrote and endured no blocks, no painfully slow processing, and certainly no lapses of confidence and ability. Good things happen fast!

*N*o *way!*

While Lin-Manuel Miranda is, indeed, the creative force behind the stunningly successful Broadway musicals *In the Heights* (2005) and *Hamilton* (2015), they were neither easy nor fast to write. In fact, they were both just the opposite.

Miranda began writing *In the Heights* as an eighteen-year old when he was struggling to figure out exactly what he wanted to do. Inspired by the idea of telling stories and seeing those stories come to life onstage, he set out to create a musical that he himself would find riveting. The vision was clear and hopeful. The actual journey? Painstaking and long.[1]

It took Miranda a full ten years to completely create *In the Heights*. Ten years![2] He had fallen in love with movies and performances when he was young, and his dream was to be a part of creating those kinds of films and performances that so inspired his own heart and mind. Think of how often you or I might be inspired by something or might have an idea pop into our heads or hearts. Or a hope, a possibility, an opportunity spring to light in us. Sometimes, those ideas come and go—more distractions or short-lived dreams

FROM WEAK TO PEAK!

Even though novelist Edith Wharton won the Pulitzer Prize for Fiction—one of the highest honors a writer can attain—in 1921, she claimed that "I had to fight my way to expression through a thick fog of indifference, if not tacit disapproval."[3]

from which we wake and shake our heads and say, *Nah, that doesn't actually jibe with what I really want to do or be.* Sometimes, however, those ideas come and just won't let go of us. We see inspiration for them everywhere around us, almost as if the universe itself is constantly reminding us, *Hey! Remember that this is something you really wanted to do/make/pursue!*

The desire to create wouldn't let Miranda go. He has shared that when he was nine years old, he saw the original Disney film *The Little Mermaid*. He was so awestruck by the music and the story that he went to see it a second time. But the second time was not enough, and so he went a third time. But even *three times* was not enough, so he persuaded his parents to come and see it, and he brought them two *more* times. The effect of the songs and the story on Miranda was dizzying, and it opened his world to what could be possible through music and story. He said, "I think Sebastian the crab had a big amount to do with it. The fact that this calypso number happens under the water just knocked my socks off when I was a kid. It had, like, this power over me. I would perform that thing. I would jump up on my desk in fourth grade and sing that song."[4]

I would jump up on my desk in fourth grade and sing that song.

—Lin-Manuel Miranda

Starting in fourth grade, the rhythm and rhyme of musical power in performances just took hold of him and wouldn't let go. But rather than fight his gut instinct, Miranda rode it. He jumped up on that desk and sang his heart out. It's also worth noting that this fourth-grader was singing his heart out to *The Little Mermaid*.

The.

Little.

Mermaid.

Still, Miranda was willing to boldly proclaim his joy!

Consider how intense bullying and ridicule are right now if anyone in your school dares to break from the accepted path. What are the unspoken rules for different genders in your school? For people who have different levels of money? Different styles of clothes? What if a fourth-grade boy in your school were to admit to loving a Disney princess movie? Would that be accepted and applauded?

Your gut instinct shows you what truly delights you. Think of nine-year-old Miranda sitting in that dark movie theater, his heart lighting up at Sebastian's sea song. What kinds of things make your own heart light up? What makes you delight in this life? The most courageous step you can take is to bring that delight out from hiding and show it to others—to step up on whatever version of a desk you've got and let other people see that you love what you love, that you are moved by what you are moved by, and that you won't back down because someone else says it's uncool, it's stupid, it's only for one gender, or anything else like that.

Miranda kept hold of his love for rhythm and rhyme, and by the time he was working on the songs for *In the Heights*, it took everything he had. He would sit and sing lyrics out loud as he crafted words, play around with language, and then revise and try again. And again. And again.

NOT DIMINISHED... FINISHED!

Daveed Diggs recalls that throughout his childhood, as the son of a Jewish mom and an African American dad, he never truly felt like he belonged. Diggs eventually fell in love with poetry, which became a conduit for his emotion and his creative ability. It would still take years before Diggs eventually met Lin-Manuel Miranda and rapped his way into Miranda's smash hit *Hamilton*.

Ten years later, when *In the Heights* debuted on Broadway, it was a massive hit. It managed to continue its run from 2005 until today, and now a blockbuster film is in the works, to be released in June of 2020. Consider, during that ten-year span of creation, how many times Miranda might have been tempted to stop, to quit, to doubt whether anything he wrote was ever going to see the inside of a theater. To stick with an idea for ten years because your gut keeps telling you it's crucial to finish is powerfully beautiful—and rare! Good things develop slowly, not at the speed of Instagram—but instead through billions and billions of instants. Every instant becomes another step closer toward a bigger mission. Many people look at this kind of work and label it *failure*. After all, we are used to *thinking* that success happens quickly because we only see it when it happens! We often worship instants of glory rather than long hours working in secret. But for Miranda, those long hours working in secret created a stage hit that blew off the roof.[5]

HAVE GRIT—DON'T SPLIT!

Laura Numeroff, prolific author of the bestselling children's picture book series that began with If *You Give a Mouse a Cookie*, at first didn't think she had a success on her hands. The original manuscript was rejected more than a dozen times before it was eventually published and became a smash hit.

And the same trend continued with *Hamilton*. Miranda shared that it took him six years to create *Hamilton*. Four years faster than *In the Heights*, but still ...six years! He noted that he once spent an *entire* day working on *only two lines* for the musical.[6] Most of us would hear that and think it was a failure of a workday. What if you had to write an English essay, and you spent a full day working on it, and then had two sentences to show for all your work? Now, I'm not talking about opening up a document but then spending the whole day on Instagram or Snapchat or Twitter, and then writing two quick sentences at the very end of your day. That's not work. That's distraction! I mean, what if you spent the whole, *actual* day working on two sentences—just writing, rewriting, choosing new words, getting the consonance and assonance to sound just right, rethinking the message and the meaning behind those words, then trying again. And when you finish those two sentences, you realize how many hours and hours you've poured into them.

If you then took those two sentences to your teacher and said, *Look! I've just spent eight hours writing these two sentences!* they might not be exactly glowing with praise for you. Think of your state standardized test. When it comes to the writing portion, what if you calmly raised your hand and said, *Excuse me . . . um, I'd really like to craft some beautiful lines, and it might be tough, so I'd like to spend about eight hours on two sentences. Do you think the standardized test judges will be cool with that?* My guess would be an emphatic . . . *no.*

In our world, working slowly and with great focus and determination isn't always celebrated. A lot of people want quick results, and when something doesn't happen fast or make a big splash right away, it's sometimes judged to be a failure.

You can't control the success of a thing. You can't say, "I'm going to go write an award-winning musical," that's not how it works. You know, your goal is to just make something that feels as true to what you set out to do as possible.

—Lin-Manuel Miranda

But Miranda's journey tells a different story. And his sixteen years working on two Broadway plays reveal that the quiet moments of following your gut, along with hard work and determination, hold great potential, no matter what anyone else thinks. He said, "You can't control the success of a thing. You can't say, 'I'm going to go write an award-winning musical,' that's not how it works. You know, your goal is to just make something that feels as true to what you set out to do as possible."[7] What you can control is the time and the dedication you put into what you believe.

You can't always control how fast something happens, and you can't always control the reception it gets. But you can climb up on your proverbial desk, belt out the songs that delight your heart, and then work hard to create your own.

What desk awaits your feet, and what song desperately needs your voice to belt it out?

NOTES

1. Leah Fessler, "A Tweet Lin-Manuel Miranda Wrote in 2009 Shows the Struggle behind His Genius," Quartz at Work, November 18, 2018, https://qz.com/work/1467163 /hamilton-creator-lin-manuel-miranda-shared-the-struggle-behind-his-genius/.
2. Fessler, "A Tweet Lin-Manual Miranda Wrote."
3. Rose Leadem, "These Artists, Authors and Leaders Battled Self-Doubt Before They Made History," *Entrepreneur*, November 9, 2017, https://www.entrepreneur.com /slideshow/304340.
4. Lin-Manuel Miranda, "Lin-Manuel Miranda on Disney, Mixtapes and Why He Won't Try to Top 'Hamilton,'" interview by Terry Gross, *Fresh Air*, NPR, January 3, 2017, https://www.npr.org/templates/transcript/transcript.php?storyId=507470975.
5. Fessler, "A Tweet Lin-Manual Miranda Wrote."
6. Fessler, "A Tweet Lin-Manual Miranda Wrote."
7. Fessler, "A Tweet Lin-Manual Miranda Wrote."

10

JOHN CENA

At his birth, John Cena's biceps were so big that extra doctors and nurses had to rush into the room simply to hold his arms up. It took seven doctors and nurses to carry the future professional wrestler and movie star to a table to check his vital signs, but the table wasn't even big enough to hold him. It was the start of a burgeoning career. By the time he was twelve, Cena had wooed and won the favor of every single student in his Massachusetts school, engendering praise and adoration from all of them. No one ever thought about criticizing, critiquing, or—never!—bullying him. Instead, his stature and reputation grew until he made his appearance on the professional wrestling circuit, wowing audiences just as he had done his whole life. His message? A clear one: real men are tough.

*N*o *way!*

Growing up in a family of five boys in West Newbury, Massachusetts, John Cena had a life that differed greatly from what wrestling fans and movie audiences might surmise. While his brothers were relentlessly competitive and rough, Cena wanted to get beyond a need to compare himself to them and to the world around him. He wanted to somehow find a way to live a life that was about more than winning—but about trying new things, stepping outside of what you're used to, and truly being who you are.[1]

This was no easy task. As a child in school, Cena endured bullying often. There were two bullies, especially, in his high school who really gave him a hard time. He was often taunted for his size and made fun of for attributes about his personality that he felt were just a part of who he was.[2] For many boys growing up, the pressure to be tough can feel enormous. Among my own middle school students, many young men stay after class to share with me that they feel so much pressure, so much fear, and so much anger or sadness about situations in their lives—with their dads, with bullying, with not measuring up—and yet they feel lost for where to go or how to do anything different. Cena can relate to this struggle.

Trying to empower himself, he began lifting weights and

HOLD THE BOLD!

An immigrant to the United States from the Democratic Republic of the Congo, Dikembe Mutombo ended up becoming a star National Basketball Association (NBA) player and someone who worked tirelessly through many struggles not only to help himself but to help others worldwide. He has said, "I was born in a house where my mom and dad always left the door open. . . . In my household there was no stranger. My mom gave food to anybody." This kindness has permeated his life during and after the NBA.[3]

playing football, but he never felt as though he truly fit the "tough guy" persona that many boys and men believe they must embody. Instead, he always felt like a sensitive and deeply emotional person, which explains how—years later—he was able to talk about his uncertainty, fear, doubt, or other emotions from the stage of a professional wrestling match, from the screen of a Hollywood movie, or in an interview with a magazine or website. Cena has said that he gets it when people see his size or his wrestling persona and automatically think he's tough as nails and gritty. Cena understands that people wonder about him and other "tough guys," "Are they really that jaded and hard-edged, or are they actually human beings? I'm a human being, I really am. I'm much more of a softie than I am Clint Eastwood in 'Dirty Harry.'"[4]

I'm a human being, I really am. I'm much more of a softie than I am Clint Eastwood in "Dirty Harry."

—John Cena

This journey beyond the trap of trying to be a "tough guy" has also led Cena well beyond the scope of the wrestling ring. Even though he holds the record for the most matches ever won in World Wrestling Entertainment (WWE), he has also played a stay-at-home dad in the movies and has written and published a children's book, *Elbow Grease*. Cena has argued that it's deeply important for people to see that just because someone looks massive and muscular, this does not preclude their being sensitive and wanting to love and care for others. Additionally, due to his past of being bullied, Cena is also troubled by the tragic lie that those who *don't* look big and muscular aren't strong. They are.

Their strength lies in so many areas that traditional notions of toughness ignore! This message comes powerfully to life in his picture book, *Elbow Grease*, when Cena's main character—a truck named Elbow Grease—wants more than anything to win the big race, to be the best. Spoiler alert: he loses. But the courage is in the attempt.[5]

Losing doesn't necessitate a lack of strength or a lack of belonging. Instead, with his book, Cena wants young people to learn early that "it's okay to be different. And it's okay to be you."[6] The truck in Cena's picture book mirrors his own journey and his own hopes for young boys—and kids of all kinds—to understand that toughness alone is not really winning. Instead, being yourself within a culture that tries to bully you into being something you're not is the *real* victory.

It's okay to be different. And it's okay to be you.

—John Cena

At this point in his life, you might think that Cena has it all and has accomplished it all. He's a record holder as a professional wrestler, a movie star, and a published author. However, Cena is quick to share that he continues to fail and flounder and that what makes life worthwhile is the very act of trying new things and taking on new challenges. After two of his first movies—*The Marine* and *12 Rounds*—miserably failed according to movie standards (making back very little money of the production costs and being attacked harshly by many movie critics), Cena could have walked away from the challenge of acting. Instead, when another opportunity opened for him, he tried again. Why? He shared that failing and trying again is the very recipe for how he wants to live his life: "I've swung and missed so many times, I'm glad nobody is keeping track except me. I think with failure comes embarrassment and comes humility. A lot of the reason we spend valuable minutes wandering away from purpose is because we're always afraid about what people will say and what people will think ... I stopped caring about what other people thought and started caring about, like, what am I going to do that's going to make my life happy and make my life effective?"[7]

PLUCK ENOUGH!

After playing football at the University of Miami, Dwayne Johnson signed up for the NFL draft in 1995. The only problem was, no team picked him. After going back home to live with his parents, he learned that not making the pros might have been a good turn, since in 1996, he took on his role as The Rock in the wrestling arena.

A lot of the reason we spend valuable minutes wandering away from purpose is because we're always afraid about what people will say and what people will think.

—John Cena

This profoundly beautiful question is something you need to ask yourself too: *What am I going to do that is going to make my life happy and make my life effective?* People will always be ready to attack and judge your attempts at anything worthwhile. If you give them a microphone to detail your failings, they will often gladly accept the opportunity! However, if you try something difficult and fail, but the act of the attempt helps to bring joy and meaning to your life, then moving forward with it again is the very definition of courage. And courage in this capacity leads to the sensation that you are, indeed, fully alive.

It is also worth noting that Cena doesn't simply ask what's going to make a life happy. We can all get lost daydreaming about things that we *think* may make our lives happy, but really won't. As I write these words, I envision that a massive slice of banana bread, with a huge hunk of butter on it—no, *two hunks of butter!*—will make me very, very—*No! Three hunks of butter!!!*—very, very, very happy. And I also envision that ants who grew just a bit beyond their normal size—let's say they are one-foot-tall ants—entered this library and offered to massage my aching feet right now. Wow, yes, happiness. And I also envision that being able to sleep for ten hours straight and not wake up to a crying baby would be sublime. Yes, astoundingly happy!

Yes! And I also envision—

You're right. I apologize. I've lost the thread of what really matters here, which is that, quite simply, we can lose the thread of what really matters if we focus only on what we think makes us happy. We can get lost in a lot of things that don't relate to any deeper purpose for our lives.

And so, the second part of Cena's question is so crucial: *what makes my life effective?* For Cena, working hard, trying again, and helping others' dreams come true is a huge part of how he answers this question himself. One way he does this is through the Make-A-Wish Foundation, which processes seemingly impossible wishes from chil-

CRAVE THE BRAVE!

At the 2016 Olympics, gymnast Simone Biles accomplished an unprecedented feat: wining four gold medals in a single Olympics. Then, in October 2019, she earned the distinction of earning the most World Championship medals in the history of the sport: twenty-five. She even has four official gymnastics moves named after her! However, her journey to get there included feeling embarrassed about her body (and being teased over it) and learning to cope with and accept her diagnosis of ADHD.

dren coping with severe difficulty or medical prognosis and helps those wishes to come true. To date, Cena has made more than six hundred wishes from children through the Make-A-Wish foundation come true—beyond what any other celebrity has done through this organization.[8]

Sometimes, competing with others to be the best isn't the best indication of your own strength. Instead, managing to use your own voice, your own body, your own personality and vision and emotion in the most authentic way possible *is* the very definition of success. Like Cena, you may be taunted for it, you may fail by trying it, and you may be categorized wrongly because of it. But none of this can prevent you from asking that profound question of yourself: What makes my life happy and effective? As you seek and try to find the answer, be ready to make mistakes and get criticized along the way. After all, no matter how big your biceps are or how many times you win, this is *still* the only path to being and becoming who you really are.

★ The Flop Files: **Michael Phelps** ★

Consider how *amazing* you would feel if you won an Olympic medal. Now imagine that it wasn't just *any* Olympic medal but a *gold* Olympic medal.

The glory!

The fame!

The joy!

Now, imagine that it wasn't just one Olympic gold medal, but twenty-eight Olympic gold medals. That would be enough glory, fame, and joy to last far more than a lifetime, right?

Not so much.

Olympic swimmer Michael Phelps reached all those heights over the course of five Olympic appearances between 2000 and 2016. Along with his twenty-eight Olympic gold medals, he also broke records, captivated audiences, and generated the support of an entire nation at his back.

But none of this could touch the severe depression and anxiety Phelps was battling. Sure, he seemed to be living any athlete's dream on the outside, but on the inside, he didn't even want to be alive anymore. Following his victories during the 2012 Olympics, Phelps shared, "I didn't want to be in the sport anymore . . . I didn't want to be alive anymore."[9] Even though he had won eight gold medals at those 2012 Olympics, they did nothing to assuage the depression he was battling.

Phelps shared that he stayed in his room for five days, eating almost nothing and barely sleeping. He felt like nothing was worth it, and there was no way out.

On the outside, we can present so many images of what it means to succeed, and yet inside, we can be breaking and struggling and fearing and feeling as though we are completely alone. Phelps felt like this. Even as his face graced national newspapers and magazine covers, his heart was breaking.

Finally, Phelps made a truly victorious decision: he would start therapy. This meant he would need to talk about his emotions, bring up memories and experiences that he had tried to bury and forget about. Instead of pretending that everything was fine (and had always been fine), the Olympic swimmer would have to have a whole new kind of courage: the courage to face his feelings. He reflected, "I was very good at compartmentalizing things and stuffing things away that I didn't want to talk about, I didn't want to deal with, I didn't want to bring up—I just never ever wanted to see those things."[10] He finally refused to stuff his emotions, refused to pretend they weren't real.

Because of this brave decision, Phelps began to slowly come back to life. The more he worked through his emotions, the more connected and available he became for his kids and his wife. He now says that the joy he feels in talking about his own journey through darkness, and helping others to see that they are not alone, is far more powerful than any medal ever was. Real victory—real success—for Phelps was not in winning twenty-eight Olympic gold medals but rather in working to save lives—his own, and others—by getting real about depression and anxiety, and by enjoying the family he and his wife are growing.[11]

NOTES

1. Ned Ehrbar, "John Cena Reveals He Was Bullied as a Kid," CBS News, June 29, 2017, https://www.cbsnews.com/news/john-cena-interview-bullying/.
2. Jordi Lippe-McGraw, "John Cena Admits:'I Was Bullied,'" *Huffington Post*, April 14, 2017, https://www.huffpost.com/entry/john-cena-admits-i-was-bullied_b_58f10639e4b048 372700d7d7.
3. Maggie Fazeli Fard, "Dikembe Mutombo: The Giver," *Experience Life*, April 2014, https://experiencelife.com/article/dikembe-mutombo-the-giver/.
4. Sandy Cohen, "John Cena Shares His Love for Kids and How They Inspire Him," Associated Press, March 19, 2018, https://apnews.com/9a2a7bc01e734295a1bc9f44b5b03619.
5. Delfina V. Barbiero, "John Cena Tackles Toxic Masculinity in 'Elbow Grease' Children's Books," *USA Today*, June 4, 2019, https://www.usatoday.com/story/life/books/2019 /06/04/john-cena-childrens-book-elbow-grease-motozilla-bookcon/1335778001/.
6. Barbiero, "Joh Cena Tackles Toxic Masculinity."
7. Cohen, "John Cena Shares His Love for Kids."
8. Conchita Margaret Widjojo, "John Cena Has Granted Over 600 Make a Wish Foundation Wishes—More than Any Celebrity in History," *People*, November 6, 2019, https:// people.com/movies/john-cena-has-granted-over-600-make-a-wish-foundation-wishes -more-than-any-celebrity-in-history/.

9. Susan Scutti, "Michael Phelps: 'I Am Extremely Thankful That I Did Not Take My Life,'" CNN, January 20, 2018, https://www.cnn.com/2018/01/19/health/michael-phelps-depression/index.html.

10. Scutti, "Michael Phelps: 'I Am Extremely Thankful.'"

11. Karen Crouse, "Michael Phelps Is Losing World Records, but He's Gained Other Treasures," *New York Times*, August 19, 2019, https://www.nytimes.com/2019/08/19/sports/michael-phelps-records-family.htm.

11
JOAN OF ARC

Growing up in Domremy, France, in the early fifteenth century, Joan la Pucelle (as she was called at the time) was a quiet, unassuming girl. She only began to study military matters in her twenties, and by the time she was aiding Charles VII on his mission to be crowned the king of France, Joan had already earned three advanced degrees in military strategy, theology, and communication. Plus, she had numerous chances to train and practice so that she would also be physically fit to lead troops into battle all over France. Many people immediately saw eye to eye with her and agreed to lend their support. Additionally, when Charles VII was finally crowned, all tension quieted, and everyone decided to get along. The English left France, France was united, and Joan decided to retire at the age of sixty-seven years.

*N*ot!!!

Even though Joan la Pucelle *is* credited with establishing Charles VII as the King of France, she did so as a teenager, with no training or degrees, and no royal or wealthy heritage. The story of who, exactly, Joan was is rife with mystery and a series of events that seem—even to those of us who relish seemingly improbable tales—ultimately impossible.

As a young girl, Joan of Arc (as she is now known) would break the barriers of what would seem possible to both the people of her day and the people of ours. The impossibility of her life—at every single step—would have seemed to make her destined for immediate glorification. Instead, this truly astounding, world-changing leader was betrayed, punished, and destroyed for her courage and conviction. It would take five hundred years for this grave failure to be overturned and for Joan's place in history to be re-established.

Now, we know Joan of Arc as a world-renowned figure whom many adore and admire. So, just *how* did she go from being a normal young teen to an epic leader, then to an attacked heretic and failure, and finally, to the figure we now hear so much about?

The year was 1428, and Joan was living with her parents and two brothers in a town called Domremy, in France. The town was on the border between France and what was then called the Holy Roman Empire. Her dad was a tenant farmer, which meant he

FAIL...THEN PREVAIL!

Queen Laxmibai ruled a northern part of India called Jhansi in the mid-1800s. At the time, the British were attempting to expand their rule into this area. Laxmibai failed at trying to peacefully persuade the British to leave, and so she joined the resistance and led her army herself as a warrior queen in 1857.

rented land from someone who had a whole lot more money than Joan's family did. In renting the land, Joan's dad (and, by extension, her mom and her two brothers and herself) farmed it, then sold crops and goods to stay alive and continue work. In other words, Joan's family was not wealthy. They also had no connections to great leaders or royal families of the day.[1]

At the time, there was a whole mess of confusion surrounding France. The English wanted to rule France, and there were some French citizens and leaders who essentially said, *Cool beans! Let's just let the English be in charge, okay? We'll have our own people to lead locally, but let's just chill out and say the English king, Henry VI, is our go-to guy for power. Okay?*

> ## HOLD THE BOLD!
>
> In 1955 in Montgomery, Alabama, a woman named Georgia Gilmore decided that she had had enough of being told to enter and sit in the back of the bus by white drivers. Two months before Rosa Parks refused to move her seat, Gilmore boarded a bus at the front, and the white driver told her to get off. She recalled, "I told him I was already on the bus and I couldn't see why I had to get off."[2] Gilmore continued her work in civil rights, becoming an integral part of the 381-day Montgomery Bus Boycott.

Particularly in northern France, such were the sentiments. And even in some of the nearby towns and villages around Joan's Domremy, many of the French felt similarly. However, Joan (and most in her town) believed that Charles VII was the rightful heir to the throne of France, and they wanted him to be crowned king at Reims, the majestic city in France where royal coronations were held.[3]

In 1428, the general confusion and bitter disagreement about who should rule caused battle after battle. Kids often fought in the battles, and in Joan's village—like in many others in the area—children regularly came home with faces and bodies marred with horrific injuries and covered in blood. Every night, uncertainty ensued. No truce or compromise seemed likely for the future.[4]

Enter a sixteen-year-old girl.

That same year—1428—Joan's town saw up close the misery of battle, when soldiers loyal to the English attacked them for siding with Charles VII. Leaving town for their safety, Joan's family later returned when all calmed, but the episode left an indelible memory on Joan. From this traumatic confrontation with possible death and horrific fighting, Joan decided to fight back.[5]

She claimed that she was in the garden that her family cared for when, all of a sudden, she began to hear voices. Joan believed these voices to be from God and from saints. A devout Catholic believer, Joan had grown up attending Mass, the service for Catholics, and praying and performing all the requirements of her faith. Sincerely believing that these voices were telling her to ensure that Charles VII was made king at Reims, Joan essentially said, Okay, let's do this.[6]

At about sixteen years old, Joan left home. (Historians disagree about whether Joan was born in 1412 or 1413—so right now, if you've got a coin handy, flip it up in the air and see where it lands; if heads, then Joan was born in 1412; if tails, then Joan was born in 1413. Okay? Ready, set, *go*! Did it? Great. Now, write me a quick email and let me know, and when I get your email, we'll continue on with the book. Go for it. Wait, what? That's not going to work? Because I need to finish writing so that you can keep reading? I see your point. In other words, it's impossible? Just about as impossible as what Joan is about to do? You got it.)

Here's the first impossible moment of a truly impossible story: Joan journeyed three hundred miles *through loads of enemy territory* to eventually arrive at the castle in Chinon where Charles VII happened to be hanging out, waiting for all this power-disputing to figure itself out.[7]

Three hundred miles!

Today, we might jump into a car or take a plane ride and travel three hundred miles fairly quickly. But in the early 1400s, going three hundred miles as a sixteen-year old girl *alone* and traveling basically at night to stay hidden (yup, she did so in the *dark*) through loads of enemy territory—well, the absurdity of this one point alone would be worthy of an epic Hollywood movie, or a fabulous YA novel, or at least worth you and me stopping here, closing our eyes, and truly trying to envision how hard this would have been.

Sixteen years old.

Alone.

Traveling through places where people would want to kill her. (Remember that children fought in these wars, and Joan was on the *wrong* side along this route!)

> ## NOT DIMINISHED... FINISHED!
>
> Qui Jin, living at the turn of the nineteenth century in China, refused to bind her feet and defer to men, as was customary at the time. Instead, she learned to sword fight, spoke her mind freely, and became an activist leading others to resist the Qing government. She was killed for her strong stance, but to this day, thousands visit her grave and are inspired by her courage.

Three hundred miles.

On foot.

But as if all that wasn't absurd enough, and didn't seem to make Joan destined for failure, the next part of Joan's journey truly was impossible. She persuaded all the proper officials (imagine a whole slew of security guards, then multiply that by a really, really big number) to let her see Charles VII. She had no wealth, no royal connections, and no power.[8]

Yet, she convinced one of the most powerful leaders in France to let her come and talk with him about her ideas for winning the war.

Historians—to this day—still throw up their hands and say, *AAAR-GHLAFLOTTTREPITTTITY!!!!!!! We just don't get it!*

(If you've ever had the chance to study in a library near any historians, this phrase is an oft-repeated one. They use it fondly whenever they come to a part of history that utterly confuses them. You might try using the phrase yourself, the next time you are taking a really tough test in school. If that test happens to be in history class, and your teacher truly loves history, they will probably look at you fondly with a great grin of recognition.)

However it happened, Joan finally convinced everyone at the castle at Chinon to let her talk with Charles VII. But they had one little trick up their sleeves to ensure that Joan really was sent by God—as she claimed. Before they let Joan into court, Charles VII hid himself amid lots of the others at court instead of remaining on the ostensible seat of authority, in the front. He reasoned that if Joan was being honest, she'd enter the court and immediately pick him out from the crowd.[9]

Did she?

The next absurdly impossible point: she did.

Bam, there you are Charles VII—I see you!

Charles VII sheepishly (I imagine) came out from the crowd like a kid who had just been found in a rousing game of hide-and-seek. Joan proceeded to tell him, basically, that God told her that he needed to lead the charge against the English and all those loyal to the English. Joan would help with the military stuff. If he did so, Joan promised, Charles VII would eventually be crowned king of France at Reims.

And we are now up to the absurdly impossible point number four (go back and count if you don't believe me!): Charles VII said, *Cool beans. Let's do this.*

Okay, he didn't quite say it like that, and it wasn't quite that quickly, but Charles did grow to trust Joan and eventually allowed her to make hugely strategic battle decisions—including the decisive event of leading the French troops into battle to retake the city of Orléans, which had been under siege by those loyal to the English. Doing so provided the French with enough momentum to allow them to enter the city of Reims (previously controlled by those loyal to the English) and officially crown Charles VII. On July 17, 1429, during this coronation, Joan leaned down to her old hide-and-seek pal, Chuck, and whispered, "Gentle king, now is executed the will of God, who wished that the siege of Orléans should be lifted, and that you should be brought into this city of Reims to receive your holy consecration, thus showing that you are a true king, and he to whom the kingdom of France should belong."[10] (However, I bet what Joan really wanted to say at this exact moment was *Cool beans, Chuck! Remember when we first met last year, and I convinced you to follow me? TOLD YOU SO.*)

Joan—now a seventeen-year-old girl—had literally accomplished the truly impossible. Charles VII sat on his throne, proclaimed as the King of France, and in only about one year. Joan had led troops into battle, gotten wounded in the shoulder with an arrow, and stood up to prosperous, powerful, and older generals who had disagreed with her strategic military decisions. And yet Joan had been right basically every time. Her decisions had led to this truly historic and impossible moment.

And here's where it would be very cool (*cool beans* level of coolness) to stop the chapter and say that you and I should sometimes attempt things that seem impossible because, hey, we never know! I could write a little paragraph here to inspire you to chase down big dreams and possibilities, even if they seem absurdly impossible.

However, we can't do that this time.

Because what happened next continues Joan's truly impossible journey.

Instead of receiving great praise and unending loyalty and comfort due to her courageous leadership, Joan was captured by those loyal to the English crown. She was tried for heresy—and, among other crimes, for the crime of wearing men's clothes (seriously). Those with immense power in the Catholic Church questioned her for seventy days, kept her in a cold, dark cell, chained her, and sometimes put her in the blocks (hands and feet into wooden holding compartments). They demanded that Joan deny she heard anything from God; they demanded that Joan say the only way anyone could talk to God was through the powerful men of the Catholic Church; and they demanded that she stop wearing all those men's clothes![11]

Joan—as you can probably surmise—said, essentially, *No way*.

And so, this group of powerful Catholic men decided that this teenaged girl should be executed by them tying her to a tall wooden stake and then setting her on fire.

In the flames, Joan refused to deny what she believed she had done and heard and the mission she had attempted.

It would be almost five hundred years before the Catholic Church essentially admitted, *We were wrong*. But they eventually did. In 1920, under the rule of Pope Benedict, the Church decided to take a drastically different approach to the seemingly impossible life and works of Joan la Pucelle: they made her a saint. The Pope canonized her, making her a true heroine in the Catholic Church and a model as Saint Joan of Arc.[12] Against incredible odds multiple times, Joan relied on her inner belief that she was doing what she had to do, risking her life every step of the way. Why would she risk so much? She claimed that "one life is all we have and we live it as we believe in living it.

But to sacrifice what you are and to live without belief, that is a fate more terrible than dying."[13]

One life is all we have and we live it as we believe in living it. But to sacrifice what you are and to live without belief, that is a fate more terrible than dying.

—Joan of Arc

Hers is a story that *does* seem impossible. Absurdly impossible. And though its ending is deeply tragic, her life manages to profoundly confound even the most brilliant historians today because they wonder just *how* it could even have happened.

Joan should have been a failure. Instead, she succeeded as a military leader beyond anyone's wildest expectations or imaginations. And yet, the powerful Catholic Church, along with potent political will, chose to destroy her. Joan's fall was not by her own choice, but rather it was decreed for her.

Sometimes, the most powerful people and groups in society fear what they cannot understand. Joan's rise to prominence befuddled the powerful status quo all around her, and so they ensured her failure. They forced her failure.

Have you ever done something you felt pretty dang proud of—something that surprised even you? But then right afterward, somebody tried to knock you down for accomplishing it? My past seventh-grade students often heard me discuss the phenomenon of catching deep-sea crabs: they are held in buckets without covers. Though they are capable of climbing out, escape is never a concern for those who catch them. Why? As soon as one attempts to escape, the others pull it back down. Freedom and success can sometimes arouse anger, jealousy, or fear in others.

Joan's story failed while it was still so early on! Her story failed not because of her own choices, though, but because of the fear and jealousy of others. In perhaps the most ironic twist of history, however, when the Catholic Church recognized its failure five hundred years later, Joan could finally succeed, once more, in not just her own eyes but in the eyes of the world too.

Though she was a teenager, though she had no money, and though she had no royal or political connections, Joan deemed all of that inconsequential and instead decided to change the world on her own terms.

NOTES

1. Yvonne Lanhers and Malcolm G. A. Vale, "St. Joan of Arc," *Encyclopædia Britannica*, December 2, 2019, https://www.britannica.com/biography/Saint-Joan-of-Arc/.
2. Klancy Miller, "Overlooked No More: Georgia Gilmore, Who Fed and Funded the Montgomery Bus Boycott," *The New York Times*, July 31, 2019, https://www.nytimes.com/2019/07/31/obituaries/georgia-gilmore-overlooked.html.
3. Owen Jarus, "Joan of Arc: Facts and Biography," Live Science, July 19, 2013, https://www.livescience.com/38288-joan-of-arc.html.
4. Jarus, "Joan of Arc."
5. Jarus, "Joan of Arc."
6. Jarus, "Joan of Arc."
7. Lanhers and Vale, "St. Joan of Arc."
8. Jarus, "Joan of Arc."
9. Jarus, "Joan of Arc."
10. Jarus, "Joan of Arc."
11. Lanhers and Vale, "St. Joan of Arc."
12. Lanhers and Vale, "St. Joan of Arc."
13. Joseph Hartropp, "'One Life Is All We Have': The Surprising Sainthood of Joan of Arc," *Christian Today*, May 16, 2017, https://www.christiantoday.com/article/one-life-is-all-we-have-the-surprising-sainthood-of-joan-of-arc/109214.htm.

12
SOCRATES

Socrates was an ancient Greek thinker who basically became famous by walking around and talking to the air (and whoever would listen). It was fairly easy to become a renowned thinker/air-talker. Socrates realized at a young age that this was his life's true vocation. Perhaps it was due to his massive long white beard, which he first began growing around the time he started kindergarten (age five). Or maybe it was his proclivity toward rambling on and on and on . . . or maybe it was even his massively good looks and epically awesome fresh-scent smell, since Socrates was known to be the heartthrob of his day. Whatever the case, Socrates put on his fancy, gold-plated bathrobe, started walking around, talked a lot, and *bam*: wisdom. That's the true path of enlightenment: gilded bathrobes, chilling out, long beards, and good looks.

*N*o *way!*

Trying to figure out exactly who the *real* Socrates is could be likened to trying to figure out the precise length of the fingernail on your left pinky. Or as difficult as trying to freeze orange juice in the sun on a summer day. Or as difficult as trying to use *only* duct tape to build a fully functional, solar-powered automobile.

It's hard.

But there is some general agreement among scholars about some key facts of the life of Socrates, first among them being that Socrates lived from approximately 469 until 399 BC. So, he lived to be about seventy years old. It is also generally agreed that Socrates was very strange. People in Athens, Greece, where he roamed the marketplace freely talking to strangers, thought he was strange. And people today, who still love learning about him, continue to think he was strange. And we know that he didn't have a specific job, was not interested in becoming a politician and getting elected to government (as many in his day were if they were interested in education and ideas), and managed to eschew any kind of leadership role. Socrates didn't even write down a single word![1]

So, if Socrates was a man who lived over two thousand years ago, wasn't elected to any kind of leadership position, didn't want to be famous or powerful, and never wrote down a single word, why do we still remember, honor, and quote him relentlessly today? How could Socrates have managed to change the way a lot of people in the world think, by never aiming to do so?

Having trouble answering those questions? Good. You should be! Consider everything you've learned from all kinds of people and places about how to make an impact. Want to be a successful leader in business, the environment, sports, government, or any other area?

The endless message is clear enough: *be loud!* And many people *have* achieved great, important, and beautiful aims by being loud. Maybe by garnering loads and loads of followers on Twitter, or by launching a massive website, or by creating their own YouTube channels. However, as writer Mike Jung pointed out in his essay "Speak Up" from the book *Break These Rules,* "We don't all need to suck the air out of every room we walk into or treat conversation as a gladiatorial sport. We have methods of making our presence felt that are quieter and more contemplative, but no less powerful. In other words, there's more than one way to speak up."[2] Sometimes, leadership and impact isn't about chasing numbers, microphones, or social media hits. Instead, success can be quieter too.

This is the kind of impact Socrates had on people of his day—and ours. A quiet impact. Well, quiet in *some* ways. Because even though he didn't crave a political or educational title, and he never wanted—or got—any money, he managed to be metaphorically loud in some other, very interesting ways.

First, he smelled.

He smelled *awful.* Socrates had argued with his peers and with anyone who would listen that lots of clothes were superfluous. Why waste money and interest on lots of clothes and possessions? Furthermore, why even bother changing your clothes? Or washing them?

FROM WEAK TO PEAK!

Before Kerry Washington became a star in the hit television series *Scandal*, she was fired from two other television show pilots (first episodes of a show). The shows moved forward, but both times, Washington did not. She was told by experts in show business that she had to change a lot of things about the way she looked, but Washington refused. Instead, she said, "I didn't really change those things that people told me I had to change."[3] And she made it as herself.

Socrates was so deeply after thinking about what really mattered in life—what he considered to be the truth—that he never bothered to change or wash his clothes. In this way, people knew when Socrates was around! Yet they still flocked to him to hear his epic conversations, hungry to watch him question others about what they found important, then slowly analyzing why this is so, in order to eventually draw out truths about life and holes in other people's excuses for why culture and society should simply remain unchanged.[4]

Second, Socrates was considered to be the exact *opposite* of the standards of attractiveness for men of the fifth century in Athens, Greece. It has been reported that "Socrates was profoundly ugly, resembling a satyr more than a man—and resembling not at all the statues that turned up later in ancient times and now grace internet sites and the covers of books."[5] Instead of adhering to the route other men of his day had taken to gain popularity and a following by trying to make his face and body fit some kind of cultural standard, Socrates was viewed by his peers to be the opposite of that cultural standard. No one was calling Socrates handsome, hot stuff, or zinger man, if that third label was ever used (then or now). Instead, he was viewed with disdain for his looks. And yet? You guessed it: he was still followed, garnered the biggest audiences to listen to his conversations (Socrates refused to call them *teachings*), and had the biggest impact on the most students.

NOT DIMINISHED... FINISHED!

Charlotte Brontë, author of novels such as *Jane Eyre* and *Villette*, became one of England's best-loved novelists. However, this wouldn't have been a predictable result. When she was only twenty years old, she sent some of her writing to a respected author named Robert Southey. In his reply, he said, "Literature cannot be the business of a woman's life."[6] Thankfully, Brontë rejected his advice.

Socrates was profoundly ugly, resembling a satyr more than a man—and resembling not at all the statues that turned up later in ancient times and now grace internet sites and the covers of books.
—Debra Nails, philosophy professor and Socrates scholar

Third, Socrates rejected the traditional forms of teaching. In Athens during the fifth century, many teachers convened in public areas—such as the marketplace—and lectured, trying to impart what they believed they had learned. Education was seen as the filling of empty cups back then (and, you might argue, still now by some people!). The role of teachers in fifth-century Greece was to take all the knowledge they had accumulated and basically pour it into students (those who supposedly had zero, zip, zilch knowledge). *Bam!* Learning! However, Socrates thought this method of learning and growing was ridiculous. Instead, he believed that students already came with fascinating kinds of knowledge and insight and that a real thinker would question them, engage them in conversation, and they would learn by responding to these questions. Conversation and thinking—deep thinking—were the paths that enabled genuine learning. Therefore, Socrates refused to allow himself to be labeled a teacher. He didn't want people to associate him with what he viewed at an utterly useless model for learning and growth. Because of this strange kind of conversational learning, Socrates's influence and audience grew. However, the only reason we even *know* about Socrates is that his non-teaching teaching was so amazing that one of his students, a guy named Plato, was inspired to write down everything Socrates said and share it with the world![7]

So, Socrates became loud by being soft. He became legendary by seeking only to influence the people with whom he conversed. His reputation has endured because he sought to ensure that he had no fancy plaques or leadership positions. Ironically, Socrates became a world-changing philosophical figure even though he never sought that, never published any bestselling works, and never did *anything* to ensure that his legacy or ideas would live on.

He talked to people. He wore unwashed clothes, the same stuff day and night, never made any money, and refused to just get on with what his culture and his time period deemed best. In one particularly poignant conversation, Socrates quipped, "I prefer nothing, unless it is true."[8] Socrates could not be shaken by the lure of money, fame, or power. And so, when government officials in Athens accused Socrates of not abiding by the rules of the gods, and for corrupting the youth of the city, Socrates refused to deny any of his explorations into what he viewed as truth. A trial was convened and lasted thirty days, during which time Socrates questioned his questioners and revealed them to have little reason—either logically or morally—to find him guilty of any crimes.

Yet they did. Socrates was sentenced to death, and on the day of his death—to be conducted by drinking poisonous hemlock—

FAIL...THEN PREVAIL!

Diagnosed with a terminal illness, and already having undergone thirty surgeries, teen Shantell Pooser has been fighting tough medical predications her entire life. Pooser's mom has refused to accept rejection of her daughter: she has written to over forty hospitals asking for help, and she keeps pleading with their insurance company to pay for her daughter's medical care. Pooser eventually was able to fulfill her wish to be an honorary flight attendant, as well as to meet First Lady Michelle Obama.

Socrates told friends and others gathered around, "If you take my advice, you will give but little thought to Socrates but much more to the truth."[9] To his dying day, Socrates wanted others to pursue truth, rather than loyalty to a person or persona.

If you take my advice, you will give but little thought to Socrates but much more to the truth.

—Socrates

Socrates achieved a kind of success that is incredibly rare—both in his era and in our own. Instead of amassing followers and influence, he sought to think deeply and live authentically. He wanted to try to figure out what really mattered in life, he advocated for equality of the sexes, and he was willing to endure ridicule and face death if it meant seeking after what he regarded as truth.

Now, I am not suggesting that you stop washing your clothes, wear only a single outfit to school (or at your home school group, or anywhere else you might go every day), and resist any chance to speak into a microphone. Like the other figures in this book, Socrates provides one unique example of someone who made a huge impact on the world. However, Socrates could teach us a few things about success. If you're feeling overwhelmed by the burden of creating ever more social media posts and followings, or you tend to be much more introverted and have no desire to rousingly raise up your voice amid a huge crowd, it doesn't mean that you can't succeed in a powerful mission that changes everything. Like Socrates rambling around town, talking with others about what matters, refusing to concede to lies and excuses, there are other ways to make an impact and to make a difference. Volume doesn't have the market cornered on changing the world.

I prefer nothing, unless it is true.

—Socrates

It might not be the kind of success that your teacher, peers, or even parents recognize. But sometimes there are triumphs beyond certificates, plaques, and honors. Sometimes, you and I make a difference by the quiet ways we live our lives, chasing after truth, and thereby resisting the status quo of any culture or era.

★ The Flop Files: **Mary Shelley** ★

When you hear the word *Frankenstein*, what do you imagine? A green monster with deep black hair, maybe bolts coming out of the side of his head and walking in zombie-like fashion toward . . . you?!

When Mary Shelley wrote her now-epic novel *Frankenstein* in 1816, that depiction couldn't be further from the heart of her story, or from the story of her heart. Shelley was the daughter of an audacious and bold justice-oriented pioneer named Mary Wollstonecraft. Her mother unabashedly denounced the ways in which conventional English society at the time cornered and relegated women to the roles of mother and servant. Instead, Shelley's mother fought for equality and recognition for women.[10]

Shelley would attempt to follow in her mother's footsteps, even though her mother died during childbirth and her father would disown her. Shelley's dad, Charles, was repulsed by his daughter's decision to run away with a married man—the poet Percy Shelley—and he refused to recognize his daughter anymore. Dealing with the deep shame of her father's rejection, Mary Shelley departed England and would attempt to write amid her love affair, eventually meeting up with the poet Lord Byron.[11]

Eventually, living away from her England roots, Shelley felt freer and freer to write. One evening, Lord Byron played a game in which he challenged the three to see who could craft the creepiest ghost story. This was the catalyst for the eventual creation—and later publication—of Shelley's first novel, *Frankenstein*. Contrary to common belief today, the novel bears the name of the scientist who created a new man, and not the name of a demented monster. Victor Frankenstein, in Shelley's novel, aimed to create a living human, did so, and then was supremely disappointed in what he had done. The creator rejected his creation.[12]

Following the same storyline as her novel, the public, by and large, rejected Shelley's novel too. As scholar and writer Charlotte Gordon has noted, "After multiple rejections, the novel was published in January 1818, and in one of the great ironies of publishing history, *Frankenstein* would earn no royalties. Sales were so weak that there was no indication it would become one of the bestselling English novels of all time."[13]

Amazingly, a novel that is now often required reading, and an author whose life is fodder for fascinating explorations and inspirations, was decisively rejected by the very society for which it was produced! At first, Shelley's brilliant creation was rejected and ignored, and she never profited off the massive financial success it would have.

NOTES

1. Debra Nails, "Socrates," The Stanford Encyclopedia of Philosophy, Spring 2018 Edition, ed. Edward N. Zalta, https://plato.stanford.edu/archives/spr2018/entries/socrates/.

2. Mike Jung, "Speak Up!," in *Break These Rules: 35 YA Authors on Standing Up, Speaking Out, and Being Yourself*, ed. Luke Reynolds (Chicago: Chicago Review Press, 2013), 104.

3. Jaleesa M. Jones, "Kerry Washington Has Zero Time for Hollywood's Beauty Standards," *USA Today*, April 11, 2016, https://www.usatoday.com/story/life/entertainthis/2016/04/11/kerry-washington-has-zero-time-for-hollywoods-beauty-standards/82908622/.

4. Nails, "Socrates."

5. Nails, "Socrates."

6. Lyndall Gordon, "Yours Insincerely, Charlotte Bronte," *Independent*, July 22, 1995, https://www.independent.co.uk/arts-entertainment/books/yours-insincerely-charlotte-bronte-1592617.html.

7. Nails, "Socrates."

8. John M. Cooper, ed., *Plato: Complete Works* (New York City: Hackett Publishing Company, 1997), 14.

9. Nails, "Socrates."

10. Charlotte Gordon, "Mary Shelley: Abandoned by Her Creator and Rejected by Society," Literary Hub, January 25, 2018, https://bookmarks.reviews/mary-shelley-abandoned-by-her-creator-and-rejected-by-society/.

11. Gordon, "Mary Shelley: Abandoned by Her Creator."

12. Gordon, "Mary Shelley: Abandoned by Her Creator."

13. Gordon, "Mary Shelley: Abandoned by Her Creator."

13

PHIONA MUTESI

In order to become a chess master and one of the best players in her entire country of Uganda, Phiona Mutesi had the best chess tutors in the world. Many around her noticed her natural brilliance for the game and immediately nurtured it by allowing her the time, space, and sustenance necessary to single-mindedly pursue chess. From the start, Mutesi almost never lost a match, nor was she ever derided for her gender. She learned early on how to play patiently and with great focus and became quite accustomed to traveling far and wide for extensive tournaments. Now in college in the United States, Mutesi still adores chess, and is adamantly working on become a grand master, the highest possible level attainable for a chess player.

*N*ot quite!

Okay, Mutesi is indeed a remarkable chess player, one of the best ever in her home country of Uganda. But her journey toward this epic triumph is anything but simple and is not without failures, obstacles, confusions, and a deeply surprising change in path.

Mutesi was born in the Katwe section of Kampala, the capital city of Uganda. Katwe is known countrywide as one of the toughest parts of Uganda, and many families struggle daily simply to survive. Harriet, Mutesi's mother, has shared that the family has endured a state of near-constant struggle simply to remain safe and fed. Once, Harriet had to move Mutesi and her siblings because they had been robbed, and she feared for their safety. Other times, they moved because the structure in which they were living was about to disintegrate. By the time Mutesi was fourteen years old, the family had moved five times, to different parts of Katwe. Mutesi helped to bring in some meager amounts of money by selling maize from atop her head in the marketplace, but that provided scant food for her entire family.[1]

PLUCK ENOUGH!

It's hard to imagine that a young man growing up in eastern Turkey, whose main job was taking care of sheep, would one day immigrate to America, start his own company, and also show how some of the basic premises of American business practices are actually wrong. But that's just what Hamdi Ulukaya did. The founder of Chobani, a top-selling yogurt in the US, has said that the role of a CEO should be to take care of employees and give back to the community, rather than to focus on what a business can get.

However, a meeting that might never have taken place caused a huge change in Mutesi's life trajectory. One day, as her older brother Brian left home, Mutesi decided to follow him to see where he was going. She hoped it would be someplace where some kind of meal would be waiting! Through twists and turns she followed him, until he stopped at a small terrace to join other kids who were moving small black and white pieces all around a board. The first time, Mutesi only watched from afar, struggling to find the courage to enter and see if she could join.[2]

But during Mutesi's second visit to the chess group, the coach and teacher, Robert Katende, noticed her and invited her in. He encouraged her to learn how to play the game of chess and to join in with the other kids. Katende himself had come from a struggling neighborhood similar to Mutesi's and was there in Katwe attempting to find avenues for kids to connect and learn. He had started by teaching football (what we call soccer) but had expanded to chess when he realized that many kids were not interested in playing football.[3]

CRAVE THE BRAVE!

When Tropical Storm Imelda slammed Beaumont, Texas, on September 17, 2019, Satchel Smith, age 21, was working at the Homewood Suites in town. As the storm raged and flooded the area, Smith ended up being the *only* person on staff who made it in to work at the hotel, and for thirty-two hours *straight*, Smith fought through all of the storm's onslaught and power outages to keep people safe, warm, and fed. Guests would later say his actions were selflessly heroic.

Mutesi hesitantly entered, began learning, and even *did* get a meal—just as she had hoped. But she got a lot more than food too. She had been introduced to a new way to find joy, to challenge herself, and to express her fierce intellect and prodigious fighting spirit. She took to chess immediately and soaked up all she could from her coach, as well as enjoying challenging every other kid in the chess group. Finally, she made it to facing off against the chess champion of their group, an older boy who had never lost. Mutesi said that the other sixty kids from the group all gathered in close, watching the match expectantly. She recalled, "The other boys around, they were telling him, 'How can a girl beat you? You can't allow that.'"[4]

But Mutesi wasn't in the business of allowing a boy—no matter how good he was at chess—to tell her what she could or could not do. She won the match, earning her first (unofficial) title as a chess champion. The triumph gave Mutesi a new feeling of empowerment and confidence—like she could do anything she wanted. She explained, "After winning [against] this boy, I'm, like, 'I can beat any other boy in the whole world!' Back in Africa, the society—the way it trains us—it trains us to be, like, 'We women are nothing. Boys are the ones who go to school. The girls are supposed to be home.'"[5] Mutesi was not about to allow this kind of societal message to seep into her heart or her mind, though. Instead, she kept learning as much as she could about chess, and she began traveling in wider and wider circles to play more challenging opponents.

After winning [against] this boy, I'm, like, "I can beat any other boy in the whole world!" Back in Africa, the society—the way it trains us—it trains us to be, like, "We women are nothing. Boys are the ones who go to school. The girls are supposed to be home."

—Phiona Mutesi

However, as her sphere of competition grew, so did her aggressiveness. Mutesi recalled that, initially, her strategy for chess involved trying to finish off her opponents as fast as possible. Toward this end, Mutesi attacked her chess opponents with the full force of her budding knowledge and maneuvering, only to end up losing her first approximately fifty matches. Failing over and over again, yet sensing her own abilities to be a master at the game, Mutesi finally relented and allowed Coach Katende to teach her how to play with force but also with patience.[6]

The new style suited her well, as she quickly rose in national prominence. She, along with two members from the Katwe chess club coached by Katende, were able to earn the right to play in Africa's International Children's Chess Tournament in 2009, in Sudan. Sixteen highly competitive teams from across the continent competed for the distinction of winning the championship. Mutesi was about thirteen years old at the time, while many other teams included older players and those with more experience in the game. However, Mutesi led her team to victory, and they returned to Katwe triumphant and to a loud hero's welcome.

SWERVE WITH NERVE!

Vogue magazine editor Anna Wintour was once fired from her job at *Harper's Bazaar* where she was working as a junior editor in the fashion department. She didn't let the job loss stop her for long, and now Wintour is also the artistic director of Condé Nast— the parent company that owns *Vogue*, as well as a host of other magazines.

Mutesi's meteoric rise in the field of chess continued, and she traveled farther and farther, even competing in an international competition in Siberia, Russia. However, even while her story began to attract attention, and her chess won her fans worldwide, she and her family still struggled with the necessities of life. A book about her life garnered some income, which eventually allowed Harriet to move the family to a small home surrounded by land and space.[7]

But something was still missing. Instead of Mutesi's story becoming one of single-minded devotion and focus toward becoming a

grand master in chess, Mutesi made arguably an even more courageous decision. As she struggled with continuing to find joy in
the game and wondered whether she was doing it because of what
everyone around her was telling her or because it was truly what she
wanted to do with her life, Coach Katende helped her discern her
path forward by asking her a crucial question:"I notice people expect
you to do this, but what are you expecting yourself to be doing
in your life?"[8]

---

*I notice people expect you to do this, but what are you expecting
yourself to be doing in your life?*

—Coach Robert Katende

Rather than continue on and seek to attain the title of grand
master, Mutesi accepted a tuition scholarship offer to attend classes at
Northwestern University, in Seattle, Washington. Her coach's question challenged her to figure out her own path, rather than to abide
by everyone else's expectations of her. Attaining a college diploma
was one of Mutesi's own important goals, and she chose to try and
silence the voices of others long enough to pursue that. As she currently works on her degree, she still faces a steep learning curve,
explaining that it took her four days of very slow typing to eventually
finish a two-page paper for a class, which her peers wrote in about ten
minutes. It's hard work. She doesn't always feel like a winner. But she
feels good about the decision she has made and says that she is exactly
where she wants to be.[9]

Your passion for something you love may help you rise from
difficult circumstances. Look around for people like Coach Katende—

someone who can offer you support and teach you the basics of an area you might love. And consider the nature of surprise and coincidence that might unlock a path forward for you. Ever considered playing a drum in the marching band? Designing a clay pot? Dancing ballet? Or, like Mutesi, playing chess?

The path toward your passion may not be clear, and it may not be prescribed by the route you're currently on. Be ready to be surprised. Even so, as you pursue something you love and enjoy, may you also have the kind of bravery Mutesi demonstrates in being willing to let go of something to pursue new challenges, even if other voices tell you that you must be crazy to do so.

Just because something is hard, that is no indication of whether it's right for you or not. Sometimes the right thing for you to pursue is the hardest. Sometimes it will entail you failing fifty times before you taste triumph. Sometimes, it will entail you leaving something at which you have been victorious to pursue something that overwhelms you all over again. In these moments, let Coach Katende's question be a helpful compass for your decision: I notice people expect you to do this, but what are you expecting yourself to be doing in your life?

★ The Flop Files: **Queen Victoria** ★

Lead an entire government starting at the age of eighteen years old, standing under five feet tall, dealing every day with men who want to wrest power away. Lose your partner at the age of forty-two. Survive seven assassination attempts over the course of your reign.[10]

Does that sound like a job description you'd be interested in signing up for? For Queen Victoria, this was part of her story as the monarch of Great Britain from 1837 until 1901. During these sixty-four years, Victoria managed to speak eloquently and powerfully and find ways to keep her government together. When men were the predominant political force in Great Britain (and in much of the world), Victoria played a powerful role. Never one to back down from asserting her own opinion, she is currently the second-longest-serving monarch ever to rule Great Britain, superseded only by Queen Elizabeth II, who broke the record in 2015. While the seven assassination attempts on her life proved that everything she did wasn't always popular, Queen Victoria managed to survive them all, and she lived into old age, even though she carried with her the deep grief of losing her husband, Albert, in 1861. For forty years, from his death to hers, Victoria wore black every single day, as a way of mourning her husband and demonstrating the deep bond of passionate love they shared.[11]

Sometimes, a grief you endure or a pain you face may remain with you long after the event has passed. It does not mean you still can't accomplish amazing feats in your life. Your sadness does not have to perfectly and completely flee. It is okay to embrace the full humanity of who you are—all your emotion, experiences, struggles, joys, and hopes—and use it as you continue to grow and work in this world. Queen Victoria models a kind of leadership and strength that doesn't hide from the painful emotions and experiences of life but, rather, keeps moving forward even while remembering that life may not be easy, perfect, or always feel happy.

NOTES

1. Tim Crothers, "Chess Queen of Africa," *Guardian*, August 28, 2016, https://www.theguardian.com/global/2016/aug/28/chess-queen-of-africa-phiona-mutesi.
2. Crothers, "Chess Queen of Africa."
3. Crothers, "Chess Queen of Africa."

4. Eilís O'Neill, "After Achieving Chess Fame, 'Queen of Katwe' Takes New Path," WBUR, January 11, 2019, https://www.wbur.org/onlyagame/2019/01/11/queen-of-katwe -phiona-mutesi-chess.

5. O'Neill, "After Achieving Chess Fame."

6. Crothers, "Chess Queen of Africa."

7. Crothers, "Chess Queen of Africa."

8. O'Neill, "After Achieving Chess Fame."

9. O'Neill, "After Achieving Chess Fame."

10. Chanel Vargas, "15 Fascinating Facts You Didn't Know about Queen Victoria," *Town & Country*, January 8, 2019, https://www.townandcountrymag.com/society/tradition /a14510744/queen-victoria-facts/.

11. "Victoria," *British Royal Family* (official website, managed by the Royal Household at Buckingham Palace), accessed August 25, 2019, https://www.royal.uk/queen-victoria.

14
STEPHANIE KWOLEK

To invent the seemingly magic material we now know as Kevlar, Stephanie Kwolek knew just what she was looking for. With incredible focus, she knew she wanted to create a substance that could be used in firefighters' boots, bridge cables, sporting equipment, hurricane safe rooms, and first responders' vests. Single-mindedly, she pursued this aim with a never-ending series of closer and closer products, until she finally created Kevlar. Her entire life mirrored this pronounced, perfect plan to develop a product. Kwolek always knew she wanted to be an inventor and never detoured from this lofty goal.

Hold on there! Not so fast!

While Stephanie Kwolek, according to her mother, was indeed a perfectionist, that didn't mean that the famed inventor never made mistakes or that she never failed. Just the opposite. One of Kwolek's most notable failures led to her best and most used invention, Kevlar. However, the invention only happened precisely *because* Kwolek created something that initially failed, but, rather than toss it aside, she took a deeper look at the mistake to find something truly astonishing. How did Kwolek reach this pinnacle of success through failing?

Kwolek was born in 1923 in New Kensington, Pennsylvania; her parents were both immigrants from Poland. Her mother loved sewing and fabrics, and Kwolek immediately joined her mother in pursuing this passion, even claiming that she wanted to be a fashion designer when she grew up. Her father's passion included the outdoors, and he would bring his young daughter with him on long, rambling walks through the fields and forests near their family home. Their meandering explorations allowed Kwolek's mind the space to freely make connections, think about what she saw, ask questions, and take samples and specimens. Kwolek would gather these small bits of nature into journals, then write about them, explain them, and analyze them. The synthesis of both her parents' affinities helped Kwolek develop a remarkable zeal for her eventual job.[1]

During her college career at Margaret Morrison Carnegie College, which was then a women's branch of Carnegie Mellon University, Kwolek became fascinated by the study of chemistry. After graduating, she began looking for a temporary job as a scientist. One of the places she interviewed was DuPont, a massive company that

NOT DIMINISHED... FINISHED!

Charles Darwin attempted to go to college for a medical degree, but he didn't keep up with the work, dropped out, and eventually began pursuing his real passion: the study of nature. Even though his own dad thought he was a failure, Darwin originated the theory of evolution and changed the world forever.

was already known for developing chemically engineered materials like nylon and Teflon.[2] Ever throw on a raincoat before you head outside for school or to play? Or maybe get your basketball or soccer uniform ready for an exciting game? Then you've had plenty of experience with DuPont, as many of us wear clothes made of nylon quite often. Take a minute and check out your tag—you might even be wearing a shirt with some nylon in it now!

Kwolek arrived at her interview with DuPont in 1946. She had planned to use her chemistry degree for a while but was already thinking about pursuing medicine as an end goal for her career. Therefore, she saw this job interview—and others like it with companies similar to DuPont—as an initial way to make a living. In the initial job interview at DuPont, Kwolek's confidence and straightforward demeanor shined. When her prospective employer, W. Hale Charch, told her at the end of the interview that she would be notified within two weeks if she had gotten the job, Kwolek requested that he tell her sooner, as she already had another job offer in hand! Her future boss and mentor responded to Kwolek's confidence with a decision that solidified Kwolek's work at DuPont: he asked his secretary to enter the office and immediately dictated an official letter offering Kwolek the job on the spot.[3]

She accepted.

Kwolek's temporary job continued, year after year, as Kwolek found herself doing a bit of what both her parents had taught her: she

HAVE GRIT—DON'T SPLIT!

Now a director of the department of Product for Developer Tools at Microsoft and similar departments at other organizations, Amanda Silver was once told by a professor in college that she was just no good at computer science and that she should leave the major to find something else to study. She didn't.

spun fibers (methodical sewing of a sort!) and analyzed the different combinations of specimens created (channeling her father's nature walk explorations) to try and create useful new compounds and materials. Polymer chemistry, as this line of work is called, enthralled her, and what Kwolek had planned on doing for only a few years turned into a lifelong career and passion.[4]

Have you ever started something with the plan of only dabbling in it to then find that you loved it? Have you ever tried a new sport, club, or activity that you figured would be short-lived but found you had an indelible and incredible taste for it? Kwolek's career choice ended up being somewhat of a happy mistake, diverting her original plans, yet using skills she had been practicing and growing all her life.

In 1965, nineteen years after she graduated from college and began working at DuPont, Kwolek was involved in the company's goal to replace the steel wires that were being used in car tires. The company had forecasted an explosion in gas prices, and scientists at the company conjectured that tires that weighed less—were lighter but just as strong—could help increase gas mileage. They set to work.[5]

Day after day, Kwolek dissolved elements and spun fibers in an attempt to re-create the steel wires in tires yet make them lighter. Kwolek would dissolve polymers—big chains of molecules—and take the dissolved substance and use a machine to spin it into a new substance. Under high heat—four hundred degrees—the polymers would dissolve, but once Kwolek and other scientists tried to spin the dissolved materials into fibers, they would be far too bendy and not nearly as strong as steel. Usually, the process created clear liquids when the polymers were dissolved, which is what scientists expected and assumed would consistently occur.[6]

One day, however, Kwolek dissolved a whole slew of polyamides, hoping this batch might yield some pretty cool results. So, she was severely bummed out by the not-so-cool results. The liquid that came out of the machine wasn't even clear this time! Rather than getting closer to a jackpot solution, Kwolek assumed she was getting further away. You see, up to this point in the field of polymer dissolution, liquids always came out clear. This seemed to be one key indicator that a scientist was on the right track.[7]

This time? *Definitely wrong track.* The liquid that came out was white and milky, and Kwolek's knee-jerk reaction was to throw it away and try to dissolve a new polymer.

Toss it!

No good!

A big mistake!

Instead, Kwolek's decision in that moment, in no uncertain terms, literally changed history. It also changed her life and the trajectory of DuPont.

SWERVE WITH NERVE!

Even though penicillin's creation was a lifesaving boon worldwide, it wasn't long before antibiotics inundated medical offices and prescriptions. The solve-all solution eventually caused resistant bacteria to develop, as well as other problems in people who did not finish or overused their treatments. Antibiotics are at times a massive success and, at others, a failure that has sent scientists back to consider new solutions!

Instead of throwing the liquid away because it did not fit precisely into the bounds of the previously accepted body of knowledge regarding this strand of chemical engineering, Kwolek saved it.

And then she spun it.

Kwolek watched it progress through the machine that helped the liquid spin into fibers, and the result was both welcome and shocking. She hadn't solved the problem of steel in tires. Instead, she had mistakenly invented something much more far-reaching, widely useful, and seemingly miraculous. Kwolek would later recall, "I never in a thousand years expected that little liquid crystal to develop into what it did."[8]

I never in a thousand years expected that little liquid crystal to develop into what it did.

—Stephanie Kwolek

In short, Kwolek had invented a material that was *four times stronger than steel.* You read that right. What another scientist might have thrown away as a silly mistake, straying from the norm, Kwolek saved and spun and created a new material that could take down steel in a head-to-head matchup. Had Steel and the New Material actually gone head-to-head, it might have looked something like this . . .

Steel: Mirror, mirror, on the wall, who is the *strongest* of them all?

New Material: Um . . . ahem . . . well, I don't mean to interrupt your conversation with your mirror, but—

Steel: Then don't! I love my mirror. I am very involved with my mirror, and this is how I start every day as Steel. My mirror reminds me that I am the toughest, most durable, strongest material ever created, and that I—

New Material: Ahem . . . uh, yeah, about that? I seriously don't mean to be rude. I mean, interrupting is not exactly my type of deal, and I realize I'm the new kid in the lab. I get all that. But actually, I'm kind of strong myself.

Steel: How strong?

New Material: Pretty strong.

Steel: *How strong?!*

New Material: Okay, okay, I am very strong.

Steel: I said, *how—*

New Material: Okay! Fine, I'll tell you. I am four times stronger than you.

Steel: Are not!

New Material: Am too.

Steel: Are not!

New Material: Am too!

Okay, you get the point. It took a while to completely develop the new material, but DuPont immediately recognized that Kwolek was onto something truly big. They gave her an entire lab and an entire support team, and she led them to fully develop what we now know as Kevlar. And while you may have thought nylon was pretty cool (and swishy! If you checked and you are wearing a nylon shirt, or shorts, or jersey, or coat, feel the swish!), Kevlar quickly became pretty cool too. People used the mighty new material for bridges, firefighters' boots, first responders' equipment, hurricane safe rooms, sports equipment, and—to come full circle—even race car tires.[9]

Kwolek the inventor turned her years wandering the woods with her father, her time sewing with her mother, and a deeply inquisitive mind into an enthralling breakthrough and new, useful material. Another person may have thrown away the milky substance and chalked it up to failure since it looked nothing like what was expected to be produced.

But breakthroughs don't always follow a familiar pattern. Discoveries, scientific or otherwise, don't always stay to a script.

Some mistakes you've made—or have yet to make—may lead you to something profoundly important and new. They might look like failures on the surface, but if you save them and spin them a bit, you too might discover that there's some magic there, and you may be exactly the one to sew it all together.

★ The Flop Files: **Penicillin** ★

The year was 1928, and Alexander Fleming was ready for a nice vacation from his work in London at St. Mary's Medical School. He took off for Scotland that summer and had a wonderful time but came back to London and the hospital to find his lab dirty and disorganized. Grumbling, he set about cleaning up the lab space . . . and discovered—among the mess—something that would drastically alter the course of human history.

In some of the petri dishes in his lab, Fleming found a mold called *Penicillium notatum*. Rather than set to work wiping the yucky mold away and getting back to his job, Fleming observed that the strange new mold was performing an interesting task: it was slowing and even stopping some of the reproduction of the bacteria in the dishes.[10]

Startled by the realization, Fleming flew into a mold-growing burst! Instead of cleaning up his lab, he tried to mold it over. What had started as a mess soon became a test—and a very important one at that!

His subsequent trials proved the accuracy of his initial findings, and Fleming began to write and speak about the strange development. He said of his medical breakthrough-by-mistake, "When I woke up just after dawn on September 28, 1928, I certainly didn't plan to revolutionize all medicine by discovering the world's first antibiotic, or bacteria killer. But I guess that was exactly what I did."[11]

However, it would still be many years before what we now know as penicillin would be readily usable, or helpful, to people. In

1940, twelve years after Fleming's fascinating discovery, two other researchers, Howard Florey and Ernst Chain, tested a form of the penicillin on mice. All fifty in their lab had bacterial infections, but only twenty-five received the supposed antidote, penicillin. The twenty-five mice who did not receive it died, and the twenty-five who did went on to recover.

These results were as staggering as Fleming's initial finding, and another scientist, Norman Heatley, came on board in 1941 to help figure out ways to mass-produce the antibiotic.[12]

Penicillin went on to drastically reduce the amount of deaths due to bacteria and infections, having an immediate and widespread impact worldwide. But what if Fleming's lab had been a little cleaner, a little tidier? Mistakes and messes can sometimes lead us to paths of profound possibility, even if it still takes us years to get there.

NOTES

1. Kiona N. Smith, "Stronger than Steel: How Chemist Stephanie Kwolek Invented Kevlar," *Forbes*, July 31, 2018, https://www.forbes.com/sites/kionasmith/2018/07/31/stronger-than-steel-how-chemist-stephanie-kwolek-invented-kevlar/#3929a27e1c3e.
2. Smith, "Stronger than Steel."
3. "Stephanie L. Kwolek," Science History Institute, last modified December 9, 2017, https://www.sciencehistory.org/historical-profile/stephanie-l-kwolek.
4. Smith, "Stronger than Steel."
5. Smith, "Stronger than Steel."
6. "Stephanie L. Kwolek."
7. Smith, "Stronger than Steel."
8. Aaron Nathans, "Kevlar Inventor Stephanie Kwolek, 90, Dies," *USA Today*, June 20, 2014, https://www.usatoday.com/story/money/business/2014/06/20/kevlar-inventor-stephanie-kwolek-dies/11133717/.
9. Smith, "Stronger than Steel."

10. Howard Merkel, "The Real Story behind Penicillin," *PBS NewsHour*, September 27, 2013, https://www.pbs.org/newshour/health/the-real-story-behind-the-worlds -first-antibiotic.

11. Merkel, "The Real Story behind Penicillin."

12. Merkel, "The Real Story behind Penicillin."

15
ROBERT INDIANA

With millions of copies of his artwork floating around the world, Robert Indiana has a name that is synonymous with success in the art world. Throughout his time developing now-famous works of art, Indiana lived to the age of eighty-nine, when he passed away surrounded by throngs of fans, friends, and reverent art critics. Paid millions for the use of his most iconic work of art, the word *LOVE* (crafted with the *L* and the *O* on top of the *V* and the *E*), Indiana enjoyed life in his multiple homes—including mansions in New York City and Cape Cod. By success standards in the art world and even in the business world, Indiana was a smash hit.

*N*ope.

Originally named Robert Clark, the artist changed his last name to Indiana after he moved from Indiana to New York to try and make it as an artist. Once there, he realized that he wasn't the only Clark trying to break into a highly competitive art scene, so he changed his last name to help himself stand out. If the name change didn't help him stand out, a work of art he designed in 1964 sure did.[1]

LOVE was a design Indiana first used on the front of a Christmas card he sent to friends that year. After making and sending the card, he realized how much he liked it, so he kept making versions of the same work. He tried new colors and sizes and continued creating and displaying the work everywhere he could—sometimes even depositing statues in public places for others to see.[2]

At once a simple and profound work of art—it has the ability to draw a viewer's eye and emanate a sense of lightness and depth—Indiana soon saw the public go mad for his rendition of LOVE. In 1965, the Museum of Modern Art in New York commissioned him to make a Christmas card with his LOVE on it that *they* could use. The subsequent year, 1966, an art gallery in New York invited him to do a whole show of various artwork using the motif he had created with LOVE.[3]

Then the US Postal Service, not to be outdone by art museums and studios, decided they, too, wanted to spread the word about love. So, they paid Indiana a one-time fee of $1,000 to create an eight-cent postage stamp for them. The stamp, when it was released in 1973, was so wildly popular that the US Postal Service decided to print 330 million copies of the stamp.[4]

Wow—330 million copies!

FAIL...THEN PREVAIL!

Artist Claude Monet was frequently harshly criticized by critics and peers alike, yet his impressionist style is now celebrated the world over (and it's worth mentioning that even a small painting of one of his flowers is worth millions upon millions of dollars).

At this point in the chapter, if you're reading closely, you might be wondering something:

You: Hey, uh, Luke, not to barge in here at all since you're the author and I'm the reader . . . but . . . you know, it sure seems like this Chicago guy—
Me: Indiana, you mean?
You: Yep, Indiana. Just wanted to be sure you were listening to me . . . Well, this Indiana guy, seems like he had an awful lot of success. Where's the failure? Where's the rejection of all his artwork, the over and over being knocked down, the struggle, you know?
Me: I'm glad you asked. See . . .

What's fascinating about Indiana's journey is that he *did* make it big. He succeeded. He moved from Indiana to New York with the hopes of making it big in a highly competitive art world. He worked hard. People took notice. He created amazing art. Museums and studios took notice. Even the postal service took notice!

But instead of being the end of Indiana's journey, this was just the beginning. Because his success ended up becoming what he later termed his biggest mistake. His success led to his failure.[5]

As LOVE spread far and wide, people couldn't wait to get it on their T-shirts, make their own versions of it, put it on book

FROM WEAK TO PEAK!

Nitrous oxide, which helps patients to relax and numbs them from pain, was originally used in the early 1800s at parties to make people laugh. However, at one of those parties, a dentist named Horace Wells watched as one of his friends, who happened to have taken nitrous oxide, got a large and bloody cut on his leg. But the friend wasn't complaining about any pain! Anesthesia was mistakenly born right then, in 1844.

covers, sell postcards and bookmarks and little signs and place mats and everything else you can possibly imagine that can hold a print of a piece of art on it. That seems like a good thing, right? That seems like a *great* thing, right?

LOVE *bit me. It was a marvelous idea, but it was also a terrible mistake. It became too popular; it became too popular.*

—Robert Indiana

It might have been, if two things were different. First, Indiana never copyrighted the work, so technically he didn't own the design. Therefore, even though *his* image was now racing around the globe—and being translated into every possible language, sometimes by him and sometimes by others—he wasn't getting much money for it. A royalty is an amount of money an artist, musician, or author makes when someone else uses their creation. And people were using Indiana's creation a whole lot. But since he never copyrighted it, he wasn't getting royalties for all of those uses.[6]

The other thing that led his breakout success to turn into a failure was that Indiana became so deeply intertwined with the LOVE art, critics and the art world started to think of him only in that way. Instead of being open to or considering all his other work, they started to see him as a commercial artist who simply had one great idea. They no longer took him very seriously. Indiana put it like this: "*LOVE* bit me. It was a marvelous idea, but it was also a terrible mistake. It became too popular; it became too popular."[7]

By 1978, Indiana had decided that he could no longer stay in the New York art scene, and he hoped that by moving away to a tiny island in Maine, he might be able to rehabilitate his image and create new art contributions that would be taken seriously. Suddenly, instead of spreading LOVE wherever he could, Indiana began to hide from it. He shunned crowds and art shows, didn't go out much, and mainly stayed in his studio and home off the coast of Maine. He reasoned, "It's much better to be exclusive and remote. That's why I'm on an island off the coast of Maine, you see."[8]

It's much better to be exclusive and remote. That's why I'm on an island off the coast of Maine, you see.

—Robert Indiana

Slowly, people heard less and less from Indiana, even though he kept creating. And even though many of his LOVE statues still grace parks around the country, and stamps, and postcards and bookmarks and T-shirts and—you get the picture—Indiana's name doesn't.

In strange twists, the day right before he died at age eighty-nine, a new lawsuit regarding some of Indiana's artwork was filed, and there are accusations that Indiana's caretaker was keeping him on the island, or keeping other people out.[9] Was Indiana reclusive and shunning connections with even friends by the end of his life, or was he being held hostage by the person he had

SWERVE WITH NERVE!

In 1894, brothers John and William Kellogg were busy boiling some wheat to prepare it to make dough. They mistakenly let it cook for too long, and what came out was far too flaky and crunchy. So, the brothers baked it instead and turned their mistake into the cereal we now call Kellogg's Corn Flakes.

hired to take care of him in his older age? We may never know the full story. However, we will continue to see the massive displays of LOVE all around us.

Sometimes, what at first seems like a great success can bring more heartache than hope. While LOVE did indeed bring immense joy and hope to many around the world, it also brought struggle and failure to the very artist who created it. Though Indiana sought acclaim and popularity, it may have been these two very things that caused him to flee society and crave a place and a space where he could once again create without the weight of popularity. You've heard the cliché "Be careful what you wish for"? Indiana may be a cautionary tale of that counsel. His story is not unlike those of other famous creators who fled the spotlight after their works became megahits, including writers like Harper Lee (*To Kill a Mockingbird*) and J. D. Salinger (*The Catcher in the Rye*). Sometimes, fame and fortune aren't all they're cracked up to be. And sometimes, there is more than one kind of success!

★ The Flop Files: **George Speck (Crum) and Catherine "Kate" Speck Adkins Wicks** ★

In an upscale, classy restaurant called Moon Lake Lodge Resort in upstate New York, two gifted cooks, who also happened to be brother and sister, worked in seamless unison preparing all kinds of specialties for diners. George Speck (Crum) and Catherine Speck Adkins Wicks were hard at work one night when a complaint came in to the kitchen from a diner.[10]

A customary food at the time was potatoes sliced and fried, typically called french-fried potatoes, because the practice was first developed in France. This style of cooking potatoes made its way to America thanks to Thomas Jefferson, who thoroughly enjoyed them in France, and asked them to be made for him in America too. The trend traveled, and many restaurants began serving them. (As a side note to this side dish: if you've ever wondered how french fries became all the rage in America—now you know!)

But one customer in Saratoga Springs, New York, in 1853 complained to Crum that the potatoes were far too thick for his liking. Not known as a patient man, Crum became visibly frustrated that anyone would complain about his cooking, and so he began cutting up the potatoes into extremely thin slices, then frying them far too long in a bunch of grease, and finally he heaped some salt on them.[11]

Take that!

Thinking the concoction would be disgusting, and a fitting way to show his disdain for the complaint, Crum was shocked to learn that the complaining customer thought the exact opposite. These potatoes were divine. Amazing. Astounding.

Soon, guests began requesting the oddly thin–sliced, fried, and salted chips. Crum continued cooking them, and soon he had a new name for the mistakenly invented snack: Saratoga Chips.

That's *one* version of the story. But because we don't have exact records, and only word-of-mouth stories that have been passed on down the generations, the other version involved Crum's sister, Kate Wicks.

In this alternate version, Wicks was hard at work in the kitchen, frying doughnuts. She figured she would prep some of her other work at the same time and began cutting potatoes. As she did so, one thinly sliced portion of a potato mistakenly fell into the vat of oil, and bam: the first potato chip was born![12]

While historians aren't exactly sure which version is correct, either way, one thing is for sure: the potato chip was invented by mistake. A snack that currently makes over $6 billion a year for snack companies, and which almost half of all Americans eat, never would have existed without an angry customer and a temperamental cook, or another cook attempting to do a lot of work all at the same time.

What was a mistake became one of the country's favorite snack foods and one which you probably ate today, or yesterday, or . . . right . . . *now?*

NOTES

1. Elizabeth Botten, "Archives Reveal Touching Stories on the Life of Robert Indiana, the Man Who Invented 'LOVE,'" *Smithsonian*, May 30, 2018, https://www.smithsonianmag.com/smithsonian-institution/robert-indiana-was-man-who-invented-love-180969201/.
2. Jori Finkel, "Robert Indiana, 89, Who Turned 'Love' Into Enduring Art, Is Dead," *New York Times*, May 21, 2018, https://www.nytimes.com/2018/05/21/obituaries/robert-indiana-love-pop-art-dies.html.
3. Botten, "Archives Reveal Touching Stories."
4. Finkel, "Robert Indiana, 89."
5. Finkel, "Robert Indiana, 89."
6. Will Higgins, "We Love Pop Artist Robert Indiana, even If He Didn't Always Love Us," *Indianapolis Star*, May 22, 2018, https://www.indystar.com/story/entertainment/2018/05/22/robert-indiana-one-coolest-and-quirkiest-hoosiers-ever/632030002/.
7. Karen Michel, "Robert Indiana: A Career Defined by 'LOVE' No Longer," *Weekend Edition*, NPR, January 5, 2014, https://www.npr.org/2014/01/05/259408158/robert-indiana-a-career-defined-by-love-no-longer.
8. Michel, "Robert Indiana."
9. Finkel, "Robert Indiana, 89."
10. "George Crum," Lemelson–MIT, accessed October 2, 2019, https://lemelson.mit.edu/resources/george-crum.
11. "George Crum."
12. Kim Severson, "The Best Chip? The First One Out of the Bag," *New York Times*, July 4, 2007, https://www.nytimes.com/2007/07/04/dining/04chip.html.

16

ALL-AMERICAN GIRLS PROFESSIONAL BASEBALL LEAGUE

When, in 1943, the first women's professional baseball league began, it was due to a social awakening about the need for equality among women and men. Fans were ecstatic about the possibilities. The women who played in the league were treated with respect, and their uniforms and team names signified that deep respect: uniforms that allowed them to do all the things that baseball players need to do— sprint, slide into bases, and dive. Some of the best team names in the league were the Rockford Tigers, the Milwaukee Grizzlies, and the Fort Wayne Sharks. Even after World War II was over, professional baseball for women continued and, as we all know, to this day is a hugely popular and proud part of American culture—encouraging young girls who love the sport to work hard and dream big as they strive to make the big league.

*N*ope.

The All-American Girls Professional Baseball League (AAGPBL) *was* a remarkable undertaking that *did* create vast new possibilities for women to be seen as equal on the sports field and enabled women who loved baseball to earn more money than the men in their families. Additionally, the women who played revealed resilience, pride, power, and purpose in profound and inspiring ways. However, after fifteen years of existence, the league was canceled due to society's lackluster support and appreciation of it. Additionally, during its run, the league faced severe bias and numerous obstacles—including some that came from the founder of the league himself![1]

In 1943, as World War II raged on, a big name in baseball got to thinking. What name? If you stop reading this book right now and find your way to a gas station or a CVS or a Walgreen's or a local corner shop, then chances are you'll *still* see this big name on the racks by the front cash register: *Wrigley*.

Back yet?

Did you buy a pack?

Pull a stick from the stack.

Now chew on *this* while you chew on *that* . . .

Charles Wrigley was the owner and founder of the massive Wrigley's gum brand, which, as your teeth are telling you right now, still exists today. But Wrigley was rich for another reason, too: he owned the Chicago Cubs baseball team. And in 1943, Wrigley began to get a little scared. See, his fear kept jabbing him with the suggestion that too many men were getting shipped off to war, to fight the rise of Adolf Hitler and the Nazis, and he worried that his team, the Cubs, and baseball in general would lose too many men to war. His profits might go down, and so he concocted a new scheme to keep baseball going, and to keep bringing in the money.[2]

HAVE GRIT—DON'T SPLIT!

Manon Rhéaume became the first woman to ever play in an NHL (National Hockey League) game. As a goalie, she played for Tampa Bay in the preseason and stopped seven out of nine goals, on September 23, 1992. Her long journey to this moment was filled with a lot of rejection, as she recalled, "There were so many times in my life that people said 'No' to me because I was a girl."

He would start a professional baseball league for women. Now, this was an amazing opportunity and a huge blessing to many women across the country who had a deep love of baseball and a passion for the sport. Women such as Shirley Burkovich and Maybelle Blair found the opportunity to be almost too good to be true. Both women absolutely loved baseball, and they never considered that there would be a way to make a healthy amount of money doing exactly what they loved. Burkovich said, "I got $55 a week. That was more than my dad was making. He worked in the steel mills. It wasn't the money—I was just so happy, just to have the opportunity to play baseball."[3]

I got $55 a week. That was more than my dad was making. He worked in the steel mills. It wasn't the money—I was just so happy, just to have the opportunity to play baseball.
—Shirley Burkovich

By the year 1948, a professional sports league that many had doubted would even last a single year was thriving. That year, an estimated 1 million fans filled the stands to see talented, hardworking women play an iconic American sport. Blair said that the feeling was almost indescribable—to be out on a baseball field playing for fans, when only a decade earlier such a vision seemed impossible: "I got on my spikes. . . . And I walked out, and I saw that field. And I says, 'Oh, my god—I am going to get to play baseball.'"[4] It was a dream that she didn't even know she had, and yet it had come true.

Even while the league advanced huge strides for women and provided an amazing doorway for players like Blair and Burkovich, Wrigley didn't have an entirely justice-minded, clear motive for establishing— or running—the league. As noted earlier, money was a big motivator, and even though the women were playing the sport they loved with a passion, Wrigley still ensured that they were viewed in a different way than the men playing professionally. How so?

HOLD THE BOLD!

Mo'ne Davis wasn't about to hear *no* regarding anything she could do with a baseball. In 2014, her seventy-mile-per-hour fastball led her team, the Philadelphia Taney Dragons, to the Little League Championship. Davis was the first girl to ever pitch in the final and to win the championship. The following year, Spike Lee made a documentary about her journey called *I Throw Like a Girl*.

One major way Wrigley ensured the women were viewed as different is built into the name of the league itself: the All-American Girls Professional Baseball League. The talented players who filled the team rosters were not called *Women* by the league's owners—first, Wrigley and later, Arthur Meyerhoff.[5]

Another way that a different standard was set for the women compared to the men was the uniforms they were asked to wear. Men's uniforms in the 1940s—and still today—provide covering for the entire length of the legs, thereby helping protect their skin as they undertake slides and dives, both necessary athletic feats of the sport. However, for the AAGPBL, women were given extremely short skirts as part of their uniforms. This ensured they would be viewed by fans first as women, rather than first as players.[6]

And third, the team names that owners developed for the various squads appeared to also defer to traditional—and deeply unjust—perspectives of women's abilities in sports. Some of the team names that reveal this bias—and show the huge disparity between the naming of female and male baseball teams—include Grand Rapids Chicks, Rockford Peaches, Racine Belles, Chicago Colleens, and the Fort Wayne Daisies.[7] (Contrast those names with some of the men's baseball team names: Pittsburg Pirates, Detroit Tigers, Atlanta Braves, Colorado Rockies, and San Francisco Giants). The message from the owners, it seemed, was clear: *Even though we are encouraging women to play baseball, and paying them well to do it, we don't want you fans to forget that they are still Daises, not Tigers! They are still Peaches, not Giants!*

Finally, an exploration of the rules of conduct that the women had to follow while employed by the league provides a stark contrast to what we now view as equality, empowerment, and self-expression. For instance, the very first rule that the players were required to follow was "ALWAYS appear in feminine attire when not actively engaged in practice or playing ball. This regulation continues through the playoffs for all, even though your team is not participating. AT NO TIME MAY A PLAYER APPEAR IN THE STANDS IN HER UNIFORM, OR WEAR SLACKS OR SHORTS IN PUBLIC."[8] So, a woman like Blair or Burkovich was not allowed to wear shorts or pants in public and was instead always required to dress in a "feminine" way.

Still not convinced of the heavy bias the players endured? How about rule of conduct number four, which ordered the players to remember that "all social engagements must be approved by chaperone. Legitimate requests for dates can be allowed by chaperones."[9] So, if you played for the AAGPBL and you wanted to go out and meet up with a friend (have a social engagement) or go on a date, then you would have to make a formal request to your team's chaperone and then get the request approved before you would be able to go out.

Or how about rule of conduct number fifteen: "Players will not be allowed to drive their cars past their city's limits without the special permission of their manager."[10] So, if you had a car, you would not be able to leave the city unless your team manager gave you special permission to do so, ensuring that you would remain close by and, by extension, under easier surveillance and control.

PLUCK ENOUGH!

Margaret Abbott was the first American woman to win an Olympic gold medal—she did so in 1900 for golf when the events took place in France. However, Abbott never knew she had even competed in the Olympics, let alone that she won. It was only the second Olympics, and the failure of the Olympic committee to label and properly document the event led Abbott to live her entire life thinking that she had simply competed in a variety of golf tournaments—the 1900 event in France being just one of them. It wasn't until the 1980s that this information was discovered!

Even with *all* of the built-in bias and inequality of the first professional baseball league for women, players still used the opportunity as a chance to showcase their remarkable talent and grit. They still displayed courage, the drive to excel, and a passion for the sport that did, indeed, help fans flock to see their games. However, by 1954, as the men's league had overcome any effects on it from World War II, the attendance for the AAGPBL was greatly diminished, a trend that had continued from the apex of 1948. Even though the league never again reached the million mark for ticket sales, the legend of the league lives on, in part thanks to the big-budget film *A League of Their Own*.[11]

I got on my spikes. . . . And I walked out, and I saw that field. And I says, "Oh, my god—I am going to get to play baseball."

—Maybelle Blair

The All-American Girls Professional Baseball League was conjectured to be an immediate flop—critics argued that no one would be interested in watching the games and that women just couldn't be great baseball players. Both these criticisms were squashed by the fifteen seasons of the league. But over time, attendance and interest *did* wane and eventually fall flat. While it initially enjoyed a far greater deal of success than anyone had predicted, in the end, the AAGPBL was not sustainable. Society, investments, and support for the league floundered, and with it, the hopes of a sustainable and permanent professional baseball league for women floundered too.

Additionally, the league itself also perpetuated some of its own failures, even as it advanced a powerful new playing field for women. Built-in bias still made its way onto that field, even as it opened doors for a new possibility that even the players themselves hadn't fully fathomed. How might *you* work to open the door to a new possibility that others can't quite yet fathom? Who might *you* invite to step into the game—or your lunch group, or your chess club, or your gaming community—even if others, at first, laughed off your conjecture? And how might you do so while engendering equality rather than bias?

NOTES

1. "All-American Girls Professional Baseball League," *Encyclopædia Britannica*, July 11, 2019, https://www.britannica.com/topic/All-American-Girls-Professional-Baseball-League
2. "All-American Girls Professional Baseball."
3. Karen Given, "75 Years after the Women's Pro League, Bringing Baseball Back to Girls," WBUR, August 17, 2018, https://www.wbur.org/onlyagame/2018/08/17/women-baseball-mone-davis.
4. Given, "75 Years after the Women's Pro League."
5. Given, "75 Years after the Women's Pro League."
6. Given, "75 Years after the Women's Pro League."
7. "AAGPBL Teams," All-American Girls Professional Baseball League Players Association, https://www.aagpbl.org/teams.
8. "AAGPBL Rules of Conduct," All-American Girls Professional Baseball League Players Association, https://www.aagpbl.org/history/rules-of-conduct.
9. "AAGPBL Rules of Conduct."
10. "AAGPBL Rules of Conduct."
11. Vincent Canby, "For the Girls of Summer, Pop Flies and Charm School," *New York Times*, July 1, 1992, https://www.nytimes.com/1992/07/01/movies/review-film-for-the-girls-of-summer-pop-flies-and-charm-school.html.

17
CARVENS LISSAINT

Growing up reading the lines of Shakespeare aloud from his high-rise apartment home, Carvens Lissaint always knew that he was destined for greatness on Broadway. Early on, he matriculated into some of the finest private schools in the country, enjoying quick success for his dominating and mesmerizing stage presence. Rooted in what many theater and acting experts term "high arts," Lissaint always felt respected for his love of hip-hop and slam poetry and consistently felt welcome to include these in his performances and his work in his graduate school for acting. This pedigree of moving from one triumph to another eventually helped Lissaint land his most prominent role ever: playing George Washington in the Broadway hit *Hamilton* at the Richard Rodgers Theater in New York City.

N

o way!

While Carvens Lissaint did eventually land a starring role as George Washington in the massively successful, Tony award–winning Broadway hit *Hamilton*, by Lin-Manuel Miranda (read about him in chapter 9!), getting there was anything but a story of success, ease, or clarity.

Lissaint's mother and father immigrated to America from Haiti, and he grew up in a section of New York called Washington Heights—interestingly, where Miranda's first Broadway hit, *In the Heights*, takes place. Growing up, Lissaint consistently struggled in school. The traditional education system didn't work for him, and he felt himself always slipping away into his imagination. Instead of rote, boring learning, Lissaint felt a desire and a drive to use his imagination and get truly engaged with his own learning. Instead, school turned him off, and his plummeting grades documented that path.[1]

Do you ever feel like, no matter what, you can't get yourself to focus at school? Or that what you're learning does not seem to connect with who you are and with the world you see (or the world you imagine!) around you? While many adults respond to any queries about school with a trite *It's just the way things are*, you're not alone. Many imaginative, energetic students wonder if learning could look different, feel more alive, create more opportunity to wonder and to wander. Lissaint was in this group.

However, Lissaint's father was determined that his son would get a good education and use it to change the family legacy. Working two jobs, Lissaint's dad was a picture of constant, unending grit. He would work all day until 2:00 AM, sleep for four hours, and then wake up and repeat the cycle. His message to his son was clear: work hard in school, earn a living, and break the cycle of working constantly to make ends meet.[2]

Managing to finish high school, Lissaint had already fallen in love with slam poetry. One evening, a coaching community he was working with brought everyone to see a slam poetry performance, and Lissaint said he knew instantly that what was happening onstage was the way he wanted to spend his life. He felt alive—like the performance on the stage ignited a deep part of who he was. [3]

Attempting to follow this dream of being a performance artist—and rejecting his father's advice to find a more stable, financially secure path—Lissaint started community college immediately following high school. However, something still didn't fit, and while he stuck with and struggled with the program for a year, he finally dropped out. He had literally flunked community college.[4]

Sound like what you expected from a star of one of the biggest Broadway hits of all time? Consider the times when you've received an F on a school test or project, or flubbed a performance, or been cut during a sports tryout. You tried your best, but you flunked. You tried, and you failed. Like Lissaint, there may have seemed like no path forward.

SWERVE WITH NERVE!

Getting his start as a mechanic, Alfie Boe loved to sing on the job. Word got around, and another mechanic shared how good Boe was with a contact involved in the music industry. Boe eventually ended up joining the English National Opera and, later on, landed the starring role of Jean Valjean in *Les Misérables* on Broadway.

Over the next three years, that sense of failure remained close by as Lissaint continued to struggle. Rather than quitting his passion for performance art and reverting to a more financially stable job, Lissaint took a bigger risk. He continued writing his own slam poems and performed them on trains and in other public places for cash. He would sing and rap and play his poetry with all the zest and zeal he could fathom and hope that people would offer enough cash for him to buy a meal, a train ticket, and maybe—if he was really lucky—a ticket to a Broadway show to keep him inspired. Meanwhile, Lissaint was homeless. He stayed the night with friends when he could, and other times he bought a ticket to the subway and simply rode the train all night long, back and forth.[5]

As Lissaint struggled to find his path forward, the Richard Rodgers Theater—where *In the Heights* was playing when Lissaint was in his twenties—was a symbol of hope. Whenever he had enough, he would buy a ticket to watch the show about his own neighborhood. He heard poetry that sounded like his own, heard rhythms and lyrics and resonances that made him feel like he was not alone. Those performances gave him hope and helped him to continue believing that one day he, too, might be on a stage like that.[6]

And so, he kept trying. He applied to New York University's (NYU's) School of Drama. And he was accepted!

Bring on the success!

Struggle? See you later! Now we enter the triumph stage of Lissaint's life!

Right?

Right?!

Not quite.

FAIL...THEN PREVAIL!

Esteemed movie director, writer, and star Tyler Perry, known for films like his Madea series, tried for years to stage plays he had written. He said, "From 1992 until 1998, every show I put on flopped. No one showed up, and I lost all my money."[7] Now, Perry regularly records blockbuster sales of film version based on many of those failed plays from the 1990s.

Even though Lissaint was accepted into the drama program, his academic record was not strong enough for him to be an NYU student, and so he was not actually accepted into the school. Lissaint's ability—his imagination, his skills, his talent, his passion—were all there, but still failure persisted.

Finally, Lissaint was accepted into St. John's University, also in New York City, with a complete scholarship. The doors had finally opened after his long saga of hard work and seemingly endless failure, rejection, and obstacles. Now, at long last, his path would be cleared to do what he loved and to show other people exactly how powerful and poised he could be.[8]

Yeah?!

No.

While in acting school, Lissaint longed to be able to perform poetry that he believed had high value and deep worth, but his professors constantly rejected his pleas. Instead, they claimed, "high art" consisted of poetry by the likes of William Shakespeare. Hip-hop didn't qualify. Slam poetry didn't count. Lissaint has elaborated, "Voice and speech teachers told me, 'You should stop doing spoken-word poetry, it's inspiring your regionalism and your dialect too much. We're afraid you'll never be able to work in the American theater because of your speech, because you do that rap thing.'"[9]

Voice and speech teachers told me, "You should stop doing spoken-word poetry, it's inspiring your regionalism and your dialect too much. We're afraid you'll never be able to work in the American theater because of your speech, because you do that rap thing."
—Carvens Lissaint

Instead of listening to their rejection, Lissaint did what he had, by now, made a practice of doing: he proved them wrong. He worked with determination to master as many forms of art and expression as he could—from Shakespeare to hip-hop and everything in between. And once he finished his undergraduate degree at St. John's, Lissaint *did* get into and attend NYU, for graduate school.

And then, *finally*, when *Hamilton* made its debut on Broadway, Lissaint auditioned and earned the title of stand-by—someone who would be ready to go onstage should certain actors be unable to perform at the last minute. From there, Lissaint earned the role of George Washington for the traveling production of *Hamilton*, and from there, yes: he earned a starring role as George Washington right on Broadway, at the Richard Rodgers Theater.

One night, his father saw him perform. "My father wept in my arms at the stage door for a good minute and a half," Lissiant said. "He wept uncontrollably and held me. It was probably the first time he's ever held me like that in his life."[10] He had proven to a long line of people, including his father, what his own determination and passion could accomplish.

FROM WEAK TO PEAK!

Elena Ricardo spent ten years of her childhood in rigorous and intense training as a gymnast, hoping to make that her career. However, at age sixteen, things didn't work out, and she switched to theater. Ricardo eventually landed a starring role in *Mamma Mia!* on Broadway.

My father wept in my arms at the stage door for a good minute and a half. He wept uncontrollably and held me. It was probably the first time he's ever held me like that in his life.

—Carvens Lissaint

While Lissaint became very familiar with both failure and struggle over the course of his journey, he never let it deter him from the deepest passion he had: to work as a performance artist. Even though he didn't have the pedigree of a private school or elite training, he never let that fact shame his own fire or dull his own dreams. He pushed forward.

Failure was not the destination of Lissaint's life journey, even though he may have stopped at its station a few times. He stayed on the train and kept riding it—sometimes all through the night to stay warm and dry. Just because the train you might happen to be on makes a stop at failure's station doesn't mean you have to get off the train. Stay on board; keep riding. Who knows where you'll stop next?

★ The Flop Files: **Bette Nesmith Graham** ★

In 1954, Bette Nesmith Graham was doing her best to provide for her son through her work as an executive secretary in Dallas, Texas. The job wasn't her dream, and it did not pay especially well. Originally, Graham had wanted to be an artist, but quickly learned that she wasn't able to provide for her son through that means. Secretarial work had been simply a way to pay the bills. [11]

But she watched—mesmerized—how window painters at her office would simply use a dab of new paint here or there to cover up any mistakes they made when they were working. Meanwhile, while *she* worked typing up the company's letters on IBM typewriters, if she were to make a mistake, she'd have to throw away the entire page and start over! [12]

As she watched the window workers, then looked at her own typewritten pages, which were sometimes almost complete before she made an error, the proverbial lightbulb went off. What if she could devise a solution much like the window painters used to handle mistakes? What if there were some way to cover up a tiny typewritten mistake on her paper so that she wouldn't have to re-create the *entire* page all over again?

There was.

At home in her kitchen, Graham worked with her blender and tempura paints to concoct a combination that matched the color of the paper at her office. The result? Whenever she made a mistake, she would apply a dab of what she called MISTAKE OUT and then keep going, rather than scrap the entire page and start over. Her concoction was so good that her boss couldn't even tell the difference![13]

Even though Graham had dropped out of high school and had to stop pursuing her original dream as an artist, she had found a way to allow creativity to find her, and she flew with it. Word spread of this divine new creation, and other secretaries began asking her for some of this seemingly miraculous MISTAKE OUT. It wasn't long before she started paying her son Michael and his friend about a buck an hour to help her mass-produce it and sell it to others. However, Graham didn't have enough money to pay the $400 fee to patent her own invention.[14]

Imagine that! She had to continue to create it in her own home and couldn't even take full credit for it because she couldn't afford the cost of, well, paying the government to officially take credit for it.

That would soon change, however, as demand kept climbing, and Graham was fired by her boss for her side job of making MISTAKE OUT. Being fired, though considered a failure by some, was the catalyst that pushed Graham to fully devote herself to her creation. And she did. Eventually, MISTAKE OUT became Liquid Paper; she got the money for her patent, built a factory, hired twenty workers, and the rest is history.

The company grew, demand continued to soar, and finally, in 1979, Graham sold her company to Gillette for $47.5 million. What had begun in reaction to frustration over redoing work and as an observation from a daydreaming mind had eventually been converted into a massive enterprise that not only changed the way hundreds of thousands of people did their work but also dramatically changed Graham's own life.[15]

NOTES

1. Zachary Stewart, "Once Homeless, Carvens Lissaint Rides Out West with *Hamilton*," Theatermania, March 31, 2018, https://www.theatermania.com/broadway/news/carvens-lissaint-rides-out-west-with-hamilton_84623.html.
2. Stewart, "Once Homeless, Carvens Lissaint Rides Out."
3. Stewart, "Once Homeless, Carvens Lissaint Rides Out."
4. Laura Bassett, "You Can Star in 'Hamilton' and Still Fear for Your Life as a Black Man," *Huffington Post*, January 7, 2019, https://www.huffpost.com/entry/carvens-lissaint-broadway-hamilton_n_5c2d0cd6e4b08aaf7a955162.
5. Stewart, "Once Homeless, Carvens Lissaint Rides Out."
6. Bassett, "You Can Star in 'Hamilton.'"
7. Carolyn M. Brown, "Tyler Perry on How to Find Success after Failure," *Black Enterprise*, November 25, 2014, https://www.blackenterprise.com/tyler-perry-on-finding-success-after-failure/.
8. Stewart, "Once Homeless, Carvens Lissaint Rides Out."
9. Bassett, "You Can Star in 'Hamilton.'"
10. Bassett, "You Can Star in 'Hamilton.'"
11. Andrew R. Chow, "Overlooked No More: Bette Nesmith Graham, Who Invented Liquid Paper," *New York Times*, July 11, 2018, https://www.nytimes.com/2018/07/11/obituaries/bette-nesmith-graham-overlooked.html.
12. Zameena Mejia, "How Inventing Liquid Paper Got a Secretary Fired and Then Turned here into an Exec Worth $25 Million," CNBC, July 13, 2018, https://www.cnbc.com/2018/07/19/inventing-liquid-paper-got-a-secretary-fired-and-then-made-her-rich.html.
13. Chow, "Overlooked No More: Bette Nesmith Graham."
14. Mejia, "How Inventing Liquid Paper."
15. Mejia, "How Inventing Liquid Paper."

18
CRISTINA MARTINEZ

To create South Philly Barbacoa, her amazing popular restaurant in South Philadelphia, chef Cristina Martinez was given many highly prestigious grants from the United States government. Recognizing the tough terrain she had traveled to emigrate from Mexico, her bosses in the United States treated her with dignity and respect before she opened up her own business, which she did in a massive, epic, spectacularly big way. Martinez floated effortlessly from one success to the next and proves just how simple it is to create both an amazing dish and an amazing life.

*N*ot!

Featured on season five of the hit TV series *Chef's Table*, Cristina Martinez has a story that is anything but easy or without both failure and struggle. While she did, indeed, start her own hit restaurant, South

Philly Barbacoa, the journey to get there—and the journey to keep it going—is marked by rejection and intensely hard work, not ease and simplicity.

Originally from Mexico, Martinez married at seventeen years old but quickly found that relationship to be unhealthy and toxic. Her husband's family, too, mistreated her, and Martinez began to hope for a better future for her daughter, Karla, whom she had at nineteen years old. As Karla grew, Martinez realized that she wanted her daughter to be able to attend boarding school, earning an education that would prepare and help her to thrive. To be able to pay for the tuition, Martinez crossed the border from Juárez, Mexico, to the United States in the hopes of finding a job that would allow her to support her daughter.[1]

FROM WEAK TO PEAK!

Akio Morita and Masaru Ibuka were partners who established the massive company Sony, which we now know as a force for digital and technological creation. When the partners were starting out, one of their first products, in 1945, was an electronic rice cooker. The only glitch was that the rice always came out burned, and their product sold fewer than one hundred units. Sony, of course, would sell far more products as the company grew.

But this border crossing was a treacherous, deeply dangerous gamble that Martinez took in order to try to create this better life for herself and to be able to support her daughter's school hopes. For more than fourteen days, Martinez and those in her group trekked through the desert, under constant danger of physical harm. Water and food were scarce, and with parched throats and hopeful hearts, Martinez and her companions took one plodding step after another. There was a constant fear of dehydration, collapse, being discovered and captured, or after every risk, not even making it to America.[2]

Finally, and against all odds, Martinez stepped foot onto American soil, and with it felt her heart surge at the prospect of finally giving her daughter what she longed to provide: safety, security, school, hope, and a future. Martinez had fled an abusive husband, his controlling family, and had finally set foot on solid ground—ground on which she could build a new life.[3]

That's when Martinez began working in a variety of restaurants, getting her start by slicing vegetables. She worked hard, did everything that was asked of her, and showed incredible promise, causing her various employers to consistently promote her to higher ranks within the various restaurants in which she worked.[4]

It would be great, here, to be able to report that this trend continued, and Martinez was able to leap from one growing success to another to another, until she could open her own restaurant. But that wasn't what happened. Instead of reaping the benefits of all her hard work within the various kitchens she worked in, Martinez discovered new challenges to conquer and a life in America that was not easy in the least. Her undocumented status meant that she lived in constant fear of being caught and deported. Consistently sending money home for Karla's school, her work gave her a newfound freedom and empowerment, but her undocumented status made her a target and a scapegoat for many who refused to understand her plight and the plight of so many others like her. Martinez longed to be recognized as legitimate and stop living in fear.[5] Therefore, as an undocumented immigrant simply trying her best to create a better life for her daughter, Martinez approached one of her employers—at an Italian restaurant where she was working in Philadelphia—for help with her application for a green card. But instead of providing a letter to document Martinez's hard work, consistent effort, and meaningful contributions to the restaurant, the employer fired her.[6]

Can you imagine what this must have felt like for her? Here she is—in her greatest moment of need—putting trust in someone she's worked so hard and diligently for, and being let down completely. Instead her boss washed their hands of her, pushing her out the door rather than helping her stay in the US to continue her employment. Hearing about her predicament made little difference to her employer despite Martinez's loyalty, obvious expertise, and passion for food.[7]

Just like that, she was back where she started:

Her income? Gone. Her ability to support her daughter, Karla? Gone. Her stability and structure that she had worked tirelessly to create? Gone.

Martinez found herself in a no-win situation, grappling with the failure of her employment and trying to figure out a path forward as an undocumented immigrant. She and her new husband, Ben Miller, learned that it would be nearly impossible to find a way for Martinez to have legal status and remain in the US, as changing her status would involve Martinez traveling all the way back to Mexico, applying while there, and then waiting a required three years before she could even be considered to reenter the United States. Even then, chances were desperately slim that this would ever happen.

Needing money to support her daughter, Martinez used her ingenuity and her passion for food to turn her failure into something far more profound, and far more inspiring. She returned home to her

NOT DIMINISHED... FINISHED!

Cheese was invented by mistake around four thousand years ago when travelers happened to be carrying milk in a bag made of dried sheep intestine. The hot sun soured the milk, and the rennet from the dried sheep intestine helped transform that soured milk into what we now call cheese.

and her husband's small kitchen in their tiny apartment, turned on the stove, and started cooking. At first, she made quesadillas and traveled to hawk them in nearby markets to construction workers. Then, she decided to try cooking and selling barbacoa right out of her apartment. A slow-fired lamb meat recipe tinged with lime and a variety of other spices, barbacoa was something Martinez had been making since she was a little girl growing up in Mexico. Cooking it was not only a possible way forward but also a tender reminder of home. She said, "I've been cooking barbacoa since I was six years old. And still, when I'm making barbacoa, I feel something magical. I rejoice in my heart."[8]

HAVE GRIT—DON'T SPLIT!

Paul Prudhomme loved cooking, and he got an early shot at running his own restaurant when he opened Big Daddy O's Patio in 1957, where the specialty was hamburgers. However, the burgers were a bust, and Prudhomme acknowledged his failure and closed the restaurant nine short months after he opened it. He then sold magazines for a while. But cooking was his passion, and Prudhomme tried again. By 1979, he was the owner, with his wife, of a sought-after restaurant, K-Paul's Louisiana Kitchen in New Orleans, *and* the author of eleven cookbooks.

I've been cooking barbacoa since I was six years old. And still, when I'm making barbacoa, I feel something magical. I rejoice in my heart.

—Cristina Martinez

Figuring she would cook barbacoa for tacos and sell them out of her apartment, she hoped it would generate at least a little money to help as she charted a path forward. One Sunday, she gave the venture a try, spreading news of the barbacoa for sale to workers she knew and talking it up as much as she could. Wondering if anyone would come that Sunday, she got cooking.

Consider the times you may have been pushed out—saw a circle close in front of you and there was nothing you could do about it. Maybe you felt voiceless. Maybe you felt like somebody was judging you based on one tiny label slapped on your forehead rather than the depth and reality of who you really are. No matter how hard you tried to get back into that circle, they wouldn't let you in.

It might be that you were pushed out from a lunch table at your school, cut from a sports team, shunned in your class or in the hallways, or maybe even in your own family. Martinez faced this kind of closed circle in front of her, shut out of the work she had toiled at for so many years.

But instead of wallowing in shame and fear, Martinez started a fire. She cooked the lamb. One taco at a time, she fought back. With stakes incredibly high—constantly at risk for deportation from ICE or of not being able to support her daughter—Martinez saw her leap pay off.[9]

That Sunday morning, her barbacoa tacos completely sold out.

So, she did it again.

And again. And again. And again.

Word spread that Martinez made the meanest barbacoa around, and eventually she transitioned the business out of her apartment and into a cart, and then out of a cart and into a restaurant: South Philly Barbacoa.

The rave reviews continued to pour in—guests leaving her place smiling and satisfied and already looking forward to their next trip back.

Martinez did not allow the treacherous journey from Mexico to the United States stop her from trying to make a better life. Nor did she allow her firing after she asked for help to keep her down. Instead, she fought back with food.

This is something that can be achieved only through struggle, perseverance, and hard work.

—Cristina Martinez

And this is exactly what she continues to do. Martinez and her husband used the newfound status of her restaurant and its widespread and growing fame as an opportunity to talk about immigration, becoming impromptu leaders of the #right2work uprising across the country. The journey is not without fear, not without rejection, and not without failure. But Martinez, every day, makes the courageous decision to wake up, fight for her own ability to work, and help fight for others like her to have that same ability. She said, "This is something that can be achieved only through struggle, perseverance, and hard work."[10] And against all odds, Martinez is still persevering. She's still cooking.

NOTES

1. Chris Fuhrmeister, "'Chef's Table' Recap: Cristina Martinez Makes Taco Magic at South Philly Barbacoa," Eater, September 28, 2018, https://www.eater.com/2018/9/28/17909402/chefs-table-cristina-martinez-recap-season-5-episode-1-barbacoa-philadelphia-restaurant.

2. Abigail Fuller, dir. *Chef's Table: Cristina Martinez, Boardwalk Pictures*, September 28, 2018, https://www.netflix.com/watch/80216602?trackId=13752289&tctx=0%2C0%2Cc4fa6daf-7d2b-412b-8022-b6347b5687a1-85296636%2C%2C.

3. Fuller, *Chef's Table*.
4. Fuhrmeister, "'Chef's Table' Recap."
5. Fuller, *Chef's Table*.
6. "An Undocumented Mexican Chef Runs One of the Country's Best New Restaurants," *Bon Apetit*, August 24, 2016, https://www.bonappetit.com/story/south-philly-barbacoa -cristina-martinez.
7. Fuller, *Chef's Table*.
8. Fuhrmeister, "'Chef's Table' Recap."
9. Fuhrmeister, "'Chef's Table' Recap."
10. "An Undocumented Mexican Chef."

19

AYANNA PRESSLEY

When Ayanna Pressley won her primary race against Michael Capuano and then won again in the general election to become a member of Congress, the state of Massachusetts experienced shock. Pressley had seemingly come from nowhere to score a huge political win! She had no experience, and her triumph was a genuine lucky first try. Thankfully, she didn't have to work very hard, and she didn't have to experience much pain on her journey to get to this rare position of power. It also helped that the state's powerful political machine and its wide web of connections fully supported her, making her victory all but certain, and easy.

*W*hoa, whoa, whoa!

Ayanna Pressley's win was anything but certain *or* easy! In the Democratic primary election for a Boston, Massachusetts, congressional seat in 2016, Pressley *did* shock the entire state when she announced she would challenge Michael Capuano for his spot in Congress. After all, Capuano had won ten elections in a row. That's right: ten. In fact, he won so often that people stopped trying to go against him. Every two years, when it was time for the Boston district to elect a representative to go to Washington, DC, on their behalf, Capuano was simply the natural (and only) choice. Winning, for him, was entirely assumed and entirely expected.[1]

Enter Pressley.

When she announced she would challenge Capuano for the Democratic nomination for Congress to represent the Boston district, basically *everyone* with political power in the state (and some even *out* of the state) shouted *no* as loudly as they could. Some of them even threw temper tantrums to try to get her to drop out of the race and stop challenging the dude who had won over and over and over again. The mayor of Boston, Martin Walsh; a former governor of the state, Deval Patrick; and even an amazing civil rights icon from Georgia, Representative John Lewis, *all* endorsed Capuano and campaigned to help him beat Pressley in the intense race.[2]

Capuano had the ten-win track record, a whole lot of money, and huge political stars within the state and outside the state all in his corner. What did Pressley have? A powerful story and a powerful plea: she believed that those who hold power and represent their districts should share their concerns, their experiences, and their lives. Pressley campaigned on her belief that a new kind of leadership was necessary in Washington, DC. To put it succinctly, as she said herself often in speeches, "The people closest to the pain should be closest to the power."[3] Pressley should know, as she herself experienced intense trauma when she was growing up. For much of her childhood, her dad was in prison, and she also underwent the horror of sexual abuse.

These traumas may have threatened to destroy her as a child, but she somehow managed to turn this pain into a plea for power, believing that government should work to help people, give them a voice, and understand what people truly need to grow, overcome, and succeed.

The people closest to the pain should be closest to the power.
—Ayanna Pressley

Instead of the people electing officials just because they've been in power a long time, Pressley believed that officials should have experiences that can help them empathize with the voters they represent. With this message as the core of her campaign, Pressley's popularity grew. Her words began to resonate more and more with the crowds to whom she spoke, and when the primary arrived, it was she who had performed the seemingly impossible feat.

Even though the powerful political establishment of Massachusetts had rejected her, now that she had won, the powerful political establishment of America would certainly be respectful and more supportive, right?

Not so fast. The highest political power in the country,

FAIL...THEN PREVAIL!

In October of 2019, Eliud Kipchoge, from Kenya, broke a barrier that most experts thought was impossible: he ran a marathon in under two hours. Kipchoge flashed through the 26.2-mile course in Vienna in a time of 1:59:40. That means he ran each mile, on average, in under five minutes. The journey to get there was far from easy: he tried in 2017 but didn't make it. To prepare for his 2019 attempt, Kipchoge spent four months in almost complete solitude, only sleeping, eating, and running.

the president of the United States, in fact did just the opposite of respecting her. Even though Representative Pressley was born and raised in America, because President Donald Trump was upset by the strong voice she used to argue her ideas, he told her (and three other congresswomen) to "go back" to their countries. All of the congresswomen Trump attacked were women of color and were women unafraid to use their voices to declare their ideas boldly. Pressley, however, was used to dealing with others in power trying to silence her, and she refused to let the attack from the highest power in the country level her.[4]

PLUCK ENOUGH!

Alexandria Ocasio-Cortez was predicted by almost every political expert in the country to badly lose her race in the Democratic primary representing New York in the US House of Representatives against longtime incumbent Joe Crowley. She shocked everyone and won.

Instead, she continued speaking out, using her position to defend herself and the others whom the president attacked. Part of what prepared her to weather such a racist insult was her own upbringing and her long experience in politics in the city of Boston. Rather than being a lucky winner in her primary against Capuano, she knew her victory had been years and years in the making. She had first served in the Boston City Council, starting in 2009, as the first African American woman ever to hold that office. In her role there, she advocated for girls and women in the city, establishing a committee to support and help them and their needs. She also helped to create new policies for the public school system regarding how it worked with pregnant students or those with children.

When she finally went on to win office as the US representative, she was a groundbreaker there too, serving as the first African American woman ever elected to Congress from the state of Massachusetts. The only other woman to hold national office representing Massachusetts is Senator Elizabeth Warren. Pressley, in other words, had gotten used to being the first and to being a fighter. Along the way, people didn't always agree with her proposals or her policies, but that didn't mean she'd stop fighting for them. Her rallying cry to those in her district— and now to the nation—is this: "Change isn't waiting any longer. We have arrived, change is coming and the future belongs to all of us."[5]

Change isn't waiting any longer. We have arrived, change is coming and the future belongs to all of us.

—Ayanna Pressley

Instead of bowing to powerful people who might support others or, worse, who attack and demean her, Pressley pressed forward, overcoming a traumatic childhood to show how one can transform pain into empathy and use power to create hope for others rather than more for oneself. In her short time in Congress thus far, Pressley has already become a national voice for fascinating legislative hopes, including advocating for better gun safety and for lowering the

CRAVE THE BRAVE!

The first African American to be cast in the lead role in *Phantom of the Opera* on Broadway, Norm Lewis had quite a circuitous route to get there. He initially worked as an advertiser for a newspaper in Florida, doing some singing on the side. Eventually, he took a job as an entertainer on a cruise ship. Lewis's boss thought his voice was *so* good that he told him he should risk it all and maybe make it big. Lewis did (on both counts).

national voting age from eighteen to sixteen. Her aim is to lend a microphone to people who have felt silenced for far too long.

And so far? It's working.

★ The Flop Files: **William Wilberforce** ★

The fight to abolish something as cruel and tragic as the slave trade should have been easy in the United Kingdom, considering that slavery was *already* illegal there, right?

Wrong. In fact, getting rid of the slave trade in the 1800s proved to be seemingly *impossible*. But one person continued trying, year after year, even though the bill he brought to parliament continually failed. William Wilberforce was a surprising candidate to have such a lasting impact on the legacy of laws in the United Kingdom. Rather than nurturing dreams of becoming a well-known politician, Wilberforce originally thought he would join the church, preaching the Christian faith rather than yelling loudly about policies in the halls of Parliament. But on the issue of the transatlantic slave trade, Wilberforce found a way to practice both. He believed that his faith was completely incompatible with the kidnapping and torture of other human beings, so he began to lead a kingdom-wide awareness campaign to convince people that the slave trade should be abolished. Ships flying the British flag were still involved in the buying and selling of human beings, and Wilberforce wanted the world to see that the United Kingdom would no longer stand for this abhorrent practice.[6]

It didn't help matters that in the fledging United States, slavery was not only alive and well but also the primary way in which the economy of the new country was established and grown.

Wilberforce brought his bill to abolish the slave trade to the floor of Parliament first in 1789, and it failed.

Then he brought it to the floor again in 1791, and it failed again.[7]

He continued speaking, writing, traveling, and spreading his message about the destruction of people and families and how the slave trade so strongly contradicted his own faith. At times, people were receptive to his message. At others, people were apathetic, and at worst, people worried about the effects on their own financial wealth instead of the morality of the trade.

Eventually, in 1807, after an astonishing eighteen years of trying to pass a bill abolishing the slave trade, Wilberforce eventually was able to secure a majority of votes in Parliament and finally pass the bill.[8]

Even though the struggle almost broke him—both mentally and physically—Wilberforce persevered through failure after failure, believing that his cause was just and the need severe.

NOTES

1. Katharine Q. Seelye, "Ayanna Pressley Upsets Capuano in Massachusetts House Race," *New York Times*, September 4, 2018, https://www.nytimes.com/2018/09/04/us/politics/ayanna-pressley-massachusetts.html.
2. Seelye, "Ayanna Pressley Upsets Capuano."
3. Seelye, "Ayanna Pressley Upsets Capuano."
4. Julie Hirschfeld Davis, "House Condemns Trump's Attack on Four Congresswomen as Racist," *New York Times*, July 16, 2019, https://www.nytimes.com/2019/07/16/us/politics/trump-tweet-house-vote.html.
5. Seelye, "Ayanna Pressley Upsets Capuano."
6. "William Wilberforce," *Encyclopædia Britannica*, September 5, 2019, https://www.britannica.com/biography/William-Wilberforce.
7. "William Wilberforce."
8. "William Wilberforce."

20
MOHAMAD AL JOUNDE

Since 2011, the country of Syria has been engulfed in a dangerous civil war that makes daily life there constantly unstable and uncertain. However, one young man, named Mohamad Al Jounde, was able to easily deal with the danger of war and help other kids in the process. Before he had even turned sixteen, he started a school, which authorities respected and made sure to safeguard. Luckily, too, his family was able to remain together even as the war raged on. Seeing that hopeful actions can create new paths for peace, Al Jounde and his family never had to leave Syria, and instead factions on both sides have seen his work and decided to stop fighting.

*I*f only. If only!

Mohamad Al Jounde was twelve years old when he began to realize the power of photography and play to help kids endure ongoing trauma and to heal from it. He saw the civil war's effects on himself and his own family, as well as on kids all around him. Having little money to make drastic, wide-scale change, Al Jounde began doing the only thing he could: he walked around with his camera and took pictures, helped and taught other children how to take pictures, and played with them too. The healing power of play and art proved transformational for so many of the children with whom he connected, especially considering that many of them had never truly known safety or security of any kind. They had grown up in the shadow of war, always hearing the sounds of violence and destruction, forcing them to fear rather than to relish each new day. Al Jounde aimed to change that by teaching them that beauty could be seen in the faces of people all around them.[1]

HAVE GRIT—DON'T SPLIT!

As a refugee in Montana, after escaping civil war in Liberia, Wilmot Collins was met by racist messages scrawled on the side of his home. But instead of allowing this hateful rejection to stop him, Collins removed the graffiti, with the help of some neighbors. He chose to serve his new home country in the US military, then became the first black mayor of Helena, and in 2020 ran for the US Senate to represent Montana.

Photography had done just that for Al Jounde himself, so he wanted to spread what his own heart had so desperately needed. While there was so much violence and fear all around him, Al Jounde's dad knew his son needed some way to see hope, so the two went and visited a Syrian photographer named Ramzi Haidar, who would teach Al Jounde the essentials of the art of photography. This mentorship proved to be a lifesaving experience for Al Jounde, as he reflected, "I didn't go to school for two years, but when I started learning photography it ended the emptiness in my life—it helped me express myself and show people how I live."[2] Photography became a tangible way forward—a small action that he could take to retain hope when everything seemed so dismal and despairing all around him.

I didn't go to school for two years, but when I started learning photography it ended the emptiness in my life—it helped me express myself and show people how I live.

—Mohammad Al Jounde

Al Jounde's parents had been powerful models of this stance too. Even though danger was everywhere, his parents believed that taking action was a crucial way to keep hope alive. It wouldn't be enough to hide and hope things changed; they believed they had to do something—however small—to maintain oxygen for the fire of hope in their hearts. Therefore, both Al Jounde's mother and his father were involved in the revolution in Syria. They were activists who fought for a more just, equal, and representative ruling power in Syria, as well as community activism and organization. And so, for this stance, they became targets of the governmental regime in power. After his mother began getting death threats, the family knew that they had to leave before irreversible tragedy struck.[3]

HOLD THE BOLD!

A Medal of Honor recipient from World War II, Francis Currey fought against an onslaught of Nazi tanks and attacks to help save five trapped American military members. Though he was outnumbered and at a severe disadvantage, Currey refused to flee and instead helped save the men's lives. In later years, he would become a counselor to veterans who needed help.

Al Jounde and his family crossed the border from Syria into Lebanon and began living at a refugee camp in Aley, not far from the capital city of Beirut. The refugee camp was overcrowded, had no school, had very little food, and offered few ways to make money. Even though they had made it out of Syria, Al Jounde and his family were now refugees, and still there was little hope to be found. So, Al Jounde did what he had been taught to do by his parents: he took action. He decided to start a school in the refugee camp in Lebanon, teaching photography, yes, but also enlisting four other teachers to work with the one hundred children who began attending. Because authorities would not believe that a child could actually start and lead a school, his mom put her name on the application in order to get it approved. Approved it was, and NGOs (nongovernmental organizations) began supporting the school with some funding and supplies.[4]

CRAVE THE BRAVE!

Lau Sing Kee, a Chinese American man, served with distinction in the US Army in World War I, earning the second-highest military honor (after the Medal of Honor), called the Distinguished Service Cross. Yet, after his return to the United States, he was imprisoned for helping Chinese immigrants into the country and keeping them safe amid a racist backlash. Kee received a posthumous apology from the US Senate in 2002.

Meanwhile, Al Jounde's father had fled by boat to Greece and then ended up in Sweden in an attempt to find work and support the family. For three years, life continued in this way—Mohamad, his mother, and his sister in the refugee camp, running the school, and his father in Sweden, working and sending them money. Living apart caused an immense strain on the family, but they held on to hope that they might one day be reunited.[5]

Three years later, they would be, as Sweden granted asylum to the whole family. Asylum is essentially an agreement to allow someone from outside a country to remain in that country because their lives would otherwise be in danger. Receiving asylum was incredibly freeing for Al Jounde; however, his heart remains with those refugees who live in poverty in camps without schools and with those children who are still in war-torn Syria. As of 2017, there were almost 2 million Syrian children who were unable to attend school.[6]

Even the school Al Jounde built and led while in the refugee camp in Lebanon was ultimately destroyed by the government when they decided to move the refugee camp. This destruction of the school Al Jounde had built with hope did not last, though. The Lebanese government professionally rebuilt Mohamad's school, and as of 2019, it currently enrolls over two hundred children who are refugees.[7]

Children are hiding their stories inside. It takes trust to get them out.

—Mohammad Al Jounde

Facing immense odds and seemingly impossible walls, Al Jounde responded with hope. Even when schools were closed and the failure of both heart and art seemed inevitable, Al Jounde decided to teach children himself. Though he was a refugee himself and not even an adult, he opened his own school, enabling hundreds of kids to learn and look through the lens of a camera to perhaps find beauty where before there seemed to be only tragedy.

The war in Syria still rages on. Millions of children and families are at severe risk, and many more live in dangerous, poverty-stricken refugee camps in countries outside of Syria. Some countries have tried to grant asylum—safe haven—to those desperate for security and hope. Other countries have refused to accept refugees or help those in desperate need.

Al Jounde's example shows that even small acts of hope can have profound effects. He said, "The kids from Syria in the camps don't like to talk and don't know how to express themselves or tell us about what they've been through. Photography helps them show us where they live and how they live in more detail."[8] Instead of children hiding their trauma and their pain and their very lives, Al Jounde believes that photography, education, and play offer young people ways to take small steps forward. They offer ways to remain hopeful amid a war that seems endless and terrifying. "Children are hiding their stories inside. It takes trust to get them out," he believes.[9] This trust and the bridge that Al Jounde has helped to provide for children may be small, but it is a resounding triumph against the massive failures of war. If we can follow Al Jounde's lead, and take small steps of hope, the world might indeed look very different.

Notes

1. "2017—Mohammad Al Jounde (16), Syria," KidsRights, accessed September 10, 2019, https://kidsrights.org/advocacy/international-childrens-peace-prize/winners/mohamad-al-jounde/.
2. Helen Nianias, "'I Knew People Who Had Harder Lives than Me'—The Syrian Refugee Child Who Started a School," *Guardian*, December 22, 2017, https://www.theguardian.com/working-in-development/2017/dec/22/i-knew-people-who-had-harder-lives-than-me-the-syrian-refugee-child-who-started-a-school.
3. Nianias, "'I Knew People Who Had Harder Lives than Me.'"
4. Nianias, "'I Knew People Who Had Harder Lives than Me.'"
5. "2017—Mohammad Al Jounde (16), Syria."
6. Nianias, "'I Knew People Who Had Harder Lives than Me.'"
7. "2017—Mohammad Al Jounde (16), Syria."
8. Nianias, "'I Knew People Who Had Harder Lives than Me.'"
9. "2017—Mohammad Al Jounde (16), Syria."

21
MINDY KALING

To make it big in the world of comedy and show business, Mindy Kaling was able to look to the many examples of women of color who had come before her, mentored her, and shown her the way. Instantly, she achieved national acclaim across America and then across the world. Her first big self-written, self-produced show, *The Mindy Project*, was a smash network success and broke every category of ratings that could be broken. And then it broke ratings categories that didn't even exist! That's how cool it was! Fitting the body type most likely to be found on the covers of *Elle*, she's even graced that cover, over-shadowing other comedians who appeared alongside her. Kaling, comedian extraordinaire, had a direct route to stardom and success.

Alternate reality!

Instead of a straight path to stardom personified by other women of color who looked and sounded *just* like her, Mindy Kaling has recalled the exact opposite. Born to Hindu parents who immigrated to the United States after living in India and Nigeria, Kaling often felt as though she was involved in a solitary endeavor to pursue comedy from her background. There were so few women who had been able to break into the male-dominated genre of show business, and there were even fewer women of color.[1] What gave Kaling the confidence, the hope, and the determination to believe she could break so many barriers and achieve success in an area seemingly so lacking in diversity and opportunity?

The answer might be found if we time travel back to when Kaling was just six years old. The year is 1985, and rather than simply be content to play with whatever toys or tea sets might have been more typically or culturally considered normal, Kaling sits with a pad and writes, and writes, and writes. What is she creating? Maybe a cool picture or practicing her letters and numbers?

Nope! Kaling said, "At six years old, I was writing comic plays at home."[2] Her mind was already envisioning characters, creating settings, and crafting dialogue intended to provoke laughter and surprise. Instead of stopping or even slowing down this insatiable and curious

FROM WEAK TO PEAK!

Author Isaac Asimov was rejected from Columbia University as a young man because he was Jewish. He would graduate from a satellite school of the university and then apply to medical schools. They all rejected him, so Asimov changed course and eventually earned his PhD in chemistry, became a professor, and then proceeded to write and publish almost five hundred books. That's right: *five hundred.* Take that, rejection!

drive for humor, Kaling only grew her desire to learn all she could about the craft of comedy, watching Comedy Central shows and sitcoms that were critically acclaimed. Were her parents concerned about this drive she was developing? Maybe. But they also knew that their daughter saw comedy with a level of insight that was far beyond pure entertainment and amusement. Kaling shared, "At fifteen years old, I was talking about how 'Frasier' was so tonally different from 'Cheers,' even though they had the same character. These were things I was interested in. So my parents were prepared. They were anxious, but they knew there was no stopping me."[3]

Relentlessly, Kaling continued to pursue both school and comedy, eventually gaining acceptance into Dartmouth College in New Hampshire. Surrounded by a majority of white people, and often many males when it came to comedy, Kaling said, "A chirpy, Indian improv comedian who was constantly talking was something of a novelty to the scores of wordless men named Brian."[4] Using humor to deal with the notion of often being the only person who looked different from everyone else in the room, Kaling practiced her comedic art, worked incredibly hard, and always made a point of being vulnerable with her honest reflections and perspectives—using comedy to couch these expressions.

A chirpy, Indian improv comedian who was constantly talking was something of a novelty to the scores of wordless men named Brian.
—Mindy Kaling

Soon, she found herself working as a writer for the American version of the United Kingdom comedy hit *The Office*. In her role as writer, she worked eighteen-hour days, churning out unparalleled ideas and quirky, seemingly impossible scenarios that had the effect of creating both deadpan humor and laugh-out-loud ridiculous surprises. Additionally, she was able to garner a role in the show itself as the character Kelly. Audiences loved her work—both as a writer and as an actor. However, the intense time commitments and the requirement to stay in a certain lane of comedy—what she could use and what she could create determined by others—began to take its toll on her. Finally, after eight years and having written twenty-four episodes, Kaling decided it was time to branch out on her own, take a leap, and see what would happen. Plus, during that entire run, she had been the *only* female writer for the show. [5]

Imagine that!

That would be like being the *only* girl from fifth grade to twelfth grade to play on a soccer team or to be in the Math Olympiad. Or it would be like being the only boy to join the robotics club or play on a basketball team. Imagine being the only one. How intimidating might it feel? How alone? Would you start to feel alienated or like maybe you don't belong? Might you doubt your ability? Might you wonder why more people who look like you weren't there? Would you wonder if something was wrong with you and why you liked the things you did?

Even if Kaling wondered about any of these fears, they didn't stop her. Instead, she proceeded to write, star in, and produce a show she tentatively called *The Untitled Mindy Project*. She wanted to create a show about a woman of color who wasn't the sidekick best friend, a role to which women of color are so often relegated in other shows and films. Instead, Kaling's idea would feature an Indian American woman who was a gynecologist and who possessed incredible spunk, confidence, and style. She wouldn't waste time with self-deprecating humor or belittling herself to make others laugh. Instead, the Mindy in *this* show would *know* she was *all that*.

With an idea that good and the brilliant mind and work ethic of Kaling as the engine, any network would be head over heels with excitement to sign the project and start shooting episodes, right?

Wrong!

Instead of scooping it up, NBC shot it down.

Kaling had devoted so much time and energy to the creation of this idea and to making the pilot (the first) episode to try and win a network with it that she couldn't believe NBC rejected it. Did the seemingly unconquerable Kaling smile and then keep right on keeping on?

Not exactly. Kaling honestly admitted, "I sat in my trailer and wept."[6] After eight successful years of writing for and starring in *The Office*, Kaling's first big outing with her own idea was rejected. Even though she had fought and worked hard to experience success in an area of work where most people were white and male, she found herself now on the outside looking in.

SWERVE WITH NERVE!

Stephanie D'Abruzzo's initial career was as a television puppeteer. Ever hear of the show *Sesame Street*? D'Abruzzo was on twenty-one seasons of the children's hit. Then she switched gears, but all that work in puppetry was not wasted: she used it to join the hit Broadway musical *Avenue Q*. She now has said, "Every experience we have offstage informs us onstage."[7]

I sat in my trailer and wept.

—Mindy Kaling

But Kaling refused to give up on her pilot episode, and she believed, deep down, that her show would be a hit if she could get a network to believe in it. Finally, one did. Fox decided to move forward with what eventually became *The Mindy Project*.

Huzzah! Hooray! End of story!

Or…not so fast. While the show garnered some wonderful reviews from critics and fans alike, Fox wasn't entirely thrilled with the results. They wanted the show's ratings—how many people tuned in to watch—to get higher each season. Instead, as the show progressed each season, the ratings decreased. And so, after three seasons, Fox canceled the show. Did Kaling sit in another trailer and cry?

Not this time, because a rejection or failure can sometimes lead to a new life. While Fox canceled the show, Hulu decided to pick it up, and so *The Mindy Project* had a rebirth of sorts running for an additional three seasons, bringing the total to six.

Kaling continues to write, produce, and act, and she has never considered stopping. A film in which she stars with Emma Thompson, called *Late Night*, is her newest project. In it she plays a role that is remarkably similar to her own life: that of a comedy writer who is the only person in the room who's not a white male. And more projects are in the works! Kaling still feels that insatiable desire to create comedy, but she has also toned down her intense eighteen-hour workdays. Instead, she

FAIL…THEN PREVAIL!

Leslie Jones is known for her work on *Saturday Night Live* and her starring role in the hit remake of *Ghostbusters*. However, this comedic feat once seemed unimaginable, as Jones spent twenty-five years doing smaller comedy shows and clubs, just hoping for a breakthrough. There were nights she wanted to quit it altogether, but she kept going, and now she's got the last laugh.

knows what she is capable of, she knows what she has achieved, and even if she hasn't won an Emmy for it yet, she—like many viewers— counts her life as a smashing success.

Never one to silence her brilliant and zany ideas just because there might not have been anyone else like her in the room, Kaling hopes that the rooms where the creativity happens for Hollywood continue to become more and more diverse. She's leading the way, and maybe that's the best definition of success there is.

★ The Flop Files: Kalani Brown ★

It's April 7, 2019. We're at the Amalie Arena in Tampa, Florida. We're watching the women's final NCAA (National Collegiate Athletic Association) championship game between Baylor University and Notre Dame University. Both teams have entered this final game with a real shot at winning—having survived long, grueling seasons in which they've posted impressive records.

It's game time!

(Hey, while we watch, do you mind if I grab a handful of that amazing popcorn you brought? Thanks!)

The entire first half, Baylor is surging, but every time they seem to break away, Notre Dame's senior star, Arike Ogunbowale, manages to perform some logic-defying move to get another two points on the board. Meanwhile, on the other end of the court, Baylor's Kalani Brown, a six-foot-seven senior center, is working her hardest to rebound and put back shots to help Baylor edge ever further ahead.[8]

In a game where everything is on the line, a little before halftime, Brown is fouled on a shot and goes to the free-throw line to shoot two shots.

She misses the first.

She misses the second.

Incredibly frustrating to miss a free throw in a game as big as this. Even *more* frustrating to miss a second free throw in a game as big as this. Play continues, and just before the half ends, Brown is fouled on a shot again, and goes again to the free-throw line.

She misses her third free-throw attempt in a row.

Then she misses her fourth.

In the biggest game of her career, as a senior, with everything on the line, Brown has just missed four free throws in a row.

Imagine the temptation to despair in a moment like this! With yet another half to play, this 0–4 foul shooting has the potential to destroy her confidence and drive for the second half. But then Coach Kim Mulkey comes onto the court and meets Brown before she can ever walk off the court. The coach helps Brown to raise her head high, then speaks powerfully and forcefully to her, encouraging her, and the two exit for halftime.

Instead of coming out in despair and shame for the second half, Brown comes out of the locker room ready to rock. Showing true mental toughness and the attributes of an amazing player, Brown helps lead her team to victory in a close 82–81 win over Notre Dame. Baylor for the championship! While she missed those four free throws, she ended up adding twenty points to the team's victory.[9]

Twenty points! That's just about 25 percent of what the team made the entire game. Plus, her hard work, hustle, decision to stay strong rather than hang her head, and hope all helped her to rise above any temptation to despair. Brown proved, tonight, that no matter how many times we may miss, it's crucial not to hang our heads but to listen close to the words of those who encourage us, to take a break, and then to come out fighting (or, um, *shooting baskets*) in the second half!

(Oh, and thanks for sharing your popcorn.)

NOTES

1. Hermione Hoby, "Mindy Kaling: 'Those Moments When You Feel an Idiot—They're Good to Write About,'" *Guardian*, September 4, 2015, https://www.theguardian.com /tv-and-radio/2015/sep/04/mindy-kaling-so-heres-whats-funny.
2. David Marchese, "Mindy Kaling on Not Being the Long-Suffering Indian Woman," *New York Times*, June 10, 2019, https://www.nytimes.com/interactive/2019/06/10/magazine /mindy-kaling-late-night-diversity-comedy.html.
3. Marchese, "Mindy Kaling on Not Being."
4. Hoby, "Mindy Kaling."
5. Hoby, "Mindy Kaling."
6. Hoby, "Mindy Kaling."
7. Amy Sapp, "8 of Broadway's Most Unlikely Success Stories," ShowTickets.com, July 29, 2015, https://broadway.showtickets.com/articles/broadways-most-unlikely-success -stories/.
8. Kelly Whiteside, "N.C.A.A. Women's Final: Baylor Is Champion with Win over Notre Dame," *New York Times*, April 7, 2019, https://www.nytimes.com/2019/04/07/sports /baylor-basketball-ncaa-champions.html.
9. Whiteside, "N.C.A.A. Women's Final."

22
PATRICIA SMITH

To become an award-winning poet whose verse splashes and crashes powerfully across every page it embodies, Patricia Smith had no mountain to climb. In fact, it wouldn't even be called a hill. Maybe a very, very *slight* incline. As she began writing journalism in the 1980s, her career steadily took off, and she went from one success to the next, in ever-widening circles of gleefully generous criticism and responses. Now, as both a professor of English and a poet, Smith stands at the peak of her career, knowing that life has never overwhelmed her or the relentless journey she has traveled to write.

*O*r not.

Sometimes, life does overwhelm us. Sometimes, in our journey, we make mistakes, and even if others try to define us by our mistakes, we can choose whether to stay rooted in those mistakes or to move forward and grow, learn from them, then exercise our courage and rise up again.

Poet Patricia Smith is a profoundly moving example of this kind of courage, and her story is inspiring not only because of what she has accomplished but because of how she chose to rise.

In the 1990s, Smith was working as a Metro columnist for the newspaper the *Boston Globe*. Life was hectic, and assignments came fast and furious. She was also trying very hard to make it as a poet, and to make ends meet too. And then, in 1998, it all seemed well worth it: her searing and vivid work as a Metro columnist was met with acclaim, even garnering her recognition as a finalist for the Pulitzer Prize in Commentary that year. Even though life was hectic and work was all-encompassing, it seemed as though Smith had made it to the mountaintop in a major way in the field of writing. But soon, her prestigious prize was rescinded, and rather than gazing from the mountaintop, Smith found herself falling down a steep trail.

See, during her time as a journalist, she had decided to invent characters and quotes in four of her columns. In the world of journalism—rather than fiction writing—this is nothing short of scandalous. And Smith suffered for what she had done when the story came tumbling out: the editor of the paper asked her to resign.[1]

NOT DIMINISHED... FINISHED!

Helen Keller was criticized and attacked by many who claimed that she had plagiarized a short story she wrote when she was eleven years old, entitled "The Frost King." The story was eventually published in a newspaper called the *Goodson Gazette*. Keller went from the pinnacle of joy to the depths of despair after the accusations, but Mark Twain consoled her in a letter, encouraging her not to let it sink her. It didn't.

At this point, Smith could have chosen to hang her head in shame and remain hidden from then on. However, she made a much braver and more inspiring choice. She admitted what she had done and eventually decided that poetry was her true and deepest calling. Would she allow her entire life to be defined by what she had done while at the *Boston Globe*?

People have to give you a chance to be who you are now.
—Patricia Smith

I can relate to Smith, as I have my own history of mistakes, albeit involving a different kind of stealing. When I was growing up, I stole stuff. Actual *stuff.* I remember going to stores and swiping whatever I could—generally comics and baseball cards, but also anything else that seemed interesting or that I thought I could snag without being seen. It wasn't until years later that, through the influence of caring and challenging mentors, I came to grips with these mistakes. I recall being in tenth grade and going back to the stores from which I had stolen when I was younger and admitting to every-thing. And I will never forget the

SWERVE WITH NERVE!

In 1979, a writer named Jacob Epstein was a senior in college when he published his first novel, *Wild Oats*. A famous writer whom Epstein revered, named Martin Amis, was writing a review of Epstein's novel when he realized that the younger writer had plagiarized portions of one of Amis's books! Epstein said it was accidental and apologized. He did stop writing novels, but he didn't stop writing! Epstein has created scripts for many television shows.

look on one shopkeeper's face and her words. She looked at me for a long time, then actually thanked me.

That's right. Stunned beyond belief, I thought maybe she hadn't heard me correctly. But she said she had. She said it took courage to admit what I'd done, and she hoped I would spend the rest of my life doing something far more beneficial for society than stealing.

Those words became a powerful lightning rod for my own journey, and I tried to take them to heart from that moment onward. One of my deepest questions became *How might I give rather than seek to always get?*

Each of us is more than the worst thing we've ever done.

—Bryan Stevenson

You, too, may have your own stories of mistakes you made. Maybe you made things up for an assignment, like Smith did, or maybe you stole things, as did I. Maybe you said something you shouldn't have said or failed to do or say something you know you needed to do or say. Here's the thing: it's important to make amends for our mistakes— to take responsibility for them and to admit them.

But it's also important to not let ourselves be defined by those mistakes. As writer and justice-seeking lawyer Bryan Stevenson has said, "Each of us is more than the worst thing we've ever done."[2] Instead, the mistakes we have made create an opportunity for us to recognize them, reveal them, and then grow from them to become better versions of ourselves. We are never finished; instead, we are constantly growing, constantly changing, constantly being offered new opportunities to define ourselves not by what has happened but by how we respond to it. The person at the *Globe* who was responsible for noticing the mistakes Smith made, Walter Robinson, would later become an editor-at-large for the newspaper. His response is much like the shopkeeper's words to me. Robinson said in an interview with the *New York Times*, "The fact of the matter is that in life, for all of us, we are judged very much by how we bounce back from adversity. In that sense, I'm really heartened by what's happened in her life."[3]

We are judged by how we bounce back.

Smith had a choice to make after her mistake. She could have relented and allowed it to engulf and define her. She did not. Instead, she chose to let loose the passion for poetry that set her heart and mind on fire.

The fact of the matter is that in life, for all of us, we are judged very much by how we bounce back from adversity.
—Walter Robinson

She wrote, and wrote, and wrote. Regarding poetry, she has said, "It's how I breathe and speak to the world."[4] How do *you* "breathe and speak to the world"? And are you willing to bounce back from a mistake—whether minor or major—to keep speaking to the world?

Smith was, and her verse began stacking up major awards, including the *Los Angeles Times* Book Prize, a Guggenheim Fellowship, a National Book Award finalist status, and even a Pulitzer Prize for Poetry nomination. To this day, Smith teaches and writes with both heart and brilliance. She said, "People have to give you a chance to be who you are now."[5] Rather than allow herself to be defined by others who might seek to turn a mistake into a definition of a life,

Smith has demonstrated incredible bravery and beauty by choosing to write the poems that she believes she needs to write.

HOLD THE BOLD!

Groundbreaker poet-novelist and author K. A. Holt was told by her English teacher that her writing style would cause her to fail, and the teacher did just that to Holt: failed her often. However, Holt would go on to publish critically acclaimed books for young adults such as *House Arrest* and *Rhyme Schemer*.

The students I have been lucky enough to work with in middle and high schools have made mistakes too. Some are like the ones Smith made; others are like the mistakes I made. But each time they came forward to work with me, to share what had happened, the experience was a powerful one. Together, we saw how they could come up out of those mistakes—bounce back— rather than remain defeated and buried under the weight of a failure.

We *all* have this choice to make. Because we are all human(!), we all make mistakes. And this means we all have to choose how we'll respond to the mistakes we make. Will we get honest and then get moving to become better, to grow? Smith reveals a path of both courage and possibility, proving that a mistake cannot define you unless you let it.

NOTES

1. Rachel L. Swarns, "Fallen Journalist Finds Solace and Success in Poetry," *New York Times*, January 25, 2015, https://www.nytimes.com/2015/01/26/nyregion/patricia-smith -finds-solace-and-success-in-poetry.html.
2. Bryan Stevenson, *Just Mercy: A Story of Justice and Redemption*, (New York: Spiegel & Grau, 2014), 18.
3. Swarns, "Fallen Journalist Finds Solace."
4. Swarns, "Fallen Journalist Finds Solace."
5. Swarns, "Fallen Journalist Finds Solace."

23

LORENZO SANTILLAN, CRISTIAN ARCEGA, OSCAR VAZQUEZ, AND LUIS ARANDA (CARL HAYDEN COMMUNITY HIGH SCHOOL ROBOTICS SQUAD)

In the world of robotics competitions, MIT (the Massachusetts Institute of Technology) is almost unbeatable. With brilliant mentors, a seemingly endless supply of funds, and some of the best aspiring engineers in the world on their team, who could triumph over *them*? The answer is a small high school team from West Phoenix, Arizona. The answer is four teenagers, three of whom were undocumented immigrants from

Mexico. The answer is unbelievable to most. So just *how* did it happen? How could it have happened? Easy. The four from Phoenix received a $1 *billion* joint grant from Apple and Microsoft. Then, world-renowned, prize-winning engineers from all over the world flew into Sky Harbor Airport in Phoenix to mentor and help the team. Finally, the United States government, realizing the potential these students had, offered support instead of intimidation.

Uh . . . no way!

Luis Aranda, Oscar Vazquez, Lorenzo Santillan, and Cristian Arcega did end up defeating MIT in 2004 in that year's national underwater robotics competition. But they did so without any of the perks or supports mentioned above. In fact, they accomplished this seemingly impossible feat with many obstacles trying to prevent them from doing just that.

Mentored by two teachers at the Carl Hayden Community High School, Allan Cameron and Faridodin "Fredi" Lajvardi, the four teenagers had almost no money, zero past experience with robotics, and no privileged or prestigious connections. Additionally, three of the four students were officially termed "undocumented immigrants." They had been brought to the United States as children, but the United States refused to recognize them as citizens. Instead, they had to live under the shadow of a

NOT DIMINISHED... FINISHED!

Alan Turing was rejected and scourged by British society and government in the early to mid-1900s because he was gay. The prime minister and the queen would later apologize and make amends, and the government would finally recognize the brilliant code-breaking work Turing had done during World War II.

constant threat of deportation—never knowing if they would ever be accepted by the country in which they had grown up.

Here you have kids that can compete and that clearly are innovative, that love to build and to fuel the country forward. . . . We need these kids, and they face these impediments.

—Mary Mazzio

As a team leader, Vazquez first had the idea to develop a team to be involved in the robotics quest. His original—and lifelong—dream was to join the United States Army, but he was not allowed to serve because of his undocumented status. Rather than throw up his hands in failure, Vazquez decided to persuade some of his fellow students at Carl Hayden to do something powerful and challenging on a different playing field. Or rather, underwater.

Though the team seemed destined for failure, they worked hard. They learned all they could, stayed after school to work on their robot, and got creative with how they both raised and spent money for their engineering feat.

While other teams against which they would eventually compete had thousands upon thousands of dollars to spend on

PLUCK ENOUGH!

At Eden Elementary School in Britain, one student's father helped conduct a science experiment to teach the students the difference between herbal remedies and traditional medicine. Children from the school brought in all kinds of family soups that are traditional to their cultures, and researcher Jake Braum learned that one soup particularly was potent at blocking the growth of the malaria parasite. Made up of fermented cabbage, the soup certainly has quite the kick!

the most state-of-the-art equipment and technology for their robots, Carl Hayden's team had to improvise. Suddenly, trips to the hardware store became missions in accounting and in making decisions about what parts they'd put into their robot based on the amount of cash they had raised.[1]

They affectionately named their robot Stinky and packaged him up for the national competition in California. While the entire team expected little of their involvement in the contest, their two mentors decided to enter them into the college-level competition rather than the high school competition. They had wagered the students were probably going to lose and thought it might be better for their sense of self to lose to the very best, in a tougher category, rather than to come last among other high school teams.

In the college-level competition, MIT was only one of the elite, experienced, and well-funded teams competing. And the course was so challenging that not a single college team's robot was able to complete the entire underwater mission.

Think about that for a moment. With the best college-level robotics teams in the country competing, in a way, *all* of them failed. None were able to successfully complete each piece of the multistep course. While the Carl Hayden Falcons were among these teams that failed to finish the course, they did raise some eyebrows with a few of their ingenious approaches and earned some points toward the eventual tally.

However, in the presentation portion of the competition, the Falcons really took flight. As one team member, Arcega, confidently told judge Tom Swean as a way to explain why they had no suave and high-profile PowerPoint slides to accompany their delivery, "Power-Point is a distraction. People use it when they don't know what to say." Swean came back immediately with, "And you know what to say?" Arcega responded, "Yes, sir."[2]

PowerPoint is a distraction. People use it when they don't know what to say.

—Cristian Arcega

Arcega did. As did the rest of the Falcons. Even though the Carl Hayden team was operating on an $800 budget, while the MIT squad had $11,000 at their disposal, it was no matter. Even though the Carl Hayden team had four members with no previous experience and MIT had twelve with plenty of previous experience, it was no matter. Even though MIT was sponsored by ExxonMobil and other large corporations—with a sticker on their robot to brand it—and Carl Hayden was sponsored by whatever local businesses and people in their community would donate, it was no matter.[3]

The Carl Hayden team had used creativity and verve to accomplish tasks that would have cost other teams a whole lot more—both in time and in money. In one of the team's most surprising moves, when water got into their battery compartment, they needed a way to soak up the water and also prevent the compartment from shorting out should water get in again. They had decided to move the battery compartment onto the robot, Stinky, before the competition because it was far cheaper than running cable all the way down to the robot from a power source up above and out of the water.

But now, as the competition was imminent, they had a new problem on their hands. Leakage. Their solution would be both a brilliant engineering feat and also a supremely embarrassing moment. Lorenzo was the one chosen to go into the grocery store and buy tampons to fix their robot's issues. Terrified of who to ask which ones he should buy, he finally got up the courage to ask a woman who looked friendly, "Excuse me madam . . . could you help me buy the most best tampons?"[4] She smiled after Lorenzo's explanation of why, exactly, he needed them and then directed him to the type that would most efficiently solve the team's problem.

The Falcons used their creativity, their eight hundred bucks, and their belief in one another to fuel a truly shocking triumph in the Marine Advanced Technology Education Center's Remotely Operated Vehicle competition at the University of California, Santa Barbara. Not only did they beat MIT, but they also beat out *every single other college team.* They came in first.[5]

And here's where it would be wonderful to share with you that these four amazing students from Carl Hayden used the triumph of their experience with robotics to segue into high-powered colleges and careers. Here's where I would love to report that the four students continued their amazing run of success. Instead, they struggled every step of the way. The United States government refused to allow them to work, which meant they couldn't make money. This meant paying for college could be tough, and though Vazquez was accepted to Arizona State, when the state of Arizona passed tougher laws to prohibit what undocumented immigrants could do, he could no longer remain at school. Others on the team started their own businesses, since the government had no law

HAVE GRIT—DON'T SPLIT!

By 2013, the WNBA (Women's National Basketball Association) team the Washington Mystics had lost so many games that their own fans sometimes referred to them as the Washington "Mistakes." However, by 2019, they were the WNBA Champions. Their six-year journey to the trophy included incredibly hard work, new coach Mike Thibault (who himself had endured his own failure of being fired from another team!), and a whole lot of hope.

against *owning* a business but did not allow them to work *for* a business. However, every day was a struggle, and ten years after the 2004 famed victory, a documentary project brought the two teams together again to talk. The MIT students were involved in high-powered, high-money-making careers, while the Carl Hayden students were finding it hard to make enough money to keep the lights on.

The difference?

One team had outsmarted, outplanned, and outperformed and outpresented the other team. But the losing team had gone on to "win" in society. Mary Mazzio, who produced the 2004 documentary project entitled *Underwater Dreams*, said that when the two teams share their vastly different paths, "It's heartbreaking. . . . Here you have kids that can compete and that clearly are innovative, that love to build and to fuel the country forward. . . . We need these kids, and they face these impediments."[6]

The team members themselves realized the immense double standard they face. After winning the prestigious robotics competition, they struggled for every step forward. Nothing is given to them, and very few doors have opened. Vazquez said, honestly, of this kind of realization about his journey, "I tried my best not to let [my legal status] stop me from doing anything. It limited me a lot. It took a lot of opportunities away. But I kind of looked the other way and put more effort into it."[7]

I tried my best not to let [my legal status] stop me from doing anything. It limited me a lot. It took a lot of opportunities away. But I kind of looked the other way and put more effort into it.

—Oscar Vazquez

Vazquez eventually went back to Mexico—even though he had a wife and daughter in the United States. He wasn't leaving them; he wanted to try to work within the system the US government had set up and hoped that he would become a US citizen so that he could freely live with his family and work in the country. The process demanded that undocumented immigrants return to their home countries and then apply for legal status from their countries of origin. So, Vazquez did just that. Even though he had won a prestigious national robotics competition, and even though he had a wife and daughter, American officials refused.[8]

So, Vazquez applied again.

American officials refused again.

Refusing to let these failures deny him the life he had already been living so well, and to which he so strongly wanted to return, he found others who were willing to help take up his cause. The *Arizona Republic* began to focus on his story, and it eventually caught the eye of Senator Dick Durbin, from Illinois, who championed his case. Finally, Vazquez was granted legal status, came back to America, enlisted in the United States Army, became a citizen, and served his country on a tour in Afghanistan.[9]

The Carl Hayden robotics team may have dealt with an underfunded, implausible, and seemingly impossible mission to win a national underwater robotics competition. But instead of shying away from the challenge, they moved forward with the hopes that what they did with a robot named Stinky in a pool at UC Santa Barbara might just show others that there was more to their story. They were not just undocumented immigrants who were part of a policy debate. They were smart, hardworking, brilliant young engineers. And they still, even now, hope the world, and particularly America, sees that.

★ The Flop Files: **The Toronto Raptors** ★

Joining the NBA (National Basketball Association) in 1993, the Toronto (Canada) Raptors were the first pro basketball team in the NBA outside of the United States. And since 1993, they have been craving to prove themselves a championship-caliber team with, well, a championship.

Until 2019, that seemed unlikely.

Year after year, the Raptors found themselves losing in the playoffs—sometimes embarrassingly so. Even in the 2017–2018 season, when the team recorded their highest-ever regular season win total at fifty-nine games, they ran into a wall named LeBron James and his Cleveland Cavaliers. In order for the Raptors to make it to a championship battle, they would have to eventually find their way past James. However, in the fourteen postseason games in which the Raptors played against the Cavs, they only won two, while James's team won twelve.[10]

That's right: 2–12.

Ever feel much like no matter what you do, you can't seem to find a way to win?

That's how the Raptors felt ending their 2017–2018 season with a loss to . . . you guessed it: LeBron James and the Cleveland Cavaliers.

However, the organization shook things up massively for the 2018–2019 season. They took chances—leaps and risks and trades that much of the basketball world thought was crazy. One of those leaps involved acquiring basketball star Kawhi Leonard from the San Antonio Spurs. To get him, the Raptors had to give away some of their own great players and their coach.[11]

But the big risk paid off. Even though the Raptors would go on to lose big games in their postseason battle, they always came back just when they seemed to be on the verge of failure. Too many times, they had felt failure. This time, they would hang on.

In a series against the Philadelphia 76ers, with each team having won three games, Leonard made a last-second buzzer beater to win the seventh, and final, game by a score of 92–90. Then, in the next series, against the Milwaukee Bucks, the Raptors were down two games to zero. When reporters asked Leonard where he would go after this devastating second loss, he responded in complete seriousness, "I'm going to Toronto for Game 3."[12] Instead of devolving into doubt or worry, Leonard focused strictly on the next step: play the next game.

That approach seemed to work fairly well, as Leonard led the Raptors to win four straight games and a shot at the NBA Championships.

In their championship series against the Golden State Warriors, rather than playing their normal way—to get as close to the edge of failure as possible and then come back—the Raptors took a lead in the series and never looked back, winning the 2019 NBA finals four games to two.[13]

Years of failure—of getting so close and then losing—had created a team that was ready to take risks, play hard, and finally cross the finish line in an improbable victory on the biggest basketball stage in the world.

NOTES

1. Joshua Davis, "How 4 Mexican Immigrant Kids and Their Cheap Robot Beat MIT," *WIRED*, December 2, 2014, https://www.wired.com/2014/12/4-mexican-immigrant-kids-cheap-robot-beat-mit/.
2. Davis, "How 4 Mexican Immigrant Kids."
3. Davis, "How 4 Mexican Immigrant Kids."
4. Davis, "How 4 Mexican Immigrant Kids."

5. Davis, "How 4 Mexican Immigrant Kids."
6. Richard Ruelas, "10 Years Ago They Beat MIT. Today, It's Complicated," *Arizona Republic*, July 17, 2014, https://www.azcentral.com/story/life/az-narratives/2014/07/17/phoenix-high-school-win-mit-resonates-decade-later/12777467/.
7. Ruelas, "10 Years Ago They Beat MIT."
8. Ruelas, "10 Years Ago They Beat MIT."
9. Ruelas, "10 Years Ago They Beat MIT."
10. Harry Lyles Jr., "A Timeline of LeBron James Dominating the Raptors in the NBA Playoffs," SB Nation, May 8, 2018, https://www.sbnation.com/2018/5/8/17326606/lebron-james-raptors-highlights-history-timeline.
11. Sopan Deb, "The Raptors' Journey to the Top of the N.B.A.," *New York Times*, June 14, 2019, https://www.nytimes.com/2019/06/14/sports/toronto-raptors-parade-nba-champions.html.
12. Deb, "The Raptors' Journey."
13. Deb, "The Raptors' Journey."

24

JEREMY STOPPELMAN

Yelp is a massive internet site where users can log in and offer reviews of businesses such as restaurants, dentists, hotels, and many more. On a monthly basis, over 139 million *different* users will post or access the site, and its founder, Jeremy Stoppelman, always knew that this was coming when he originally had the crystal-clear idea to create a site that allowed people to post and read reviews. Okay, he originally had aimed for exactly 140 million unique users each month, so he was technically a *bit* short on his goal. But that's a far cry from failure, right?! Now a multimillionaire who has had to deal with buyout offers from Google, Stoppelman has a story that goes to show that great entrepreneurs follow three simple steps: (1) Get a solid, super-clear idea of *exactly* what you want to create. (2) Create it—and don't make any mistakes along the way! (3) Reap the benefits as they come rolling in.

*S*ay what?!

While Jeremy Stoppelman is the cofounder of the far-reaching internet site Yelp and the site *does* indeed record approximately 139 million different users every month, the journey to get there was far from clear, easy, or without some serious flopping along the way.

In 1999, after he'd graduated from college, Stoppelman got his first job working for a home internet provider, @Home Network. Instead of an enthralling process of creativity and connection, the job was a flop. Stoppelman has said that he lasted only four months there, and the team he was put on to create a new product regarding internet networking never actually, well, was created. He said that the team was "dysfunctional" and couldn't get anything done. For a few weeks, Stoppelman tried hard to work and figure out a path forward, but then, he said, "I just found myself without a whole lot to do after a few weeks. I'd kind of run through all the projects that they had for me, and I didn't really know how to allocate my time."[1] Instead of starting with a burst of success and glamour, Stoppelman's career in the dot-com industry was starting with a whimper. He didn't even know what to do when he went to work all day, and the project he was slated to work on with his team was ultimately sidelined as a nonstarter.

So, Stoppelman quit in an attempt to find something more interesting and more viable. He landed next at a company called X.com, which would be the forerunner to a site you may know: PayPal. At the time, Elon Musk (yes, *that* Elon Musk of Tesla fame!) headed the company and provided a drastic and welcome change from Stoppleman's previous employer. Instead of long hours with seemingly little resolve or mission, Musk filled Stoppelman's head with wild claims and predictions, such as one idea that X.com would eventually replace all credit card companies, such as Visa and MasterCard. While Stoppelman felt like these notions were outlandish, he said they also provided a genuine and prodigious burst of creativity. They opened the door to entrepreneurship as a process of invention and possibility, of trying and failing, and of attempting to do things that might, at first, seem laughable. Stoppelman never forgot this lesson. He shared about his time with Musk and the company, "So few of us had what would be called preexisting experience. We were trying to do things we didn't necessarily know how to do."[2] Instead of squashing this uncertain attempt, the company encouraged Stoppelman to pursue things he didn't really understand, and to see what he could find or create.

FAIL...THEN PREVAIL!

Ever use Google for anything? Maybe Gmail, a search, or YouTube? If so, then you can be glad that Google cofounder Sergey Brin failed in his attempts to do a graduate program at MIT (Massachusetts Institute of Technology). Because of his rejection, Brin changed course, studied in California, and met a partner with whom he would create the tech juggernaut.

This notion and the encouraging experience eventually helped him and his partner, Russell Simmons, to take a big risk and start their own company. Their original idea was to create a site where users could log on and ask one another questions. The premise was based on Stoppelman's sense that the classic Yellow Pages—a phonebook filled with names and numbers of businesses—hadn't undergone any updating in the now-booming internet age. Stoppelman and Simmons hoped that their new idea, Yelp, would solve that problem and provide a way for people to ask one another for recommendations of where to go for various services and needs.[3]

The idea was sound and exciting. So, Stoppelman and Simmons hired a team to help them put it into practice. About the run-up to its big unveiling in October of 2004, Stoppelman said, "From the moment we got [the idea] we were extremely passionate, started building it, sinking ninety-hour weeks into coding and designing the thing.... We felt like we were super geniuses."[4]

Have you ever felt like a "super genius" of any sort? Or like you were the best player on the field or the court? Have you ever had the sense that you were going to crush it—excel at whatever you were about to attempt? You did the work, you were ready, and now was your time to shine! This mood imbued the Yelp office from which Stoppelman and Simmons had built their site in secret over those ninety-hour workweeks, and on the eve of its release, they were ready. They knew it was going to be a hit. People were craving something like this, after all, right? How could it fail? What could go wrong?

Everything.

On October 4, the site officially launched, and the buzz party began! Or not. Instead of massive interest and word-of-mouth excitement, the site fizzled. Some people did check it out, but they didn't stay too long, and they didn't spread the word about what Stoppelman had hoped would be the biggest and best new website to be unveiled.

Relatively quickly, Stoppelman went from feeling like a super genius to a super failure. He shared, "The consumer reaction? Total flop.... From the moment that we launched and started seeing the site not working as expected, it was a huge letdown. And in fact, it was a real

HAVE GRIT—DON'T SPLIT!

Andrew Moffat resigned from his teaching position at an elementary school in Birmingham, England, because some in the community were critical of his message that it is okay to be gay. Moffatt then became a leader at another school in Birmingham but still endures criticism. However, he has been nominated for the Global Teacher Prize.

struggle to keep the team together."[5] What was going to be a beautiful success story had turned into an embarrassing flop. And in a twist of irony, his Yelp teammates might have felt somewhat like Stoppelman himself had felt working for the home internet provider years earlier: like they just wanted to quit, cut their losses, and get out of there.

The consumer reaction? Total flop. . . . From the moment that we launched and started seeing the site not working as expected, it was a huge letdown. And in fact, it was a real struggle to keep the team together.

—Jeremy Stoppelman

At this point, Stoppelman and Simmons could have closed their Yelp office, called it a day, and moved on to another project. Except there was a small and intriguing result from the site launch that they almost missed. A few days before the official launch, Simmons had asked Stoppelman if they should embed some kind of review feature into the site—a place where people could write a brief comment about a business, give it some stars and a bit of info—in addition to the main question-and-answer style of the site. Stoppelman had deemed the idea a nonstarter. He didn't think people would be all that interested in simply writing their own reviews. He figured they'd flock to the site for the interaction with one another—the questions and answers. However, he told Simmons to go ahead and stick the review function somewhere in the site, as a last-minute add-on, just in case someone felt like doing one.[6]

This just-in-case, last-minute add-on ended up—as we now know—being the smash hit of the site. While the main site launch was a flop, the reviews feature was not. Stoppelman and Simmons noticed people posting up to fifteen reviews in that tiny, buried section. They seemed to love it, and they spent most of their time on the site in the review section.

So, instead of shutting down Yelp, they took this small but hopeful sign, temporarily put the site on hold, and completely redesigned it. Over the course of the next weeks and months, what was originally a tiny afterthought became the whole focus of the site. Then, in the site's rerelease, the flop was over. People flocked to it. They wrote reviews, read reviews, and kept coming back again and again and again. What

FROM WEAK TO PEAK!

An engineer named Wilson Greatbatch was just trying to find a way to record the heart's rhythm in 1956, when he accidentally made a much bigger discovery. The contraption he built was a failure—it didn't record the heart's rhythms at all. But it ended up doing something much more profound that would save millions and millions of lives: it sent small electronic shocks to the human heart to jolt it into doing its work. Today, the pacemaker is a crucial lifesaving medical device.

had quickly smoked out and turned to ashes was now completely rebuilt on the premise of an idea that had previously been seen as a failure.

Yelp grew every year, as more and more people used it, and finally, one of the most dominant tech companies in the world took notice. Starting in 2005, Google came knocking on Yelp's door, and the conversation that ensued went something like this:

Google: {Knock-knock} *Ahem* . . . is Yelp home?
Yelp: It's me. I mean, uh, I'm Yelp. Who are you?
Google: Who am *I*? *Who am I*?
Yelp: Um, yeah, that's what I just asked you. Are you, like, a repeating service or something?

Google: {Laughs loudly, checking to see if anyone else can hear the conversation} Am I, Google, like, a repeating service or something?

Yelp: Um, yeah, that's what I asked.

Google: No way, man, what would give you a crazy idea like that?

Yelp: {Speechless}

Google: All right, look, I'm a busy dude, and I've got a lot of doors to knock on today, so let me get straight to the point.

Yelp: Okay.

Google: Okay. Can I buy you?

Yelp: Can you *buy* me?

Google: Who's the repeating service *now*?!

Yelp: {Speechless again}

Google: So, it's a yes, right? Yes, I can buy you? Great. Let me get some other dudes to get the contract, so we can make it official and everything, and in case you're wondering, the answer is *yes*, I'll give you a whole boatload of money. Actually, quite a few boatloads of money. Do we have a deal?

Yelp: Whelp . . . um, I'd have to say, no, thanks.

Google: *No, thanks?!*

Yelp: Who's the repeating service after all?

So, maybe the real conversation didn't go exactly like this, but I'm pretty sure it's quite close to what you've just read. And in 2006, Google came knocking again. And in 2007, and in 2008, and . . . well, you get the picture.

But Yelp declined Google's massive (and yearly) buyout offers (and those from other major tech companies), and instead Yelp decided to go public in 2012. This enabled Stoppelman and Simmons to keep ownership of the company and ensure that it would retain its independence, rather than become a smaller part of a behemoth tech company.

Though Stoppelman's path toward Yelp's success included an aimless job he quit, and a huge flop when his idea first launched, he stuck with it and eventually cocreated a massively powerful and useful website. Reflecting on his experience, Stoppelman said, "Most of the time, when you come up with an idea, and you think you've got it all figured out, when you launch in the market, you always learn something about what works and what doesn't. Very often you do have to adapt your idea and be willing and able to adjust accordingly."[7]

When you "launch" in *life*, the same process applies as when you launch in the market: Some things will work and some won't, but you'll learn loads from both.

Very often you do have to adapt your idea and be willing and able to adjust accordingly.

—Jeremy Stoppelman

Sometimes you may feel as though you're aimlessly wandering, wasting your time. Other times, you might feel as though your idea or your ability is at the "super genius" level—there's no way you can fail. Either way, you're okay. You are where you need to be. As long as you keep attempting, your confusion may be strong sometimes, and at other times, your confidence may soar. What matters is that you keep moving forward. Keep your vision wide to see how what might have been a flop could be a clue to a future success. Then, go back to your notebook, craft a new possibility, and try again.

★ The Flop Files: **Norm Larsen** ★

In 1953 in San Diego, California, a tiny company by the name of Rocket Chemical had a single goal: they wanted to create some kind of protective substance that could be used on aircrafts, rockets, and pretty much anything that could be airborne. The need was dire: How to keep aerospace materials from rusting and becoming compromised due to water damage and other wear and tear?[8]

The entire company consisted of only three people, and this small team set to work testing and trying all kinds of different solutions for how they might be able to displace water on aerospace equipment. Led by Norm Larsen, the team used the scientific process of trial and error, creating possible formulas, then testing them out to see what the results would be.

Larsen guided the team in trial after trial (after trial after trial after, yup, trial). By the time they hit their fortieth attempt, it seemed they had the solution. It seemed to literally work magic in terms of displacing water and moisture that would build up and potentially cause rusting, mechanical failure, and other dangerous issues for aerospace equipment.[9]

As they tried to figure out what to call it, they thought it might be wise to honor their long journey to finally reach their prized solution. Since the substance was designed to displace water, and since it took the team forty tries to finally find it, they decided to call it WD-40, representing "water displacement, formulation successful in fortieth attempt."

Chances are you can find WD-40 just about anywhere—in grocery stores, most garages, lots of workshops and automobile garages, and sometime even in shelves lining apartments or homes. Rocketing from its invention in 1953 to today, WD-40 is now used for thousands of purposes—far more than Larsen and his team initially envisioned for their humble substance.

While it still works wonderfully well to prevent rust and keep mechanical parts moving safely and productively, it has also been used for a few more *unique* purposes too. For instance, it was once employed by a creative bus driver around whose bus a massive python snake had coiled itself. At a loss for how to remove the gargantuan snake, the driver applied a hefty dose of WD-40, and problem solved! The concoction also came in handy when police officers were trying to figure out how to help a thief who had become trapped in an air-conditioning vent. Naked, the thief was no longer too worried about getting away—and instead just wanted to get *out!* Police grabbed a few bottles of WD-40, and the burglar was soon free (and quite a bit slippery).[10]

Even though Larsen and his team failed thirty-nine times, those trials led them to their magic trial number forty and to a product that can do truly incredible things!

NOTES

1. Victor Luckerson, "Why Yelp's CEO Turned Down Google," *Time*, December 1, 2014, https://time.com/3611053/yelp-ceo/.
2. Luckerson, "Why Yelp's CEO Turned Down Google."
3. Luckerson, "Why Yelp's CEO Turned Down Google."
4. Daniel Wolfman and Chris Beier, "Yelp's Jeremy Stoppelman: 'What the Hell Am I Doing?'" *Inc.*, December 4, 2012, https://www.inc.com/chris-beier-and-daniel-wolfman/jeremy-stoppelman-yelp-launch-strategy.html.
5. Wolfman and Beier, "Yelp's Jeremy Stoppelman."
6. Wolfman and Beier, "Yelp's Jeremy Stoppelman."
7. Luckerson, "Why Yelp's CEO Turned Down Google."

8. Douglas Martin, "John S. Barry, Main Force behind WD-40, Dies at 84," *New York Times*, July 22, 2009, https://www.nytimes.com/2009/07/22/business/22barry1.html.

9. Martin, "John S. Barry, Main Force behind WD-40."

10. Robert Roy Britt, "WD-40: Strange Facts and Myths," Live Science, July 24, 2009, https://www.livescience.com/7818-wd-40-strange-facts-myths.html.

25
BEYONCÉ KNOWLES

To become the worldwide phenomenon known as Queen Bey, Beyoncé Knowles was lucky enough to be born into a well-to-do family whose connections to the music and recording industry were already deep and strong. A precocious, confident, and outspoken young girl, Knowles made a splash even when she was little, causing heads to turn and people to pay attention. Her mother always noted that Knowles had no problems with assertiveness, and by the time she was only nine years old, she had already won a major competition on the television show *Star Search* (think *American Idol* but more than twenty years ago). After making it bigger than big in the music and film industry, Knowles experienced even more triumph throughout her pregnancy and motherhood, proving that truly talented people don't fail or struggle; instead, they simply thrive.

*U*h . . . *rewind that . . .*

Queen Bey, as Beyoncé Knowles is affectionately known by her more than 146 million Instagram followers and fans around the world, was neither an assertive kid who never failed nor an adult who simply went from one triumph to another. Instead, her life journey thus far is a model of growth through imperfection, vulnerability, and poise. She has endured failure, rejection, and struggle and talks openly about how these experiences and events have shaped the woman she is today.

In her beautiful documentary *Self-Titled*, Knowles reflects on one of her first experiences of failure, on that episode of *Star Search* when she was nine years old. She and three other girls had come together to make up the group Girls Tyme, and they entered the competition with a fierce performance—choreographed with incredible dance moves, a hip-hop/pop rhythm that made the audience lean forward, and a seemingly unbeatable result. Knowles said that she felt like there was no way they could lose. She said, "At that time, you don't realize that you could actually work super hard and give everything you have, and lose."[1]

FROM WEAK TO PEAK!

Jay-Z, whose given name is Shawn Carter, wanted to make it in music but got rejected by major record labels right and left. Finally, as a last resort, he created and produced his own CD, made loads of copies, stored them in his car trunk, and drove around trying to sell them. He is now one of the best-selling singer-songwriters in American history.

After all performers had finished, contestants waited for the results from host Ed McMahon. Deep inside, Knowles knew that Girls Tyme would be crowned the winners. They had worked as hard as they possibly could have, put in immense effort, and developed a routine that pulsated with energy, joy, and talent, and they were ready. This was the group's breakout moment, as well as Knowles's start on the long road of success.

Girls Tyme stood onstage, to the right of the host, and into the microphone McMahon spoke those beautiful words Knowles's ears were just waiting to hear.

"The winner is . . . Skeleton Crew!"

Wait, what!?

Knowles was stunned. The group was crushed. Their pursuit had failed, and on national television. It didn't make sense. How could they have worked with all their might, believed with all their hearts that they had a fresh, unique, and mesmerizing performance, and yet still lose? This moment of failure became a defining one for Knowles, as she said that it enabled her to realize, at the young age of nine, that nothing is guaranteed and that you can work with all your might toward something, but you can't control the results. You don't always win. But if you love what you do, you have to keep going.[2]

It's a lesson that has remained with Knowles to this day, and she has had ample opportunity to practice it. Even though she went on to achieve massive stardom— including Grammy awards, sold-out concerts, audience- and

HOLD THE BOLD!

Judit Polgár, from Budapest, became a grand master in chess at the age of fifteen—the youngest person ever to achieve that level. Her ability to win and play aggressively shocked the chess world. However, from 2006 to 2009, Polgár experienced a lot of struggle and failure. She refused to allow the rough patch to stop her and has continued to play competitive chess.

critic-praised performances at major events like Coachella—that doesn't mean that her *Star Search* loss was the last time she had to grapple with rejection or struggle. But by embracing her own vulnerability and honestly facing her struggles, Knowles has become an example of how to walk through these things, rather than pretend they do not exist in the realm of pursuing success.

In her closely followed marriage to another massively talented, successful hip-hop star, Jay-Z, Knowles experienced some of the toughest rejection and struggle in her life. At one point in their marriage, Jay-Z and Knowles underwent a fraught struggle, as his infidelity crept in to threaten their bond and their commitment. This development could have completely caused their marriage to flop, as many others had in the famed halls of musical breakthroughs and breakouts. Instead, Knowles used the struggle to go deeper into who she was, find her own strength, and process what had happened in the best way she knew how: creation.

Out of the struggle, she created *Lemonade*, which proved to be a loosely based autobiographical account of her dealing with the issues in her marriage, to find and assert her own voice, and to work toward her eventual forgiveness of Jay-Z and the couple's reestablished commitment. This stage of Knowles's life surprised many of her fans and critics alike, and there was widespread acclaim heaped on Queen Bey for the authenticity and courage—not to mention the lyrical prowess and brilliance—she used to deal openly with

PLUCK ENOUGH!

Born in 1911 in Mississippi, Robert Johnson had a short twenty-seven years of life that are surrounded by mystery and a lack of recognition during his time. He seemed to have taught himself guitar, recorded twenty-four songs, and amazed all who heard him sing and play in juke joints (after reportedly being awful when he began). His talent has reached across decades, and seminal musicians like Eric Clapton and Bob Dylan have said Johnson's lyrics and musicality inspired their own work. Johnson's face graced a 1994 US postage stamp.

something that had the potential to easily become fodder for gossip magazines and bitter feuds. Instead, she used this seeming failure to reaffirm her own strength and growth and to model those attributes for others.[3]

And that wasn't all. As Jay-Z and Knowles recommitted their relationship, an exclamation point to this act wasn't all that far off: pregnancy with twins. Rather than reflecting some romanticized notion of pregnancy as a time of warmth and love and excitement, Knowles took the opportunity to talk about her pregnancy and delivery in honest, even harrowing terms. She talked about how much she weighed and about her struggles with intense fear and with many medical complications and issues. She developed preeclampsia, a life-threatening condition that endangers both mother and baby during any stage of a pregnancy. And during the birthing process, one of the babies' heartbeats stopped momentarily, necessitating that the medical professionals resort to an immediate C-section to get the babies out as quickly and as safely as possible.[4]

I think it's important for women and men to see and appreciate the beauty in their natural bodies. . . . To this day my arms, shoulders, breasts, and thighs are fuller. I have a little mommy pouch, and I'm in no rush to get rid of it. I think it's real.

—Beyoncé Knowles

This intense journey left Knowles feeling different. She felt as though her body and her mind had changed because of the process, not unlike how that experience of *Star Search* many, many years before had caused her to experience a life-altering shift in how she viewed herself and the world around her. After the birth of her twins, Knowles said, "I think it's important for women and men to see and appreciate the beauty in their natural bodies. . . . To this day my arms, shoulders, breasts, and thighs are fuller. I have a little mommy pouch, and I'm in no rush to get rid of it. I think it's real."[5]

Instead of being driven to perfection, as so many advertisements admonish us to do, Knowles began to talk about being driven to acceptance—to embracing our bodies and our ideas and our hopes as beautiful, rather than as wrong. This caused a fundamental shift, too, in the way she approached her music, the people with whom she worked, and the newfound strength of voice she used. Instead of progressing with the status quo in the industry, she began to see the kinds of change she could make by, for example, ensuring that people from under-represented backgrounds could emerge and find their triumphs too. In her explanation of this shift, Knowles shared, "If people in powerful positions continue to hire and cast only people who look like them, sound like them, come from the same neighborhoods they grew up in, they will never have a greater understanding of experiences different from their own. They will hire the same models, curate the same art, cast the same actors over and over again, and we will all lose."[6]

If people in powerful positions continue to hire and cast only people who look like them, sound like them, come from the same neighborhoods they grew up in, they will never have a greater understanding of experiences different from their own. They will hire the same models, curate the same art, cast the same actors over and over again, and we will all lose.

—Beyoncé Knowles

Winning was no longer a quest to be first place on an episode of *Star Search*. Instead, winning had become people in power raising up others who might not normally have the opportunity. Winning had become embracing her body, even if the media or culture did not. Winning had become honestly grappling with struggle, rather than hiding it and pretending everything was perfect. Queen Bey is one example of how authenticity is strength, and failure and struggle are, indeed, no final verdicts for the journeys our lives will take.

How might you *redefine* what it means to "win" on your own episode of *Star Search*? How might you *rethink* the struggles you're having right now, choosing to connect with others about them, rather than pushing them down in shame? Your strength, like Knowles's, may lie along these roads, rather than on perfect paths of success.

★ The Flop Files: **Bruce Springsteen** ★

Have you ever worked so hard at something that you felt sure you'd eventually be in first place? You heard the encouragements from others that, if you put grit and elbow grease into whatever you cared about, you would eventually win the coveted and prestigious number one spot. But what if, year after year, no matter how hard you worked, the highest you ever got was number two. Or worse, number three, or number four, or . . . well, you get the picture.

Classic rock singer-songwriter Bruce Springsteen can relate. Even though he has toured worldwide for over four decades and won an astonishing array of Grammy awards, as well as composed and recorded songs that grace radio stations and films and maybe even your parents' cars or kitchen, he has never actually had a number one hit. The closest Springsteen ever got was when his song "Thunder Road" made it to number two on the Billboard Top Hits chart.[7]

But rather than make his life a process of trying to break this rarified result, Springsteen has decided to keep rocking. Each year, he continues to compose new songs, and his concerts consistently run longer and have more energy than almost anyone else performing. Even into his sixties and seventies, Springsteen has performed concerts lasting longer than four hours.

Four hours!

Additionally, Springsteen has talked openly about his battles with depression. Specifically, in his memoir, *Born to Run*, Springsteen discussed two particularly dark periods of his life when he really struggled with depression and talked openly about his need to take care of himself, including a variety of medications that help him remain stable and move forward.

Even though Springsteen's image is gritty, tough, and strong, he is a sensitive singer-songwriter who battles many dark emotions. He is honest about these battles and honest about his journey, and he doesn't allow the struggle to define who he is or what he decides to become. He continually writes the songs he needs to bring to the world, and he is not focused on creating one that tops the charts. Instead, he's more concerned with singing a song that tops the hearts.[8]

NOTES

1. Beyoncé Knowles, "Self-Titled, Part 2: Imperfection," YouTube video, 1:02, posted by Beyoncé, December 17, 2013, https://www.youtube.com/watch?v=cIv1z6n3Xxo.
2. Alex Abad-Santos, "How Did Beyoncé Get Famous? Beyoncé Has Had to Work Hard for Her Stardom," Vox, May 12, 2015, https://www.vox.com/2014/8/28/18010406/beyonce-destinys-child-star-search.
3. Cat Lafuente, "The Stunning Transformation of Beyoncé," The List, accessed September 16, 2019, https://www.thelist.com/157035/the-stunning-transformation-of-beyonce/.

4. Julyssa Lopez, "Beyoncé Opens Up about Her Pregnancy Struggles in 'Homecoming' Documentary," *Glamour*, April 17, 2019, https://www.glamour.com/story/beyonce -opens-up -pregnancy-struggles-homecoming.

5. Beyoncé Knowles, "Beyoncé in Her Own Words: Her Life, Her Body, Her Heritage," *Vogue*, August 6, 2018, https://www.vogue.com/article/beyonce-september -issue-2018.

6. Knowles, "Beyoncé in Her Own Words."

7. Brian Griggs, "He's Never Had a No. 1 Hit. But He's the Most Honored American Rock Star Ever," CNN, September 23, 2019, https://www.cnn.com/2019/09/23 /entertainment/bruce-springsteen-birthday-trnd/.

8. Griggs, "He's Never Had a No. 1 Hit."

26
GRETA THUNBERG

If you speak loudly enough, people will eventually hear you and listen to your message. This is the story and moral of Greta Thunberg's mission. As a fifteen-year-old girl growing up near Stockholm, Sweden, she embarked on a massive and daunting journey to help her country and the world finally face up to the dangers of climate change and take action to ameliorate the problem. Much to her joyful surprise, politicians listened. First in Sweden, and then throughout Europe, and then even in America: world leaders finally came to terms with the changes humanity needs to make to protect the environment and truly change the world. Sometimes change faces blowback and pushback, but in Thunberg's case, we see that a young girl with a strong voice can succeed quite quickly.

O*r not.*

It was a seemingly normal day when then-fifteen-year-old Greta Thunberg made a decision that *would* change the world. Or at least become a blaring alarm clock to try to wake up world leaders. Many probably wish Thunberg never made this seemingly small decision. Instead of going to school, as she normally would, she decided to go to the Parliament building in Stockholm instead. She would sit on the steps. She would wait.[1]

In her mind, as a student who has been diagnosed with both autism and ADHD, it was difficult to ignore the dramatic warning about the dangers of climate change she had learned about starting in third grade as a nine-year-old. At first, adults would instruct her and her peers to do all they could to make small differences for the good of the environment. That's when Thunberg followed this train of thought to its logical end, she said. "They were always talking about how we should turn off lights, save water, not throw out food. I asked why and they explained about climate change. And I thought this was very strange. If humans could really change the climate, everyone would be talking about it and people wouldn't be talking about anything else. But this wasn't happening."[2]

CRAVE THE BRAVE!

Amy McGrath was a US Marine for twenty years and also completed eighty-nine combat missions as the first woman to fly the F/A-18 fighter jet. Flying a fighter jet had been a lifelong dream, but when she was fourteen years old and told her congressman about the dream, he responded that it would never happen because she was a girl. She is now running for a seat in Congress herself!

For Thunberg, the small suggestions prompted her to ask bigger questions, and the answers to those questions genuinely scared her. If climate change was such a massive problem, she wondered, then why did all the adults seem to carry on as if it were no big deal?

They were always talking about how we should turn off lights, save water, not throw out food. I asked why and they explained about climate change. And I thought this was very strange. If humans could really change the climate, everyone would be talking about it and people wouldn't be talking about anything else. But this wasn't happening.

—Greta Thunberg

As it turns out, this question wasn't easy to answer, and asking it didn't necessarily make Thunberg a lot of friends among world leaders. Instead of listening to adults who told her that she should go back to school, leave the steps of parliament, and let the older people handle such issues, Thunberg refused. And so, the next day, she brought her fifteen-year-old self back to those same steps in Stockholm, sat down, and waited. When lawmakers stopped to ask her what she was doing, she explained her mission: she wanted Sweden's leaders to take climate change even more seriously than they were and to follow through on laws they'd already passed, as well as pass even more environmentally friendly laws.

For three straight weeks, Thunberg continued her walkout and sit-in. Instead of going to school, she went to Parliament, and soon Swedish newscasters picked up on her determined tactics and stance. In her words and actions, she did not soften her message: climate change was an issue that needed immediate and full attention, before it was too late for the world to do anything about it. Sweden had already seen record-high temperatures, as well as an outbreak of fires, and around the world, both rising heat and flooding, as well as other severe weather systems, were occurring. In the United States, these changes in climate often drastically affect (and will affect) and hurt low-income people much more than other demographic groups.[3]

After three weeks, some Swedish leaders in Parliament had taken to her cause, applauded her efforts, but continued to stress that she really should be in school. Other leaders weren't quite so effusive with their praise or quite so tender with their recommendations. As Thunberg continued to speak out as loudly as she could—inspired in part by the students of Parkland, Florida, who staged a walkout from their school after lawmakers did nothing to stem gun violence (more on one of those students in chapter 5)—more voices attacking her rose up too.

The more her message spread, the farther Thunberg traveled to connect with others and to try to convince world leaders to take action. In August of 2019, she even sailed across the Atlantic Ocean on a yacht that produced no environmentally dangerous effects, to reach New York. However, as she reached farther outside of Sweden, critics took note and tried hard to both shame and stifle her voice. One example of many was wildly wealthy British business leader Arron Banks, who sent an ominous threat over his Twitter account as Thunberg made the yachting trek to New York: "Freak yachting accidents do happen in August," he wrote and shared.[4] Imagine a grown, wealthy businessman feeling so worried about the message of a sixteen-year-old student that he would share an only-lightly-veiled death wish for her with the entire world.

But Thunberg is used to this kind of attack from adults. Many say she does not know enough. Others say she does not present her case in the proper way. Still others are friendly toward her message of doing something about climate change but feel she is too serious and harsh in the way she demands leaders do something. Thunberg hears the intense amount of hate and criticism, and she does the same thing she started doing at age fifteen on the steps of Parliament in Stockholm, Sweden: she acts. She talks with world leaders when they'll listen, and when they won't, she protests. Most recently, in September of 2019, she led a protest right outside the White House in Washington, DC, arguing that much of the world follows America's lead, and so why not pressure the president of the United States to do something about climate change?[5]

While people attack and critique her, Thunberg is not swayed. She has said, "I see the world a bit different, from another perspective. I have a special interest. It's very common that people on the autism spectrum have a special interest."[6] This special interest allows her to continue to speak and work with immense focus. She is not deterred by the criticism of her detractors, nor is she swayed by the well-meaning advice of understanding adults who tell her that she's doing it the wrong way, or at the wrong time, or in the wrong place. Instead, she holds unswervingly

HOLD THE BOLD!

Engineer Lonnie Johnson discovered the great force behind high-powered water guns one night while experimenting in his bathroom. However, it took a full *seven* years of trial and error and marketing before the product, which was originally marketed as the Power Drencher, started to become a hit. Eventually, the name was updated to the Super Soaker, and it has been a bestselling toy since!

to her goal of getting world leaders to address the dangers of climate change and help enact policies that will truly make a difference. As she works tirelessly to make these demands, she continues to try to embody them in her own life: she no longer eats meat, she refuses to fly on airplanes, and she rides her bike everywhere. Even Thunberg's family, who support her mission, have an electric car they only use when there are no other options.

I see the world a bit different, from another perspective. I have a special interest. It's very common that people on the autism spectrum have a special interest.

—Greta Thunberg

However, all of this time and energy Thunberg has invested has not yet yielded any drastic results. In September of 2019, President Donald Trump did not saunter out of the White House, listen to her, and immediately decide to change course on his stance on climate change. World leaders in Sweden, one of the foremost countries tackling climate change, have yet to implement the high standards for which Thunberg advocates.

But just because she hasn't tasted big success with her mission does not mean Thunberg is about to stop. Like the Parkland students who inspired her, just because powerful laws and actions haven't yet been adopted, this doesn't mean she will stop protesting and hoping. She won't stop working.

And even though lawmakers haven't taken action based on her work, others have. With

NOT DIMINISHED… FINISHED!

Not only has Greta Thunberg fought through an avalanche of criticism and attacks in order to keep challenging those in power against climate action, she has also finally gotten some structural support! The BBC Studios Science Unit will create a documentary television series exploring Thunberg's activism, hope, and journey for climate justice.

1.4 *million* followers, Thunberg has far more support than many of the government officials from whom she demands action! And many of her followers are taking actions of their own: some commit their daily lives to have less of a negative effect on the environment, and some join her in her protests to leaders around the world.

In one sense, Thunberg's mission, thus far, could be seen as a failure: it hasn't enacted the big kind of change she seeks. She has not won, in that regard.

However, her failure has caused a massive amount of new awareness about the issue of climate change; it has gotten students all around the world to join in her cause; and her words have sparked hope in the hearts of many around the world that, even though there is more work to be done, there are voices and hands ready to do it. As a powerful acknowledgment of this work, she was even named the 2019 "Person of the Year" by *Time* magazine. What some call failure and denounce as out of place and misguided, Thunberg calls making a difference. And she's in no mood to stop.

★ The Flop Files: **Angela Zhang** ★

Even though she was only fourteen years old and a high school student at the time, Angela Zhang wanted to be on a research team at Stanford University in California, and she wasn't about to accept rejection as the result.

Zhang kept contacting Stanford, asking if there were any research teams that she could join. Passionate about science, and particularly interested in medical possibilities, Zhang eventually received an invitation from Stanford to come and visit one of their labs and do preliminary research by reading and responding to articles. She said regarding the highly technical language, "I remember looking at my first article—all of the words were English, but I didn't understand any of them in conjunction. I spent a lot of time just patiently Googling each word. That was one of my first challenges—just really understanding the information."[7]

Even though the task felt daunting, Zhang kept at it. Painstakingly, she went one word at a time, then one sentence at a time, then one page at a time, working at the material until she could not only fully understand it but also competently explain it. The next step was to actively contribute to the new research the Stanford team was conducting.

Zhang joined an effort to try to figure out how to more effectively target cancer cells in the human body. Most of what constitutes chemotherapy treatment in hospitals all around the world consists of attacking *all* the cells in someone's body, hoping that the cancer cells are diminished in the process. But what also happens is that healthy cells get hurt too.

Zhang and the team at Stanford worked on how to differentiate between the two kinds of cells—those with cancer and those without. Working with an "iron oxide gold nanoparticle," Zhang and the team began to see that this nanoparticle could attach itself to cancerous cells and potentially carry the chemotherapy to *only* those cells, rather than attacking all of a body's cells indiscriminately. Of this potential, Zhang said, "So the ability to concentrate and deliver chemotherapy to only cancer cells would [help] increase the efficacy of some cancer drugs and decrease some of the side effects."[8]

Even though she had to call again and again and again, Zhang did not give up her mission to join a research team at Stanford University. And even though, when she arrived, the dense academic articles she was asked to read sent her constantly on a definition-finding mission, she didn't take that struggle as a sign of failure or that she did not belong. Instead, she continued, helped discover potentially ground-breaking new abilities for cancer treatment, and proved that you're never too young to overcome rejection and do something remarkable for the world.

NOTES

1. Rebecca Onion, "How Greta Thunberg Captured Our Attention on Climate," Slate, September 9, 2019, https://slate.com/technology/2019/09/greta-thunberg-climate -activism-scares-the-right-and-the-left.html.

2. Masha Gessen, "The Fifteen-Year-Old Climate Activist Who Is Demanding a New Kind of Politics," *New Yorker*, October 2, 2018, https://www.newyorker.com/news /our-columnists/the-fifteen-year-old-climate-activist-who-is-demanding-a-new-kind -of-politics.

3. Carmen Chappell, "Climate Change in the US Will Hurt Poor People the Most, Accord-ing to a Bombshell Federal Report," CNBC, November 26, 2018, https://www.cnbc .com/2018/11/26/climate-change-will-hurt-poor-people-the-most-federal-report .html.

4. Joshua Nevett, "Greta Thunberg: Why are Young Climate Activists Facing So Much Hate?" BBC News, August 28, 2019, https://www.bbc.com/news/world-49291464.

5. Max Cohen, "'If You Did Your Job, We'd Be in School': Greta Thunberg Joins White House Climate Protest," *USA Today*, September 13, 2019, https://www.usatoday .com/story/news/nation/2019/09/13/climate-activist-greta-thunberg-protests -outside-white-house/2310243001/.

6. Gessen, "The Fifteen-Year-Old Climate Activist."

7. Mary Cirincione, "Cancer-Fighting Harvard Student Looks to a Future in STEM," *US News & World Report*, May 12, 2015, https://www.usnews.com/news/the-next -generation-of-stem/articles/2015/05/12/cancer-fighting-harvard-student-looks -forward-to-a-long-future-in-stem.

8. Cirincione, "Cancer-Fighting Harvard Student."

27
LOIS JENSON

When a twenty-seven-year-old single mother named Lois Jenson decided that she needed a higher-paying job to support her family, the mining industry in Eveleth, Minnesota, was ready to support her. Even though mining had stereotypically been work reserved for men, in 1975, the industry began to offer positions to women, ensuring that equal opportunity to work was provided. Jenson thrived. At the mine, the male workers treated her with both dignity and respect. Though the work was grueling, the kind friendships she formed while on the job made the gritty realities of manual labor in the mine worth it. And the paycheck, which provided for her and her children, was a massive boon. Jenson broke a gender barrier that had existed for decades and did so in a community of both support and understanding.

If only!

Instead of a supportive—or even neutral—environment in the mines of Eveleth, Minnesota, Lois Jenson found an abusive, traumatic, and disgusting display of horrific treatment. When she started working for the Eveleth Mines in 1975, there were four women and six hundred men on staff. These six hundred men, rather than ensure a safe working environment, used the ratio to make the lives of these women—and others who would work there in the years to come—a living hell.[1]

Before she started working for Eveleth Mines, Jenson had been a secretary. Struggling to support herself and her family on the low wages of her secretarial work, she had heard that the mines were hiring and had seen the paycheck of another woman who worked there. It was far more than she'd ever make in her capacity as a secretary. The decision seemed like a no-brainer. As Jenson told it, "It really was about getting a better paying job with benefits. I didn't go there to bring up issues. I just wanted to make a decent life for my family."[2] Rather than starting out in the mines with a mission to be a leader or a voice for national change, Jenson had a goal that was small and simple: she just wanted to put food on the table. She just wanted to be able to work hard and make a living. That's all.

It really was about getting a better paying job with benefits. I didn't go there to bring up issues. I just wanted to make a decent life for my family.

—Lois Jenson

And in return for this simple goal, what did Jenson, and the other women working for Eveleth Mines, have to endure? The list is daunting but includes: stalking by male coworkers after work, groping by male coworkers during work, harassment—verbally, emotionally, and physically—during work, nooses put above the stations where the women were going to be working that day, and an endless array of horrific comments and threats.[3]

On Jenson's very first day of work in the mine, a male miner waited until the two of them were alone, then came up very close to her and said in a threatening tone, "You . . . women don't belong here. Why don't you go home? That is where you belong."[4] Immediately, Jenson was on guard and soon learned than in her capacity as a miner, she would have to be constantly vigilant. She could be attacked at any moment, threatened, followed, or harassed. Days on the job were an endless cycle of humiliation and fear.

NOT DIMINISHED... FINISHED!

Amy Cooper's research in her PhD program was criticized in front of peers and others by the chair of the program as not rigorous or academic enough. She would go on to receive two Fulbrights, earn her PhD, publish the rigorous book *State of Health*, and become a professor at Saint Louis University.

Yet she was making three times as much money as she had previously made as a secretary. The money was helping her family to survive, but she was slowly being crushed, her dignity and her entire life under unimaginable pressure. Finally, Jenson went to management to try to deal with this onslaught of attacks.

They did nothing.

So, she went to the union that represented the miners. Surely, they would do something to help her and the other women who were daily fearing for their safety simply because they wanted to make a paycheck, right?

Wrong. The union ignored Jenson too.

After these two massive rejections, Jenson decided, in 1984, to go even higher: she informed the Minnesota Human Rights Commission about the abuse at Eveleth Mines. That was when one of her bosses sexually assaulted her, pinning her wrists and attacking her in the electrical department at Eveleth Mines.[5]

Surely, now, *something* would be done. Surely, the women who simply wanted to work would be supported, dignified, and their attackers and harassers would be held accountable.

Or not.

While Jenson filed the complaint against Eveleth Mines in 1984, it wasn't until 1987—*three years later*—that the state demanded that Eveleth Mines pay Jenson a sum of $11,000 for the horrific abuse she had suffered and required the company to create a specific harassment policy in order to protect the women who worked in the mines.[6]

Finally . . . victory!

Or . . . not.

The company received the orders from the State and essentially replied, *Nope. We're not doing any of that.* Eveleth Mines flat-out refused to pay Jenson the money, and they refused to create a harassment policy or to in any way protect the women who were still working in the mines.

In other words, the company leaders knew about the abuse, received orders to stop the abuse—and make small amends for what had happened—and instead chose to do absolutely nothing.

Nothing.

Jenson refused to stop fighting for justice, and she refused to accept failure since the case involved both her safety and her dignity.

Two other women—Pat Kosmach and Kathy Anderson—joined the complaint, and in 1991, in a civil court, Judge James Rosenbaum decided that the women could proceed as a class. This meant that it would be the first class-action lawsuit based on sexual harassment. *Finally*, not failure, but hope. However, the hope was short-lived, as Judge Rosenbaum's other ruling in the 1991 case stated that the company, Eveleth Taconite Co., was not liable to create a harassment policy *or* to educate or in any way control the behavior of the men in the mines.[7]

In other words: the company had zero responsibility to do anything at all about the abuse that women were still undergoing on a daily basis. Furthermore, Judge Rosenbaum's ruling did not, technically, award any real victory to Jenson and her two brave peers. Rather, the ruling simply meant that the case *could* proceed as a class-action lawsuit. In 1991, even this was seen as groundbreaking. Imagine that: a group of women undergoing horrendous abuse and trauma at the hands of many, many men, and the only victory that could be secured, after seven years, was that a judge allowed the women to make their stand as a group, rather than individually.

CRAVE THE BRAVE!

Stacey Abrams ran for governor of Georgia in 2018. Had she won, she would have been the first African American woman to be a state governor. Though experts predicted she would lose by a landslide, she came unbelievably close to beating her opponent, Brian Kemp. Because the election was marred by voter discrimination, Abrams has boldly refused to concede and silence her voice and the votes of the state's constituents.

The next trial began in 1992, and this time, fourteen more women added their names to the class-action suit. Now, there were seventeen women, all shoulder to shoulder in bravery, attempting to hold others accountable for the abuse they had committed. In 1993, another small victory was decided: Judge Richard Kyle ruled that the company was liable to institute a sexual harassment policy at the mine *and* to educate and raise awareness among the men. But if the women were to be awarded any damages, a private hearing would have to ensue.

FAIL...THEN PREVAIL!

Leo Tolstoy struggled for two years in college at the university in Kazan, Russia. His grades were very low, and his teachers claimed that he simply couldn't learn. So, he dropped out. He would go on to write some of the most memorable books of all time, including *War and Peace*.

This process extended month after month, and defense lawyers for the company manipulated the hearing to excoriate the women in the class-action suit—attacked them for anything in their history they could find to undermine their credibility. Due to this painful process, many of the women who had formed the class-action groups developed post-traumatic stress disorder (PTSD), a condition that occurs when a person experiences intense stress and trauma and then is unable to stop reliving the trauma again and again. In other words, the very avenue prescribed for these women to try and obtain justice served the purpose of abusing them all over again.[8]

It wasn't until 1998 that the women in the class-action lawsuit, led by Jenson as the first to bravely stand and make her case, finally were awarded damages for their horrific abuse. That's right: *1998*.[9]

It had taken a total of fourteen years for the women to receive even a semblance of justice. What had they done with their lives, other than work hard to bring home a paycheck, just as their male counterparts had? Yet for the fact of being women, they were taunted, tormented, and attacked.

While their case may have failed numerous times, stalled at others, and received rejections at almost every turn, Jenson pressed forward. When she and the other women finally settled the suit, so they could move forward and put this tragic experience behind them, Jenson wondered if she had made a mistake. She wondered if she should have tried to go to a full trial and make it public, make the company and its workers to be held fully accountable for what they had—and hadn't—done.

But Jenson did not truly miss her chance to have the world see the injustice that had occurred over and over again for so many years. The world would know. In 2005, the film *North Country* was released, starring actress Charlize Theron as Jenson, and telling her story. When the movie came out, Jenson finally felt like a sense of justice had occurred. She said regarding those who created the film and of its effect on her: "These people treated us with respect and they gave us a feeling that what we did was important. This movie has given me my life back."[10]

These people treated us with respect and they gave us a feeling that what we did was important. This movie has given me my life back.

—Lois Jenson

Sometimes, you fight for justice against what you have had to endure. And you may feel, for a long time, like that justice is playing hide-and-seek with your soul. In Jenson's case, it seemed as though justice might remain permanently hidden. It did not. Even though it took twenty-one years from when she started working in the mine to when the film was released, Jenson was finally able to see her story told and to see those who had hurt her and the other women held accountable.

Keep telling your story. Try to be as brave as you can be as you share the ways in which others may have tried to silence you, and speak back to them, using all the means you have. It may take a while, and it may seem like you are failing over and over again, but justice has a way of eventually coming out, as Jenson's story so powerfully shows.

NOTES

1. Suzanne Goldenberg, "'It Was Like They'd Never Seen a Woman Before,'" *Guardian*, February 2, 2006, https://www.theguardian.com/film/2006/feb/03/gender.world.
2. Goldenberg, "'It Was Like They'd Never Seen.'"
3. Goldenberg, "'It Was Like They'd Never Seen.'"
4. Goldenberg, "'It Was Like They'd Never Seen.'"
5. Goldenberg, "'It Was Like They'd Never Seen.'"
6. Emma Dill, "The Sexual Harassment Class-Action Started at a Minnesota Mine That Helped Set National Precedent," MinnPost. February 26, 2018, https://www.minnpost.com/mnopedia/2018/02/sexual-harassment-class-action-started-minnesota-mine-helped-set-national-precedent/.
7. Dill, "The Sexual Harassment Class-Action."
8. Dill, "The Sexual Harassment Class-Action."
9. Goldenberg, "'It Was Like They'd Never Seen.'"
10. Goldenberg, "'It Was Like They'd Never Seen.'"

28
NEW ORLEANS SUPERDOME

The eighty-thousand-capacity stadium whose wide, circular roof looks more like a UFO than an arena came to life in 1975 after a relatively short period of design and construction. It helped that, both politically and logistically, everyone was on board with the project and in agreement about how it would proceed. The Superdome enjoyed an unparalleled run of events, and even when, on August 29, 2005, Hurricane Katrina slammed the city of New Orleans, causing destruction and tragedy everywhere, the Superdome was unaffected—becoming a symbol of stalwart perfection even within a city in crisis.

*N*o. *Absolutely not.*

The New Orleans Superdome has, indeed, come to be a powerful symbol for the city, but rather than one of perfection, it represents a kind of hard-fought hope that emerges from tragedy with wounds and scars everywhere, but not fully defeated.

In 1965, when the vision for the Superdome was first created, a genuine sense of excitement began to build throughout the city of New Orleans and the state of Louisiana. Nothing like it had ever been attempted, and many people weren't even sure such a feat was possible.[1]

Eighty thousand seats?!

That would literally be like building a completely enclosed city inside of a city.

Just for fun, try this: whatever city or town you're in right now— right now as you read this sentence right here that you are actually reading—try searching on the internet for the population of the city or town you're in. Don't have an internet connection available? Good! Screen-free, internet-free reading time, hooray! Let me check for you: okay, so you're reading this chapter in Windsor, Connecticut, just north of Hartford. At the latest census, Windsor had approximately 29,044 people.

That means you could fit the entire town of Windsor inside the Superdome. But it would still be more than half empty. So, you could double it, and you'd still have more than twenty thousand empty seats! (Okay, okay, so *you're* not reading this book in Windsor, Connecticut, but it's where I would have been reading a book like this when I was in middle school, if I could go back in time to my middle school life, yet retain the happenings of the future, so the book

> ## NOT DIMINISHED...
> ## FINISHED!
>
> Legendary rock-and-roll singer Elvis Presley auditioned for a singing group called the Songfellows in 1954. They promptly rejected him and in their reasoning said that it was because he couldn't sing.

would *still* be written, although that might be impossibly impossible because I would still be thinking failures aren't cool, so why would I be reading a book about how powerful failure can be?)

So, we've established that the Superdome is massive. And because of that, it makes sense that for five years after the project was approved, it was completely stalled. Five years of absolutely nothing because people couldn't agree on how, exactly, to build the thing, to make it work, and if the project really was viable, or if it was just a cool idea that was never destined to happen.

Finally, in 1971, the construction began, with the goal of being completed by 1974. However, more struggle and a

HAVE GRIT—DON'T SPLIT!

If you've ever tasted the awesomeness of a unique Ben & Jerry's ice cream, then you can thank the forty medical schools that first rejected cofounder Jerry Greenfield. That's right: all *forty* of the medical schools to which Greenfield applied flat-out rejected him. Where to turn? A good friend and ice cream!

bit of floundering ensued, and the stadium opening date was pushed back another year because the cost of construction was quickly extending far beyond the budget.[2]

In 1975, the doors to the stadium, at long last, opened. The roof did not cave. The walls did not buckle or bend. It truly was a feat of the imagination that had turned from a wild possibility into a very vivid reality. Upon the initial opening of the Superdome in 1975, Brian Brocato, who was an employee just starting out at the time (and who eventually became director of operations at the arena), recalled the overwhelming feeling he got when he first walked out to see its size and design. He said, "I remember the first time I walked in there. I went out on the floor, looked up and went, 'Wow.' And it still gives me a tingle today."[3]

I remember the first time I walked in there. I went out on the floor, looked up and went, "Wow." And it still gives me a tingle today.

—Brian Brocato

Over the next thirty years, the Superdome would be the setting for the most diverse list of events ever assembled. Professional football and basketball games were played here, home-and-garden shows exhibited, and touring shows and concerts performed, such as the Rolling Stones in 1981 and U2 in 2002. It was truly a place where anything could—and did—happen.

But then something tragic, which no one expected, happened. August 29, 2005, arrived, and with it, the destructive force of Hurricane Katrina. The levees of New Orleans, which had been tasked with keeping floodwaters out of the city in the event of a major storm, completely failed. They crumbled like sandcastle walls before the stunned eyes of a city, a state, a nation, and a world.[4]

Destruction reigned everywhere. People floated on pieces of their homes, seeking desperately to find safety amid a storm that had taken everything away—in the case of many others, even their lives. Thirty thousand people flocked to the Superdome, hoping it would provide refuge from the onslaught of terror outside.

PLUCK ENOUGH!

Famed Pokémon trainer Ash Ketchum spent twenty years consistently losing out to bigger, better trainers in every League Tournament. Finally, in 2019, Ash accomplished the unthinkable and became a Pokémon master when he won his first championship.

It did not. Instead, the Superdome flooded too, and water inside climbed to four feet high. The use of the Superdome had not been sanctioned, and it was part of no official plan, but people nearby fled there in the hopes that this massive structure that had become so synonymous with strength, power, and prestige could somehow save them.

It failed. It was not safe, there was not enough to eat or drink, and rather than find their freedom and security inside, people found confusion, chaos, and lost hope. The symbol of strength that had helped to define part of New Orleans for the last thirty years was tragically being erased, too, right before the country's eyes.[5]

SWERVE WITH NERVE!

Teachers ever ask you to use Post-it notes for your books and ideas? You can thank Spencer Silver for their existence, even though their creation was a mistake. Silver was trying to create a very strong, sticky substance and failed; a friend found another use for the weaker adhesive.

The federal government's failure to aid and support the effort to help those whose lives had been ravaged by Hurricane Katrina is well-documented, and in the wake of the storm, many thought that the Superdome, like much of the city, was beyond repair. It was too broken.

But slowly, hope re-emerged, and as the seemingly impossible effort to rebuild the city got underway, the Superdome was included in the discussions. Was it even possible?

Against all odds, the electrical and mechanical systems were in decent shape, and with the support of local and state government services, the help of local construction companies, the support of the NFL, and more, the rebuilding slowly began. It would eventually take more than a year and over $200 million, but on September 19, 2006, the New Orleans Saints returned to their home in the Superdome, the city came out to watch, and in a game that has come to symbolize far more than football, the Saints won and put an exclamation mark on a journey that seemed if not impossible the first time around in 1971, surely impossible the second time around starting in 2005.

I think it symbolized not only maybe the resurgence of our football team, but the resurgence of the city and the recovery and the rebirth.

—Drew Brees

On quarterbacking that first game back in the revitalized stadium, Drew Brees would recall, "I think it symbolized not only maybe the resurgence of our football team, but the resurgence of the city and the recovery and the rebirth."[6] The city of New Orleans had continued to struggle under the enormous task of rebuilding, but a place that had become a central part of life in the city was now open, flourishing, and seemed to suggest that there was life left yet. When the team went out and won that first game, it became a rallying cry for hope moving forward.

Reflecting on the transformation from a ravaged city and a destroyed Superdome to a place whose restoration proved that healing was never impossible, architect Arthur Q. Davis captured the two symbolic acts that the Superdome has come to embody. He wrote in his autobiography, "The Dome personified New Orleans even before August 29, 2005, but now, thanks to Hurricane Katrina and the Saints' remarkable 2006 season, the Dome is known the world over as a symbol of great tragedy and of almost unbelievable triumph."[7]

The Dome personified New Orleans even before August 29, 2005, but now, thanks to Hurricane Katrina and the Saints' remarkable 2006 season, the Dome is known the world over as a symbol of great tragedy and of almost unbelievable triumph.

—Arthur Q. Davis

Rising from tragedy, the Superdome now resembles a feat of hope and possibility rather than failure. Its iconic circular rooftop shows that failure—even the most heartrending kind—does not have to be final. Sometimes, the places we think need to be completely torn down and left for dead may have possibility left in them. We may need to look with the eyes of an architect, or see with a different kind of vision, but the future holds potential to rebuild from rubble if enough people are willing to take the leap.

NOTES

1. Ted Lewis, "Designed to Be 'Greatest Building in the History of Mankind' Superdome Still Amazes Even on 40th Birthday," *New Orleans Advocate*, August 3, 2015, https://www.nola.com/news/article_c1a84887-0bff-5227-a6a1-8705da8d6758.html.
2. Lewis, "Designed to Be 'Greatest Building in the History of Mankind.'"
3. Lewis, "Designed to Be 'Greatest Building in the History of Mankind.'"
4. Jeanna Thomas, "10 Years Later, the Saints Still Feel the Significance of the Superdome's First Game after Hurricane Katrina," SB Nation, September 26, 2016, https://www.sbnation.com/2016/9/26/13037146/saints-falcons-monday-night-football-2006-hurricane-katrina-superdome.
5. Thomas, "10 Years Later."
6. Thomas, "10 Years Later."
7. Arthur Q. Davis, *It Happened by Design: The Life and Work of Arthur Q. Davis*, (Jackson: University Press of Mississippi, 2009), 51.

29
GRACE HOPPER

Alter a lifetime of service in the US Navy, in 1986, Grace Hopper retired with the rank of rear admiral—one of the first few women to ever achieve that high rank in the United States Navy. She was also the oldest active service member in the armed service branches at the time, at the age of eighty years. To achieve these admirable feats, Rear Admiral Hopper had a litany of successes along the way. Her parents—both also esteemed and successful—modeled for her the way real growth and success occurs: quickly and with support! Never failing a single exam or struggling with the status quo, Hopper ascended the navy's ranks with a traditional leadership style and work ethic that everyone supported.

*N*o *way!*

Instead of forging an easy or failure-proof path forward, Grace Hopper achieved her tremendous, groundbreaking ascension by living her life according to a motto she kept: "Dare and do." It would define the choices she made over the course of her eighty-five-year life and was inspired by the example first set by her parents from the time she was young.[1]

Growing up in the early 1900s, Hopper experienced the strong stigma attached to women who chose to study and pursue mathematics. Socially, it was considered unbecoming and inappropriate for young woman to study math and instead much more proper to pursue careers along secretarial or teaching avenues. Rather than abide by this unfair stigma, Hopper's mother loved math and found ways to study and advance her own knowledge, serving as a brave example for her daughter regarding the need to pursue what you love, no matter what society tells you. Additionally, Hopper's father worked incredibly hard as an insurance broker, achieving great success, even though he had had both of his legs amputated. He would constantly encourage Hopper to debunk society's standards for women and to instead pursue what she was passionate about. This early encouragement from both of her parents helped pave the way for Hopper to challenge the status quo of American society as she rose through the military ranks.[2]

Hopper's rise would not be without failure and rejection, however.

Her first major failure came when, at the age of sixteen, she applied to Vassar College. She wanted to go on to college and earn a degree in mathematics, yet in order to be accepted, she would need to score well enough on a rigorous Latin exam. Instead of passing and joining the student body at Vassar, Hopper bombed the test, and Vassar rejected her application. Instead of joining the college of which she longed to be a part, Hopper wasted no time in continuing her education for an extra year at a boarding school and then began at Vassar one year later.

She thrived in her college courses and loved mathematics so much that she chose to continue by studying for—and earning—both a master's degree and a PhD in math from Yale University, the first in 1930 and the second in 1934.[3]

If you've ever failed in your first attempt to get in somewhere—be it a special program in your middle school, a team, a club, or even an essay contest or a dance competition—you have two choices. You can decide that it wasn't meant to be, let the drive go, and find something else to do. Or, if you love it, you can spend the next year (or month, or two years), getting stronger, learning more, becoming more prepared, and then trying again. Hopper's pursuit of Vassar would not be stymied by a single rejection, and if anything, it only encouraged her hunger to attend the following year. This

SWERVE WITH NERVE!

Robert Kiyosaki became an internationally bestselling author, speaker, and financial entrepreneur when his book *Rich Dad, Poor Dad* was published in 1993. However, long before that, two of his self-created businesses went bankrupt, and he struggled to figure out what to do.

hunger then lent momentum for her next two degrees. Hopper's PhD was especially rare, as in 1934, the vast majority of degrees were awarded to men, and relatively few women earned a degree in mathematics. Hopper was one of these few.[4]

And one of the few Hopper would continue to be. After teaching mathematics at Vassar College (yes—where she was first originally rejected!), Hopper made the unusual decision to join the United States Navy. But, like Vassar, they too rejected her initially.

Weighing 105 pounds and thirty-four years old, Hopper was told her low weight would be an issue, as it did not meet the physical requirements the navy held, and that she was already too old. Rather than accept this rejection, Hopper . . . well . . . *rejected* the rejection.[5]

Imagine that! Seriously, not just as a rhetorical exercise. Consider something from which you have been rejected. Now, imagine rejecting the rejection. Cut from the basketball team? What if you said, *I'm going to keep showing up to practice because I* love *this game so much, and I am going to get people water, dribble on the side, just do whatever I can to get better and be a part of this team.* It's hard to imagine any coach being able to resist that kind of work ethic and determination, right?

Turns out, it was pretty hard for the US Navy to resist the kind of work ethic and determination that Hopper could bring. She figured out how she could get a waiver for her weight and permission from the government to join the navy.

They relented.

She joined.

Immediately, she had a big impact. Along with other mathematics-minded service members, Hopper got to work on the Mark series

FAIL...THEN PREVAIL!

Have you ever failed a big test? You're not alone. The bar exam is a test that anyone who wants to be a lawyer must pass before they can practice law for their career. But many amazing people have bombed their first (and sometimes second) tries at the big test. Among those who failed the bar are: Kathleen Sullivan (who would later become the dean of the law school at Stanford University), California governor Jerry Brown, First Lady Michelle Obama, President Franklin D. Roosevelt, and Benjamin Cardozo (who became a Supreme Court justice!), among many others.

of computers, the first of their kind. This work often required an insane amount of focus, as Hopper and others on the team would have to remain, at times, by the massive computers to input codes twenty-four hours a day![6]

Hopper was repeatedly honored for her work in the navy, left for a while to join the private sector, and then returned to the navy when they needed her back. They had been trying to come up with a system for their payroll operations and had failed a whopping 823 times (yes, you read that right). No one at the navy could quite figure out a good standardized system with the computers, and so . . . *who you gonna call?*

Not the Ghostbusters (as much as I love them). You call Hopper.

She came back to work with the navy and remained there until the age of eighty. Before she retired in 1986, she received one of the highest promotions possible, and became one of an elite group of women to attain the rank of rear admiral.[7]

FROM WEAK TO PEAK!

In 1987, tennis player Stan Smith was inducted into the Tennis Hall of Fame as one of the greatest players of all time. He was even ranked as one of the top forty players ever by *Tennis* magazine. However, this feat wasn't easily predicted from when he was growing up. Instead, when he sought to be a ball boy when he was younger, coordinators at the Davis Cup rejected him due to his clumsiness.

Throughout her life, Hopper grew accustomed to surprising those who doubted her—whether about her career inclinations or regarding what the technology in front of her was capable of accomplishing. She once mused, in an interview, that she hoped she could live until the year 2000 so that she could be alive when computers would be even more advanced, and she could speak back to everyone who told her certain things were impossible. She said, "I want to point back to the early days of computers and say to all the doubters, 'See? We told you the computer could do all that.'"[8]

I want to point back to the early days of computers and say to all the doubters, "See? We told you the computer could do all that."
—Grace Hopper

Hopper never succumbed to the rejection of others—whether it be those who told her she didn't belong or those who may have stymied her interest or growth. Thanks, in part, to the example of her parents, and to her own seemingly endless reserve of determination, Rear Admiral Grace Hopper relentlessly pursued her passion for mathematics and combined it with service to her country.

★ The Flop Files: Janet Guthrie ★

Have you ever imagined yourself behind the wheel of a car, revving the engine, feeling the vibration, and then rocketing off in a cloud of dust? Full disclosure: I drive like I'm about ninety-five years old, and racing a car has only ever absolutely *terrified* me. But for Janet Guthrie, who was first an aerospace engineer, racing was her ultimate passion. And if race car driving is one's ultimate passion, there's no higher challenge than to qualify for, and compete in, the revered Indy 500.

So, that's what Guthrie decided she would do. Starting in 1963, Guthrie began trying to qualify for the epic race. However, there was just one problem: no woman had ever accomplished the feat, and the men who ran the race and, well, raced the race weren't about to usher in that kind of change with an open door. Instead, they fought it with everything they had.[9]

Year after year, as Guthrie continued her quest to qualify for the race, she endured a truly astounding amount of rejection from almost everyone in the racing community. They threw as many obstacles as possible in her way and mocked and taunted her constantly. One race car driver, Richard Petty, was especially brutal and consistent in his attacks on Guthrie. Once, he said about Guthrie, "She's no lady. If she's a lady, she'd be home."[10]

The message from Petty and a massive onslaught of other drivers, owners, and the media was absolutely clear: a woman did not belong on the racetrack.

But Guthrie's response was just as absolutely clear too: *Yes, I do.*

And so, she kept racing, kept trying to qualify, year after year after year. Finally, a full *thirteen years* after she began her mission, Guthrie did it. She qualified and became the first woman to compete in the Indy 500, in 1977. The epic feat occurred at the Talladega Superspeedway race, and guess who happened to also be at the race, watching?[11]

Petty.

Not only did Guthrie break through a barrier she had been dreaming about for years and years, but one of her harshest critics saw with his very own eyes as she did so. Each lap Guthrie sped around the track was like a powerful response to Petty's, well, pettiness. As her engine revved, the words it said were *Yes, I do . . . yes, I do . . . yes, I do . . .* belong here.

And so do you.

If you're facing years and years of rejection or failure as you attempt to achieve something that someone like you hasn't before accomplished, you have to believe that you belong there. Others, like

Petty, are going to shout with all their strength that you're out of your place. But they're wrong. And you prove them wrong by your time on the track. You keep revving your engine, you keep driving your laps.

And in your head—just like Guthrie—you remind yourself that you're exactly where you're supposed to be, no matter what anyone else says to try and knock you down.

NOTES

1. Rebecca Norman, "Grace Murray Hopper," Biographies of Women Mathematicians, Agnes Scott College, last modified March 4, 2019, https://www.agnesscott.edu/lriddle/women/hopper.htm.
2. Norman, "Grace Murray Hopper."
3. Norman, "Grace Murray Hopper."
4. "Grace Murray Hopper," *A Science Odyssey*, PBS, accessed September 14, 2019, https://www.pbs.org/wgbh/aso/databank/entries/btmurr.html.
5. Norman, "Grace Murray Hopper."
6. Norman, "Grace Murray Hopper."
7. Norman, "Grace Murray Hopper."
8. John Markoff, "Rear Adm. Grace M. Hopper Dies; Innovator in Computers Was 85," *New York Times*, January 3, 1992, https://www.nytimes.com/1992/01/03/us/rear-adm-grace-m-hopper-dies-innovator-in-computers-was-85.html.
9. Associated Press, "'Gentlemen and Lady, Start Your Engines,'" *New York Times*, May 22, 1977, http://archive.nytimes.com/www.nytimes.com/packages/html/sports/year_in_sports/05.22.html?module=inline.
10. Michelle R. Martinelli, "Racing Trailblazer Janet Guthrie Reflects on Indy 500 and Sexism in Motor Sports," *USA Today*, May 26, 2019, https://www.usatoday.com/story/sports/motorsports/2019/05/26/janet-guthrie-indianapolis-500-nascar-sexism-motor-sports/1242690001/.
11. Martinelli, "Racing Trailblazer Janet Guthrie."

30
HAIFAA AL-MANSOUR

As a female film director from Saudi Arabia, Haifaa Al-Mansour knew from an early age that she wanted to fight for equality in her home country. At school, when her mother would visit wearing a lighter-than-normal *niqab* (veil to cover her face), Al-Mansour swelled with pride. As her career grew, Al-Mansour consistently saw doors open where previously only men had been allowed, and as she developed some of the first short and feature-length films to be shot in Saudi Arabia, critics swooned.

*N*o *way!*

Haifaa Al-Mansour grew up east of Riyadh, in Saudi Arabia, where until 2015 it was illegal for women to even vote. Being out in public as a woman was a dangerous decision, especially without a male counterpart, and until 2018, it was illegal for women to drive in the country. Under this kind of oppressive status, Al-Mansour rose to prominence by directing powerful feature films over the most recent decade that managed to showcase female characters who struggled against such a system, fighting to reveal their voices, their strength, and their empowerment.[1]

However, Al-Mansour didn't always see this kind of fight as success. There was a time, early on, when she felt like a failure for being part of a family that pushed back against the status quo. Early on in Al-Mansour's life, in elementary school, her mother would make small acts of resistance against the status quo laws of the country. For instance, a heavy black *niqab* (veil) was required for women to cover their faces, but Al-Mansour's mother wore a lighter veil as a small form of resistance. This, and other acts by her more progressive family, caused Al-Mansour to stand out. She felt like she was a failure because of her family's decisions, like she should be embarrassed rather than proud. Al-Mansour recalled of this time period, "As a kid I was always embarrassed. This woman, I have nothing to do with her. I was always running away when she came to my school. But things like this make me stronger now. I appreciate it a lot better. What she did made me realize how important it is to be true to yourself and not to follow whatever is around you if it is limiting, if it is not right."[2]

HOLD THE BOLD!

In the forty years from 1939 to 1979, 7,332 full-length movies were created in of Hollywood. Of these, want to guess how many were directed by women? Fourteen. Kathryn Bigelow wasn't about to let those stats stop her, however, and she became the first-ever female director to win the Best Director Academy Award in 2008. She is still the only woman ever to win this award.

What she did made me realize how important it is to be true to yourself and not to follow whatever is around you if it is limiting, if it is not right.

—Haifaa Al-Mansour

Al-Mansour slowly began to see the necessity of feeling her own strength and using her own voice. Her family loved watching VHS tapes of old American movies, including those starring actor Jackie Chan, and these provided a kind of doorway through which she could consider what might be possible. As they grew older, she and her classmates were given the task of creating and performing in plays that taught about regulations for girls or about the religious requirements of prayer. Al-Mansour began to take small liberties, just as her mother had earlier on. She started to inject small moments of humor and made it a challenge to herself to see if—in writing and in performing—she might be able to make her classmates laugh.[3]

Al-Mansour decided to study abroad, at the American University in Cairo, Egypt, when she was an older teenager. This experience, plus other opportunities to travel, greatly informed her own vision of her home country. More than ever, she felt as though the strict requirements and rules for women in Saudi Arabia were silencing freedom and empowerment for girls. When she tried to rent an apartment, no one would lease to her unless her father came along and provided a man's support. When she tried to get to work every morning at an oil affiliate, she was not allowed to drive herself, and so if the male driver was late or didn't show, it drastically affected her own ability to work.[4]

She had had enough. One of the ways Al-Mansour decided to push back was to use her love of writing and telling a story through film. In 2003, she made a seven-minute-long film entitled *Who*, with an intense, drastic message. The film told the story of a man who dresses as a woman, even wearing a face veil in order to kill other women. It was strong message to a society that seemed to devalue women, and Al-Mansour received a lot of backlash after the film. She said, "I got lots of hate mail after *Who*. People said that I don't respect my own culture, that I am not religious. It's not true."[5]

I got lots of hate mail after Who. *People said that I don't respect my own culture, that I am not religious. It's not true.*

—Haifaa Al-Mansour

While the short film was viewed as a complete failure and she was rejected by many in power, others began to take notice both of her filmmaking skills and her passion to tell stories that would try to change the status quo.

This, eventually, led Al-Mansour to try something no one had ever done before: write and film an entire feature-length movie in Saudi Arabia with Saudi actors and actresses. In a country where, at the time, movie theaters were outlawed, such a task was no small feat. Al-Mansour channeled her fond memories of her green bicycle into a new story about the strength of girls in her home country, where such strength seemed to be continually repressed. The feature-length film is called *Wadjda* after the main character, a ten-year-old girl who desperately wants to own and ride her very own bicycle. There's just one problem: such a desire doesn't mesh with the rules of her country, as girls are not allowed to ride bicycles and move about freely on their own. Wadjda is determined and won't stop because of her society's rules, so she competes in a contest. Participants recite passages from the Koran in an attempt to win prize money; with it, Wadjda will buy her beloved bike.[6]

At first, all Al-Mansour had was the script and the hopes that somehow she'd find the means to make the film idea become a reality. Winning a $100,000 grant from the Abu Dhabi Film Festival helped enormously, but Al-Mansour still need to get a production company on board to help to fully fund and finish the film. Starting a formidable marketing campaign, Al-Mansour reached out to every production company she could find in the hopes that just one would agree to help her produce the film.

For a while, no one did.

Email after email created rejection after rejection.

Getting so close after writing her script during her graduate studies at the University of Australia, then developing it with the large grant from Abu Dhabi's film conference, Al-Mansour was determined not to give up now.

PLUCK ENOUGH!

In the early 1900s, every single movie director and studio owner was male. However, Alice Guy-Blaché, a young woman with incredible resolve and creative vision, changed all that. Though it took immense resolve and energy, she directed over one thousand films and opened her own studio in New Jersey.

So, day after day, she continued emailing and querying production companies. She has stated that she emailed *every single* production company in all of Europe. Finally, one said that beautiful word: *yes.*

Razor Film, in Germany, decided to take on the project, and Rotana Studios also came on board to support the creation of the film. But this wasn't the end of the setbacks and the struggle. Whereas other filmmakers might simply proceed to find their actors, cast the film, set up cameras and settings, and begin, Al-Mansour had an added challenge that truly made the creation of *Wadjda* a unique mission: the director was not allowed to be seen in public actually, well . . . *directing*.[7]

That's right. Saudi Arabia's strong societal system of how men and women function made it taboo for women to be seen out in public, openly working or

> ## CRAVE THE BRAVE!
>
> Famed actor Harrison Ford spent over a decade trying as hard as he could to become an actor. Told by movie industry leaders that he just didn't have the ability to do it, Ford persisted, and finally found himself starring as Han Solo in an epic enterprise known as Star Wars.

(especially) leading others in their work. Therefore, the director had to remain in a nearby van the entire time the film was shot, speaking into a headphone to tell others located on the set what to do and whether to reshoot a scene, change a line, change the lightning, or anything like that. But this added challenge did not phase Al-Mansour. Instead, it magnified her determination to finish the film and her belief that the film needed to exist for others to watch. She said, "I hope a father buys it for his daughter. . . . Or if a man watches it and, like my father did, gives more space to his daughter, to his wife. Because men control women's lives in Saudi. It takes a real man to be a little relaxed and allow women to be."[8]

It takes a real man to be a little relaxed and allow women to be.
—Haifaa Al-Mansour

At every turn, Al-Mansour wanted to use her voice to try and tell stories that needed to be told. And she's still doing it. Branching out from her home country of Saudi Arabia, Al-Mansour even recently accepted the offer to direct a biopic of the life of English writer Mary Shelley—the famed author of the classic novel *Frankenstein*. Al-Mansour has acknowledged that it may seem like an interesting pairing, but she can relate to the author's life in unique ways: Both are women who were judged to be incapable of producing epic feats of creativity because of their gender. Both debunked this attack with their actions.

Al-Mansour grew beyond the shame she felt as a child, the criticisms she endured along the way toward becoming a filmmaker, and the failure to get picked up by a production company in her relentless pursuit to do what she needed to do. Her films now are projected on screens across the world; her stories told in big, bold actions because of those she took herself.

★ The Flop Files: **Roxane Gay** ★

Now a bestselling author of the memoir *Hunger*, the collection of essays *Bad Feminist*, the comic *World of Wakanda*, and much more, Roxane Gay was no stranger to rejection and failure for much of her writing life.

Even though she wrote relentlessly during her twenties and thirties, Gay received mostly rejections for all her writing submissions to publishers. Even her first novel, *Untamed State*, took almost two years to sell to a publishing company. En route to getting that book to a contract for publication, Gay said she had to revise it countless times and work with two different literary agents. Even then, her years and years of hard work garnered her $12,500, not nearly as much as many other full-time jobs would have offered for work that might have taken a lot less time![9]

As she was living through her years of writing and rejection, Gay felt often like she wanted to quit—like success as a writer might never come. In fact, she has recalled, even *after* she had sold her first novel and it did not parlay into bigger success or an ability to live on her writing, she figured she had tried her best and that, maybe, it was time to move on from writing. If it weren't for a special supporter in her corner, she might have done just that.

Instead, she stuck with writing, kept producing more work and sending it out, and hoping that someway, somehow, she'd be able to make a living.

Looking back, as Gay considered what success means for a writer, she shared, "What I wish I could have told myself when I was hopeless about my writing prospects is that I should have defined artistic success in ways that weren't shaped by forces beyond my control."[10] Falling prey to a notion of success that means only one thing, Gay has reflected on how deeply this made her want to quit.

If you view success in one narrow way, then it's easy to feel as though all of your other accomplishments count for nothing. Sometimes, you might make it to the final and lose, but that doesn't mean you haven't had some success. To be honest, sometimes success can mean simply getting out of bed in the morning, putting on your shoes, and facing a day that you know is going to be—for one reason or another—really tough.

Gay made this point powerfully as she explained her own journey: "Sometimes, success is getting a handful of words you don't totally hate on the page."[11] Success for a writer—or for any person—can't be defined only by the way others respond to and value what you do. It's also about how *you* respond to and value what you do. That essay you have to write for English class? Just because you don't win an award for it (or get an A+) doesn't mean you didn't succeed.

Everything you endured to write it goes into the final product. The struggle you face is a part of the success you taste.

In Gay's case, she kept working because she loved to write and because she had a special friend stay in her corner, cheering her on. Both are crucial to keep going—especially if you're finding that success isn't looking exactly like what you'd hoped.

NOTES

1. Haifa Al-Monsour, "Haifa Al-Mansour: 'It's Very Important to Celebrate Resistance,'" interview by Liz Hoggard, *Guardian*, July 13, 2013, https://www.theguardian.com/theobserver/2013/jul/14/haifaa-mansour-wadjda-saudi-arabia.
2. Rebecca Keegan, "Meet Haifaa Al-Mansour, the Saudi Woman Challenging Riyadh—and Hollywood—to Evolve," *Vanity Fair*, May 25, 2018, https://www.vanityfair.com/hollywood/2018/05/meet-haifaa-al-mansour-the-saudi-woman-challenging-riyadh.
3. Keegan, "Meet Haifaa Al-Mansour."
4. Horatia Harrod, "Haifa Al-Mansour: I Wanted to Have a Voice," *Telegraph*, July 19, 2013, https://www.telegraph.co.uk/culture/film/starsandstories/10183258/Haifaa-al-Mansour-I-wanted-to-have-a-voice.html.
5. Harrod, "Haifa Al-Mansour."
6. Keegan, "Meet Haifaa Al-Mansour."
7. Keegan, "Meet Haifaa Al-Mansour."
8. Dan Zak, "'Wadjda' Director Haifaa Al Mansour Gives Female Perspective of Life in Saudi Arabia," *Washington Post*, September 19, 2013, https://www.washingtonpost.com/lifestyle/style/wadjda-director-haifaa-al-mansour-gives-female-perspective-of-life-in-saudi-arabia/2013/09/19/ff9b15f6-1bd5-11e3-8685-5021e0c41964_story.html.
9. Roxane Gay, "Ask Roxane: Is It Too Late to Follow My Dreams?" *New York Times*, December 30, 2017, https://www.nytimes.com/2017/12/30/opinion/sunday/ask-roxane-is-it-too-late-to-follow-my-dreams.html.
10. Gay, "Ask Roxane: Is It Too Late to Follow My Dreams?"
11. Gay, "Ask Roxane: Is It Too Late to Follow My Dreams?"

CONCLUSION

When I was a new father, and my first son was two years old, I'll never forget going for a particular walk on a particularly rainy day in a particularly rainy country, England. We were living there for a few years as my wife, Jennifer, finished her PhD. So, my son and I were out for a walk on this rainy day, and we came to a massive puddle. This was the kind of puddle you might look at and wonder, *Hhhmmm, is this a lake in the middle of the sidewalk?*

"Let's go around this way, Tyler. That's a *huge* puddle, and we don't want our feet to get soaked," I said (quite logically, in my opinion).

"We go through puddle and no get wet!" my little guy roared back (rather illogically, in my opinion).

I stopped, looked at my progeny, and repeated, "It's a huge puddle, Tyler. If we go through it, we will get wet."

Thinking I had firmly (and quite logically) put the matter to rest, I began to walk around the puddle. Of course, I assumed my son would follow.

No. He stood right where he was, in front of the puddle, and let out his fierce battle cry of a claim: "*We go through puddle, and we no get wet!*"

Then, like only a two-year old can, he proceeded to rush through the puddle. Water sprayed and splashed *everywhere*. It soaked him completely. It soaked me completely. I believe it also soaked a poor older man who happened to be near us on the sidewalk at precisely the wrong moment that day.

Tyler made it to the other side of the puddle, looked up at me with dawning clarity, and then began to sob. "*I all wet!!!!!!*"

This was his plaintive cry.

What did I do, you wonder? Did I rub it in and say, *I told you so?!* Did I comfort my wee one, cradle his soaking body in my soaking arms? Did I become angry and exasperated at his total disobedience?

I laughed. Pretty loudly.

Because, think about it: it's funny. It's actually downright hilarious to think that he could somehow rush through a massive pool of water and somehow come out the other side completely dry.

Impossible.

And yet I think that many of us try to live life this way when it comes to failure. We want to attempt cool stuff; we want to try beautiful things; we want to make a difference or chase a dream or try out for a team or let the world hear us, in our music, in our screams. We want to, simply put, *do stuff*!

Yet we have this mistaken belief that we can do stuff without getting wet—that we can run through difficult changes and somehow never fail. But life comes back at us, again and again, in a way very similar to the puddle (or was it a lake?) on the sidewalk that day in England. Life says, *If you're going to go through me, you're going to get wet. You're going to fail.*

We can't make it through life and do anything that matters without making mistakes, being rejected, encountering struggle, and yes: failing.

Failing is a part of every success, and struggle is a part of every triumph worth reaching.

The question we all face is whether we're going to walk through it. Are we going to try to find some way around doing what we dream of? Like I was trying to convince my son that day, are we going to simply go around the huge puddles in our lives? If we do, we run the risk of not learning, not growing, not seeing ourselves and the people around us and the world in any deeper ways than we currently do.

But if we are willing to walk through the water, we are going to learn a lot. We are going to learn about how strong we are. We are going to learn about who's willing to walk through the struggle with us. And we are going to learn what it takes to get soaked—and keep on keeping on.

And that, ultimately, is a big part of what matters most in life.

I hope these profiles, stories, and snippets of other people, places, and things help remind you that if you struggle, you are not alone. If you fail, you are in good company. If you've been (or are being!) rejected, this is no verdict of who you are and what you'll end up accomplishing.

So, as you stand before puddles in your life right now—whether big or small—I want to tell you the opposite of what I once told my son that day. I want you to go ahead: walk through them. I'm not going to lie and say that you'll stay dry, that everything will be fine and easy.

It won't.

But you'll find that others are trying to get through puddles too—some right alongside you!

And you'll find that you *will* make it to the other side.

And it will be worth it.

Maybe, somewhere along that sidewalk, we'll even see each other. I'll look out for you. You'll look out for me. If we do meet up, let's agree to laugh at ourselves a little too, okay? Because we're all in this together.

Every puddle in your life matters, and every time you walk through, it's going to shape you more and more into the person you want to be. Please—for my sake and for the world's sake—don't stop. I need you to chase and pursue what you care about. The world *needs* you to do this. It matters. You matter.

See you out there on the sidewalk, my friend.

OFF THE PAGE AND ON THE SCREEN

FANTASTIC FAILURES FROM THE WORLDS OF FILM AND LITERATURE!

Profound stories showcasing the importance—and frequency!—of failure populate the pages and screens of some truly incredible books and movies. If you're looking to be inspired by stories both real and imagined, then check out some of the following books and movies and be prepared to see how some amazing characters experience, face, and rise above their own mistakes, rejections, and failures.

MOVIES

Captain Marvel
In keeping with the Marvel Studio list of blockbuster superhero film hits, *Captain Marvel* breaks new ground by featuring a female protagonist, and specifically one who has no need for a romantic interest or someone else to rescue or save her. Instead, she finds her own strength

by reconnecting with her core identity. Carol Danvers, aka Captain Marvel, is serving in the US Air Force when she endures a blast that fills her with the power of a tesseract—enabling her to complete epic feats of strength and daring. However, this power is inhibited by forces that want to control her and use it toward their own ends. Danvers eventually must learn that real strength lies in falling down and getting back up—over and over again—and not in getting it right and perfect the first time. Full disclosure: I cry at the end of this movie every single time, and I use it with my college students to talk about what it means to be strong. Please watch this one!

Mona Lisa Smile

As a new professor at the prestigious Wellesley College for women, Katherine Ann Watson is rejected both by some of the students—one in particular who disagrees with the professor's progressive tactics and ideas—and the administration. Rather than acquiesce, she continues to fight for the students' right to seek their own bold careers, rather than aspire only to be what society encourages them to become.

Rudy

Daniel "Rudy" Ruettiger is a smaller-than-average football player who dreams of making the University of Notre Dame football team. Rather than listen to everyone else who tells him the dream is ridiculous, Ruettiger works as hard as humanly possible, longer and harder than any other player, and eventually makes the team. However, he is allowed only to practice with the team, not considered a strong enough player to go out on the field during games. Rather than accept this definition of his ability, he continues to work hard both physically and mentally, hoping for a chance to prove everyone wrong and show them that heart can be just as powerful as physical size.

Akeelah and the Bee

Akeelah Anderson has faced the tragic death of her father and goes through her middle-school experience getting by as best she can. However, when she's forced to compete in the school spelling bee, a unique talent—and passion—emerges. Anderson finds that she loves words, their rhythms, sounds, and configurations. With some encouragement from a mentor and coach who has his own grief to face, Anderson learns to persist even in the face of immense obstacles and fear of failure, eventually making it to the Scripps National Spelling Bee.

Draft Day

Faced with the seemingly impossible task of rebuilding a football team that has struggled in the past, manager Sonny Weaver Jr. must work wisely to select the best possible players in the NFL (National Football League) draft. However, his trades and his choices end up creating a storm of disapproval. Colleagues, media, and even the Cleveland Browns' team owner are all furious with the manager over what they see as a failure of wisdom and strategy. It remains to be seen if Weaver can turn what seems like failure into success.

Karate Kid

Both versions of this classic film are well worth watching—the original from 1984 and the remake from 2010. Each tells the story of a teen struggling to find where he belongs and feeling both bullied and overwhelmed by others. The protagonist sees his life as a failure, and he can't seem to get traction to move forward. A mentor helps him see that what the world values and chooses to notice is not always right. He helps the teen understand that, in the end, it's self-control, composure, and purpose that provide real victory, not machismo.

Black Panther

When T'Challa becomes king of Wakanda after his father dies, the land is unified under his leadership. Then, when a new heir comes back to Wakanda, demanding to be given a chance to fight for the throne, T'Challa loses the fight. His failure is compounded when Wakanda begins to fall into disarray and danger. T'Challa must forge his path from failure toward a new hope for his kingdom—even though the task is both daunting and difficult.

Star Wars: The Last Jedi

Continuing the saga George Lucas began back in 1977 (which, you remember from chapter 6, was originally ridiculed by esteemed directors like Brian De Palma and studio heads!), this eighth installment in the series is notable for the powerful ascension of Rey, who realizes that she can connect to the Force in remarkable ways. While she is often ridiculed for being nothing and coming from nothing, she proves that these attacks will not stop her from helping those she loves and continuing to try to stop the forces of hatred and fear in the galaxy.

Moana

Filled with irresistibly memorable songs created by the brilliant Broadway writer Lin-Manuel Miranda (featured in chapter 9), *Moana* explores the story of a young girl in line to be ruler of her people, who live on an island and fear straying too far from its shores. However, Moana believes otherwise. Even though she repeatedly fails or is barred from setting out on the sea, she refuses to relent in her belief that a wider adventure is necessary to save her people. Eventually, she finds a way to journey beyond where even her own father, the current ruler, has ever been. (Warning: you will not be able to stop singing these songs once you see the film. I still sing them daily, all the time, even to my college students.)

CROSSOVER (BOTH MOVIE AND BOOK)

The Hate U Give

Exploring the life of sixteen-year-old Starr Carter, this novel and movie both are groundbreaking in their resolve to showcase police violence against African American men. Carter witnesses a police officer murder her childhood friend and must find and use her voice to speak out against the injustice. Facing critics on all sides, and danger from within and outside of her neighborhood, Carter learns to do the very thing she is most terrified to do—this will risk not only her life but the lives of those she loves, but it may change her community for the better forever. This is a powerful—and highly intense—book and film.

The Hunger Games

The now-epic and worldwide phenomenon by Suzanne Collins explores the ways in which society fails in a dystopian world. By seeking power alone, people have fallen into a decrepit and tragic ritual of exploiting children as fighters to satisfy viewers' desire for violence and competition. However, Katniss Everdeen defies the odds stacked against her and attempts to turn her world from failure back to hope.

Hidden Figures

The nonfiction book, both adult and young adult versions, as well as the blockbuster Hollywood movie, tells the story of a group of women who changed the landscape and possibilities of space travel.

Working for NASA under strict, unjust racial laws, Mary Jackson, Katherine Johnson, Dorothy Vaughan, and Christine Darden fought for their respective places at the table. They made hugely significant contributions to space exploration; yet for years, their work was neither discussed nor respected. Now, this book and film changes that.

Pride and Prejudice

Jane Austen's 1813 novel—and Hollywood's many film versions—explores the life of protagonist Elizabeth Bennet. Refusing to acquiesce to the tired regulations her society had for women, Bennet speaks her mind freely and with force. However, she also reveals an ability to embrace her own mistakes in thinking, as she learns more about who people really are. A tender love story, a hilarious relational romp, and a call to be who you are, *Pride and Prejudice* is essential reading and viewing!

Harry Potter

This is J. K. Rowling's classic series about a young wizard who seems to be the definition of failure in the normal human world but proves to have immense power that, with the help of friends and mentors, saves the world. Both the books and the films are mesmerizing and showcase not only Potter's exploits as they redefine success but also those of his formidable friends, Hermione Granger and Ron Weasley. The series has the power to help us rethink what it means to be strong, what it means to succeed, and who we really are versus who society tells us we are.

Anne of Green Gables

Classic books? Check. Inspiring television films? Check. *New* graphic novel edition? Check! All three forms of this beautiful story about a bold young girl who is not afraid to let the world know that she's got opinions, ideas, and dreams are required reading and viewing. That's especially so for anyone who needs to be reminded that you're not alone if you've been told to be quiet, shape up, and fit in. Anne (with an *e!*) does not, and she helps to change her small corner of the world by resisting doing so.

Spare Parts

This nonfiction book was turned into a movie that featured George Lopez as the coach of the Carl Hayden Community High School robotics squad. The team's journey is explored in this book in chapter 23, and both the book and film versions of their story are remarkable. Detailing the team's quest to become the best robotics developers in the country, the story contains so many powerful moments where failure seems inevitable, and yet the team finds a way to move forward and eventually defeat the renowned MIT team. It is a powerful example of how brilliance and triumph can rise-up when there is a willingness to buck the status quo!

The Outsiders

The amazing novel written by S. E. Hinton when she was only sixteen was made into an amazing film directed by Francis Ford Coppola. Both versions explore the story of how two rival groups try to fit in to society and how they war against one another as they seek to find their places. Society's failure to create a system where both groups can coexist is on display, as characters learn that violence does not solve their dilemmas and that love can overcome seemingly impossible differences. Gritty and raw, the novel and film don't gloss over the pain that people feel as they try to find where they belong or the mistakes they make along the way.

BOOKS

The Crossover by Kwame Alexander

Poetry! Novel! Novel in poems! Poetic novel! Alexander's 2015 Newbery-winning book tells the story of Josh Bell (aka Filthy McNasty), a basketball star who also deeply loves words. The epic rhythms of the book match the fast-paced saga of its protagonist as he grapples with family grief and loyalty and love. While basketball plays a central role in the novel, you don't have to love—or even understand—the sport to still enjoy the book, and if you read it alone, read it out loud. I guarantee doing so will make your heart beat fast. *And,* there's even a prequel, out in 2019: *Rebound.*

Out of My Mind by Sharon Draper

Struggling with her severe cerebral palsy, eleven-year-old Melody Brooks is brilliant. The problem is, society can't see that about her. Relegated to a room in her school where she has no way of communicating with others all that she knows, Brooks slowly comes to find ways to connect with the world around her and challenge the world's notions about what it means to be bright, to be respected, and to be seen for who we truly are. Careful what time you start reading this one, as once you start, you won't go to sleep until you finish!

Roll of Thunder, Hear My Cry by Mildred D. Taylor

I absolutely loved, loved, loved reading this book with my own seventh-grade students year after year. The recipient of the Newbery Medal in 1977, Taylor's novel explores the powerful ways that the Logan children face intense racism and refuse to acquiesce to its unjust and cruel demands. Vivid and action-packed storytelling runs throughout this novel as we watch the Logan kids stand up for themselves again and again in a society that constantly threatens to silence and destroy them.

Harbor Me by Jacqueline Woodson

This amazing novel feels like poetry and falls like rain on a reader's soul. It's awesome. Sharing the story of six kids who have a rare opportunity in school, this middle-grade novel gets real, real fast. The six students have the ability to talk about *anything* they want throughout their day, and they each share their stories that range from being about a father who is behind bars to an undocumented immigrant terrified of being deported. Facing seemingly insurmountable obstacles, these teens find ways to connect with and support each other that will make you both cry and cheer.

The Memory of Light by Francisco X. Stork

This is a beautiful, harrowing novel that explores the journey of Vicky Cruz, a sixteen-year-old girl who struggles with severe depression and has attempted suicide. Unsure how to grapple with the many confusions and difficulties she faces, Cruz slowly comes to see that there is a community of people who love and support her as she tries to regain her sense of hope. The novel is fearless in its depiction of the struggle Cruz endures and shows us how perfection is never possible. By embracing and sharing openly with one another, we start to heal and help one another to take small steps forward.

Flying Lessons and Other Stories edited by Ellen Oh

This short-story anthology includes ten truly awesome stories by some of the best writers alive today. They share powerful journeys that include realistic and wildly surreal struggles, failures, and triumphs of unique protagonists. You could read the entire volume front to back or jump around and find your favorite stories, those that are most interesting to you. Either way, there's a lot to love here about failure and making mistakes—and watching how characters deal with and come back from these struggles.

Okay for Now by Gary D. Schmidt

Exploring the journey of a fourteen-year-old kid who loves baseball and birds, this novel is laugh-out-loud funny but also weep-worthy. When I read it, I did both—sometimes within a few minutes of one another! Rejected by his father and many of his peers, fourteen-year-old Doug Swieteck slowly learns how to love what he loves (as the poet Mary Oliver might tell us!) and embrace who he really is, rather than subscribe to the false ideas that he's got to be tough and macho.

Smile by Raina Telgemeier

This is an *amazing* graphic novel that my oldest son, Tyler, and I have read together over, and over, and over (and over!) again. It's the true story of the author's journey to learn to smile again after a dangerous and terrifying fall left her with broken teeth. Enduring multiple and invasive dental procedures, the protagonist grapples with whether she will ever be able to feel joy and hope again—whether the smile she once had will ever return. Warning: you will laugh and cry throughout this stunning book.

EXERCISE

CREATIVE QUESTIONS ON FAILURE, SUCCESS, AND ALL THE TANGENTS IN BETWEEN TO GET YOUR MIND MOVING AND YOUR HEART PUMPING!

1. Would you rather be known worldwide but have few close friends, or have amazingly close friendships and never make the news?
2. Given the choice, would you want to find a cure for a terminal illness or be the leader of a social movement?
3. If someone were to give you a grant of *$1 million* to do something that would benefit society, what would you do with the money?
4. You've just accomplished something truly amazing, seemingly impossible. How do you want to celebrate?

5. You've just failed miserably at something that you worked very hard for. How do you want to grapple with the failure?

6. Someone has invited you to give a special presentation to *all* the teachers in your town. What would you say to them?

7. Someone has invited you to give a special presentation to the entire body of elected officials of your country. What would you say to them?

8. You get the chance to talk to anyone profiled in this book, face-to-face. What would you ask that person? What would you want that person to ask you?

9. What do you most wish people knew about you right away when they meet *you*?

10. What do you regret?

11. What three things would you most like to accomplish?

12. If you were given the option to sail around the world for a year or to design a state-of-the-art robot with a group of scientists, which would you choose?

13. If you could be drafted into any professional sport, which would you choose?

14. If your life became a movie, what would the opening scene be?

15. If you created a book based on your life, what kind of book would it be? A picture book? A graphic novel? A memoir? A realistic fiction novel? A science-fiction escapade? Or something else entirely?

16. Of all the people you know, who would you call the most successful? Why do you think so?

17. What advice have other people given you about what it means to succeed?

18. Have you ever questioned what a teacher or other adult told you was true? What was it, and why did you question it?

19. What's the biggest lie you've ever told? How did you act/ respond *afterward*?

20. What's the hardest truth you've ever admitted?

21. If you had to choose to be any cartoon character, who would you choose and why?

22. If you had to choose to be anyone in this book, who would you choose to be and why?

23. What is one thing you wish, wish, *wish* someone would say to you?

24. What is one thing you wish no one would ever say to you again?

25. What school experience made you feel the proudest of yourself?

26. What school experience made you feel the smallest or the most ashamed of yourself?

27. Given the choice, would you rather direct a big Hollywood picture, write a big Hollywood screenplay, star in a big Hollywood movie, or have absolutely nothing at all to do with Hollywood? Why?

28. Pretend that there is a massive sports championship game. Would you rather be the go-to player, the coach, a sportswriter watching the event to write about it, a fan watching for fun, or nowhere near the game? Why?

29. If you could live anywhere in the world, where would you go and why?

30. If you had to go on an adventure for a whole year—leaving home and school—and you could only take one person along with you, who would you bring and why?

31. What's the kindest thing anyone has ever said to you?

32. What's the most hurtful thing anyone has ever said to you?

33. Have you ever watched someone else fail at something? What was it, and how did the person respond?

34. Have you ever watched someone succeed greatly at something? What was it, and how did the person respond?

35. If you could change any *one* thing about the world, what would you choose to change and why?

36. If you could change any *one* thing about the way you are educated, what would you choose to change and why?

37. If you could come up with a single question that *everyone* you asked had to respond to with complete honesty, what question would you create?

38. If you could know the *complete* truth about anything in history that has ever happened, what would you choose to know and why?

39. If you could *unlearn* anything you know right now, what would you choose to unlearn and why?

40. If you could only watch one movie over and over again for the rest of your life, which movie would you choose and why?

41. If you had to live trapped inside any book for one week, which book would you choose and why?

42. If you had to live trapped inside any movie for one week, which movie would you choose and why?

43. If you could switch places with anyone you know and live their life for a whole week, who would you choose and why?

44. If you could switch places with anyone in this book and live their life for a whole week, who would you choose and why?

45. If you could invent your own smoothie and it would be a worldwide hit—the most sought-after drink ever—what would be in it, and what would you name it?

46. If you were guaranteed to succeed, would you rather climb Mount Everest or write and publish a bestselling book?
47. If you were guaranteed to fail, would you rather attempt Mount Everest or try to write and publish a book?
48. If the *entire world* would follow *your* definition of success, what would you tell everyone it is?
49. Given the choice between being able to speed-read entire books in twenty minutes or run the mile in under five minutes, which ability would you choose and why?
50. Given the choice between attending a massive dance party or going to an orchestra concert at a symphony hall, which would you choose and why?
51. You can write a list of ten pieces of advice for every tween and teen, and it will be published on the front page of every newspaper or news website in America. What ten things do you write?
52. If you had the ability to create one rule that everyone in the world had to follow, what rule would you create?
53. If you had the ability to change one event in history, which event would you change, and in what ways would you change it?
54. Would you rather be a failed artist or a successful business-person? Why?
55. Would you rather be a failed businessperson or a successful artist? Why?
56. Your name is blasted on all the television news stations this morning. What's it for?
57. If you could be the owner of any company in the world, which company would you want to own and why?

58. If you could be the author of any book ever written, which book would you have penned and why?

59. If you could be the inventor of anything in the world that has ever been created, what would you choose and why?

60. If you could un-invent anything that has been created, what would you un-invent and why?

61. If you could choose to be master of one ability, what would you choose and why?

62. You are crying and yet also kind of laughing at the same time. Why? What has happened to get you feeling and acting this way?

63. You are cheering wildly—clapping your hands and hooting and hollering in great and astounding excitement. Where are you, and why are you acting this way?

64. You are angry, and your words come fast and strong as you look with fierce eyes at . . . *what?*!

65. Someone writes you a letter that inspires and helps you enormously with what you're dealing with *right now* in your life. What does that letter say?

66. Today's news highlights something in your past that you've done wonderfully well. What thing do they highlight?

67. Would you rather go one week without seeing or touching *any* screens or go one week without eating any sugar? Why?

68. Someone surprises you with a gift that you absolutely *love*. What is the gift, and who has surprised you with it?

69. An important adult in your life looks you directly in the eyes and says, "I am so proud of you right now." What have you just done?

70. Given the choice, would you rather pilot a fighter jet or steer a sailboat? Why?

71. If a product you invent would be sold in *one* store, which store would you want to stock it?

72. If you could create a brand-new word that would officially be added to the dictionary, what word would you create and what would its meaning be?

73. You had to stay up super, super late to finish something really, really awesome. What did you need to finish?

74. You had to wake up super, super early to do something really, really important. What did you need to do so early?

75. You are given a job where you can make $100 for every hour that you work. How many hours do you choose to work? Why?

76. Would you rather make a lot of money and absolutely *hate* going to work every single day or make a little money but absolutely *love* what you do? Why?

77. If you could live in a world where money did not exist, would you choose to do so or not? Why?

78. If you could create your very own middle school, what would it be like?

79. A dangerous catastrophe *almost* occurs, but you step in to prevent it at the last second. What has almost happened, and how did you prevent it?

80. Think of something hurtful that someone has said to you to which you never responded. Pretend you can go back to that exact moment and speak with a strong, powerful voice. What do you say?

81. If you could add one person to this book, who would you add and why?

82. Would you rather be admired and revered by children or by adults? Why?

83. If you had a choice between someone making a movie of your life or writing a book about your life, which would you choose and why? If a third option was to have neither, would you choose that instead? Why?

84. You create a number one Billboard hit song. What are the lyrics?

85. Your state government wants to create a new memorial in the capitol of the state. The governor asks *you* to decide who or what it will honor. What do you say?

86. You become the CEO of any social media platform. Which one will you lead, and will you make any changes to it?

87. If you could create a hall of fame for *any* skill or ability, and you would be the first inductee, what would it be for?

88. There is a massive (*massive*) blank canvas in front of you, as well as a big tub of variously colored spray paints. What do you create on it?

89. If you wrote a letter to a student one grade lower than yours, what would you say?

90. A television studio executive calls you and says she's interested in creating more shows that feature what students like *you* really want to see, so she asks for your opinion. What do you tell her?

91. All current fashion and style trends are completely forgotten overnight, and when you wake, you get to set the trend of what's considered fashionable. What do you choose and why?

92. Someone decides to dedicate a music video to you. What's the style of music, and why do they say it's dedicated to you?

93. Every single sticky note in the world, for one week, will be printed with a quote you love at the top of it. What's the quote you choose and why?

94. In your school or community, who do you think *really* makes the decisions? Why do you think this?

95. Given the choice, would you rather be educated in a place that is totally screen-free or a place where everything is done on screens? Why?

96. If you could give yourself three challenges, what would they be?

97. If you could give yourself three encouragements, what would they be?

98. Think of someone you care about. If you could ensure this person always remembered one key thing, what would that be?

99. Think of someone you really admire. What do you think is that person's biggest struggle?

100. If you were given a time machine, with every kind of gadget and capability, where would you go first and why? When you got there, if you could take one piece of wisdom back to your regular time and place, what would that wisdom be?

ACKNOWLEDGMENTS

Every book is the work of a community of people and never just the result of the author whose name is on the front cover. With *Even More Fantastic Failures*, the community who supported and ushered this book into life is very special to me, and I am deeply grateful to all of them.

The subject of failure has been so important to me because I have seen over and over how my own students have struggled to feel okay about themselves in the midst of, well, *struggle*. Too often, they interpret struggle as a sign of weakness rather than a sign of strength. Therefore, my impetus for creating these books came from my students. They craved stories of people who were as human as they were—people who endured fraught family situations, confusion, fear, trauma, worry, regret, rejection, and, yes, failure. I endeavored to show my students that they are not alone. Anyone who has done beautiful things in this world has had their share of struggle and failure. So, I want to thank my students, first and foremost, for sharing their own lives so honestly with me, for sharing their own concerns and struggles and heartfelt questions. Teaching high school, middle school, and now college, I see that our questions may change in structure and context as we grow older, but the content remains: *Am I okay the way I am? Does the world need me? Is there a place where I belong?* Here, I say a resounding yes to all three and an emphatic thank-you on top of that.

I also want to thank the truly amazing team at Beyond Words, especially Lindsay Easterbrooks-Brown and Emmalisa Sparrow Wood. By this stage in the game, you know how much I love working with you both. In all the writing I've done throughout my life, the projects you encourage, and the deep, thought-provoking, and progressive way in which you encourage them, is a beacon for me. Being on your team has been a joy. I appreciate the very insightful ways you've helped to bring what was a brief proposal to full-blooded life. And I'm deeply thankful for our phone conferences, excited email chains, and endless possibilities of who we would profile, how we would do it, and above all, the difference we hope these stories will make. Thank you for inviting me to be on *your* team and thank you for authentically believing in the need for this message to reach our readers. I value your incredibly hard work ethic, your brilliant vision, and your commitment to tie meaning to action. And to my sentence-splicing, phrase-dicing, maximizer of enticing messages copyeditor, Kristin Thiel! *So many times* you found key areas that needed some serious fixing and reworking, and you've pointed them out to me with grace and a genuine desire to see this book be its very best. Thank you for all of your hard work and close reading! And thank you to the rest of the amazing team at Beyond Words who helped bring this book to the world: Mike Corley, Devon Smith, Bill Brunson, Corinne Kalasky, and Brennah Hale.

To my in-laws, Susan and Wendell Anderson, who have been in my family's corner as we sought a place to live, a place to write, and a place to dream—and who encouraged us continually that we would find our way forward. Thank you for your love of good stories, your love of us, and your love of your grandsons! We're all ready to wake you up super-duper early at the very next sleepover.

To my fifth-grade teacher, who started the FLAIR writing program in your classroom, Robert Looney. Thank you for encouraging me to write my stories, and for laughing out loud when you read them (instead of telling me to write something different!). Your encouragement of creativity has inspired me as well as many other young writers growing up, looking for ways to tell stories to help us figure out how to live in this big, beautiful, strange, confusing world. Thank you for your example of deeply loving poetry and for the endless joy you brought to the classroom every single day.

To my writing mentor and supervising teacher from many years ago, when I was just starting out in room 106 with you: John Robinson. Thank you for modeling the beautiful combination of contemplation and action. You showed me how one can be deeply passionate about work as a teacher but also serious and committed to one's work as a writer. Seeing how you managed to synthesize both passions in your own life has been a beautiful boon to me in mine. Thank you for your unwavering support and love of my whole family—and for always challenging me to have that most dangerous thing of all: hope.

A special thank-you to my oldest son, Tyler. Now that you're eleven, this has been the first book that I have created in a truly different way. Different how? You were beside me much of the way through the journey of writing this book. You sat with me in the evenings at Panera, with our ginger-mango tea, and by day in the library at Endicott College. You worked on your novel, *Surfing a Tsunami*, as I researched and wrote this. And I want to honestly tell you, son, that it was a surprising joy that I never expected. Hearing your fingers tap the keys and seeing your own words grow to fill your blank pages spurred me on and, okay, I'll admit, made me cry. Hey, you know that's the way I am! But I appreciate your resolve to write and to want to write beside me. Thank you, son. I am proud of you.

To my younger sons, Benjamin, Joshua, and Samuel, thank you for reminding me constantly of the need to tickle. When in doubt, overwhelmed, confused, or worried, *tickle*! Thank you, also, for leading and including me in the many family dance parties that jogged this sometimes-foggy brain and helped it refocus. I love you, sons, so very much, and I'm grateful for all the ways—big and small—that you remind me of what matters in life. See you on the dance floor, dudes.

To my family, who has supported and taught me to see life from so many perspectives, and to laugh a little along the way. My four brothers: Christopher, Michael, Bryan, and Matthew. Each of you experiences the world through different lenses, whether as a deaf man or a gay man, as a therapist or a dad or a social worker or a seeker. Your experiences have guided and shaped mine, and I am so grateful for the fact that you've shared them with me—from when we were little kids to now that we're grown men. Thank you, brothers. And to my mom and dad: thank you for modeling that life doesn't have to be perfect to be fun, to overcome hard moments, to heal. Mom, your relentless desire to see the good is inspiring to me, and, Dad, the way you stood and applauded for me—the first one up—at that talk meant so much to me. I love you both so much.

And to my wife, Jennifer, even though I wrote about it in the conclusion of the first book in this series, you have to know that the way you raised my head up out of shame for being a thirty-two-year-old paperboy and helped me believe in who I was as a writer, teacher, and dad . . . just, *wow*. I'm so grateful that you met me in my place of shame and embarrassment, told me you loved me in that very place, and walked beside me through it. No wonder I'm ready to cry at the sheer sight of a newspaper! Thank you for the journey we've been on and the journey still yet to come. You once painted a sign that read: *Life doesn't have to be perfect to be beautiful.* Thank you so much for everything you do to help our family forge a beautiful life. I wake up in wonder and go to bed in gratitude, thanks to the woman of strength, compassion, wisdom, and love that you are.

And to you, dear reader. Yes, to you! I probably don't know you. But based on everything I've ever researched, every class I've ever taught, and every community I've ever participated in, I can guess with some sense of certainty that right now, you may feel a little confused. Or a little fearful. Or a little fatigued. Or a little ashamed. Or a little like a failure. Or a little overwhelmed. Or *a lot* of any of these things. I am grateful that you've read these words, but I have one final challenge to couple with this thankfulness. Please let the stories of these inspiring people propel you to reach out, to seek support, to ask for help, to tell your story, to speak your truth, and to believe that this world needs you. The biggest thanks I can send your way is simply this: thank you for keeping on, for not giving in to any lies that tell you you're not good enough or you're not needed.

You are.

You are.

You are.